BAD ATTITUDE/S ON TRIAL: PORNOGRAPHY, FEMINISM, AND THE *BUTLER* DECISION

Bad Attitude/s on Trial is a critical analysis of pornography in the context of contemporary Canada. The notion that pornography both reflects sexual domination and 'victimizes' women has recently found expression in law in the landmark Canadian Supreme Court decision of *R. v. Butler* (1992). Many feminists embrace this new law as progressive, but in the post-*Butler* years, straight, mainstream pornography is still flourishing, while sexual representations that challenge conventional notions of sexuality, such as those centring on gay and lesbian sex and s/m sex, are the focus of censorship. It is the censorship of sexual others that the authors critique from a legal, cultural, gay, and philosophical standpoint.

Lise Gotell examines the intervention of the Women's Legal Education and Action Fund (LEAF) in the *Butler* decision and provides an overview of socio-legal debates on pornography and censorship. Brenda Cossman examines the *Butler* decision itself and challenges the dominant reading of this case as a feminist victory. Becki Ross critically examines the expert testimony she delivered in defence of *Bad Attitude*, an American lesbian sex magazine seized by police from Glad Day Bookshop in Toronto in 1992. She details the difficulties she encountered in explicating and contextualizing the specificities, nuances, and complexities of lesbian s/m fantasy in a court of law. In the final chapter, Shannon Bell advances a conception of pornography that is not distinguishable from philosophy, using philosophy to make pornography.

Bad Attitude/s on Trial provides a new debate on pornography and feminism. It will be of particular interest to students of both women's and gay and lesbian issues, but will also be relevant for scholars of law, political science, and philosophy, as well as for anyone interested in a different, provocative view of the *Butler* decision.

BRENDA COSSMAN is Associate Professor, Osgoode Hall Law School, York University.

SHANNON BELL is Assistant Professor, Department of Political Science, York University.

LISE GOTELL is Assistant Professor, Department of Political Scienc Atkinson College, York University.

BECKI L. ROSS is Assistant Professor, Sociology and Women's Stuc University of British Columbia.

BRENDA COSSMAN
SHANNON BELL
LISE GOTELL
BECKI L. ROSS

Bad Attitude/s on Trial: Pornography, Feminism, and the *Butler* Decision

UNIVERSITY OF TORONTO PRESS
Toronto Buffalo London

© University of Toronto Press Incorporated 1997
Toronto Buffalo London
Printed in Canada

ISBN 0-8020-0687-6 (cloth)
ISBN 0-8020-7643-2 (paper)

Printed on acid-free paper

Canadian Cataloguing in Publication Data

Main entry under title:

Bad attitude/s on trial

Includes bibliographical references.
ISBN 0-8020-0687-6 (bound)   ISBN 0-8020-7643-2 (pbk.)

1. Pornography – Political aspects – Canada.
2. Pornography – Social aspects – Canada.   3. Obscenity
(Law) – Canada.   4. Feminism – Canada.   5. Butler,
Donald Victor – Trials, litigation, etc.   I. Cossman,
Brenda.

HQ472.C3B32 1996   363.4'7'0971   C96-931344-6

Chapter 5, 'On ne peut pas voir l'image,' is a development of 'Pictures Don't
Lie. Pictures Tell It All,' *Journal of the History of Sexuality* 6, no. 2 (October
1995): 284–321. © 1995 by The University of Chicago Press. All rights
reserved. Published with permission from the University of Chicago.

The last picture in chapter 5 ('The image cannot be seen') is by Scott McLeod
(reproduced by permission). All other photos are by Jennifer Gillmor
(reproduced by permission).

University of Toronto Press acknowledges the financial assistance to its
publishing program of the Canada Council and the Ontario Arts Council.

Contents

Acknowledgments

Brenda Cossman

Special thanks to Sandra Haar and Ellen Flanders, for inspiring me to take this project on and for sharing their energy and engagement around issues of pornography and censorship; to Bruce Ryder for the daily gift of collegiality and for his generosity of support, research, and intellectual engagement, which seems infinite; to Max Allen for bringing unreported cases to my attention that I would have otherwise missed, and allowing me to borrow from his tireless research in this area; to Aviva Rubin for her unwavering support when many others wondered what I was up to, and her endless enthusiasm for critical debate on these and other issues; to Ratna Kapur, for always believing in my work, and somehow always ending up at the same place as I do. And, finally, to Shannon, Lise, and Becki, for the challenge of intellectual collaboration, and whose influence on my work is unquantifiable.

Lise Gotell

The final stages of this project coincided with my first year of full-time teaching, the late stages of my pregnancy and, finally, the long-awaited birth of my son Liam. I am first of all extremely grateful to my co-authors, most especially Brenda and Shannon, for their work in pulling this book together when my life was consumed by breastfeeding and infant care. Brenda, Shannon, Becki, and I had met for many months discussing the complexities of the post-*Butler* political and social landscape, and it was through these wonderfully engaging discussions that my own contribution to this book took shape.

I am also extremely appreciative of those on the 'front line' of current struggles for sexual democracy – sex-trade workers, artists, bookstore workers, and many others.

As an academic, I have been inspired by the work and commitment of Thelma McCormack, a true mother of the sexual revolution, whose writings have promoted toleration and disdain for sexual repression.

I am indebted to my friends and family, most especially my partner Janine Brodie, our son Brodie Nutbrown, and my friend Chris Gabriel. Their love and support made it possible for me to complete my work on this book. Finally, I am forever grateful to my son Liam, who came into my life in the middle of this project and whose presence is a constant reminder of all that is important. It is my hope that he will grow up into a society that is more tolerant and democratic than our own.

Becki L. Ross

For valuable discussions I want to thank my co-contributors, Brenda Cossman, Shannon Bell, and Lise Gotell, as well as Ingrid Stitt, Gary Kinsman, Max Allen, Clare Barclay, Elaine Carroll, Jennifer Gillmor, Midi Onodera, Shonagh Adelman, Margaret Christakos, Liz Czak, Ellen Flanders, Dany Lacombe, and anonymous reviewers for the University of Toronto Press. For many years, I have been mentored by 'the big girls': Chris Bearchell, Varda Burstyn, Pat Califia, Lisa Duggan, Nan Hunter, Thelma McCormack, Joan Nestle, Gayle Rubin, and Carole Vance. To each, my deep and loving gratitude. David Jardine, Leslie Roman, Stuart Blackley, Tim Timberg, and Susan Boyd all read and commented on the manuscript. I am grateful for their generous assistance. And the Ontario Arts Council provided some timely financial support during the early stages of this research.

Shannon Bell

My gratitude and love to all those with whom I worked on sex: my co-authors Brenda Cossman, Lise Gotell, and Becki Ross, my consort Gad Horowitz, friend and long-time collaborator Kath Daymond, and photographers Jennifer Gillmor and Scott McLeod.

Special gratitude to Buddies in Bad Times Theatre – the largest Queer Theatre in North America – for providing me with a political, social, sexual, performative, deviant home from which to do pornosophy; specifically thank you to Sky Gilbert, Gwen Bartleman, Tim Jones, Tori

Smith, Ed Jackson, Brian Hui, Monyan King, Kirsten Johnson, and Sonja Mills. My appreciation to Sue Golding for her democratic excess and to Arthur and Marilouise Kroker for exceeding theory.

The four of us would like to thank our research assistant Eliza Erskine without whom we would never have completed the manuscript, Jill Grant at Osgoode Law School, and John St James, whose copy-editing skills are truly impressive. Especially, we thank Virgil Duff, University of Toronto Press executive editor, for his enthusiasm, support of the project, conversations, and sense of the important.

BAD ATTITUDE/S ON TRIAL

1

Introduction

BRENDA COSSMAN, SHANNON BELL

Bad Attitude/s on Trial is a critical analysis of pornography in the context of contemporary Canada. We examine conflicts around pornography within Canadian feminism, the growing public and legal influence of anti-pornography feminism, as well as the current climate of intensified state censorship. The regulation and censorship of sexual materials has intensified since the mid-1980s, as have campaigns by anti-pornography feminists. During the last decade, anti-pornography feminism has enjoyed remarkable success in the courts, in the legislatures, and in the realm of public opinion. Previously, debates about public representations of sexuality were polarized between civil-libertarian advocates of free expression and moral conservatives. But increasingly, a 'new' public discourse which constructs pornography as an expression and an ideology of sexual violence has become the constraining norm of the pornography debate. The notion that pornography both reflects sexual domination and 'victimizes' women has recently found expression in law in the landmark Canadian Supreme Court decision of *R. v. Butler* (1992). In February 1992, the Supreme Court of Canada ruled on the case of Donald Butler, the owner of a Manitoba video store selling 'hard core' videotapes, magazines, and sexual paraphernalia. Butler had been convicted by a lower court and charged with various counts of selling obscene material, possessing obscene material for the purpose of distribution or sale, and exposing obscene material to the public view. The Supreme Court granted Butler's appeal of the convictions and ordered the case returned to the lower court for retrial.

R. v. Butler was the first constitutional challenge to the obscenity law, s.163, of Canada's Criminal Code. The Supreme Court of Canada considered whether s.163 violated the freedom of expression guarantee in s.2(b) of the 1982 Canadian Charter of Rights and Freedoms. The Court found that although s.163 does violate the Charter, this violation is 'justified under s. 1 of the Charter' (*R. v. Butler* 1992, 452) as a 'reasonable limit prescribed by law' (Canadian Charter of Rights and Freedoms 1982, section 1).[1] The *reasonable limit prescribed by law* is informed by the equality rights guarantees in s.15 and s.28 of the Charter.[2]

In its ruling the Supreme Court not only upheld the constitutionality of the obscenity laws but also set out a new test for determining whether representations are obscene. According to the new test established by the Supreme Court, sexually explicit representations that do not include violence, are not degrading nor dehumanizing, and do not involve children should not generally be found to be obscene. This test is seen by many to signal the beginning of a new era of liberalization in the regulation of sexual representations, according to which sexual explicitness is no longer condemned in and of itself. At the same time, however, the net of criminal regulation over some sexual images has been tightened in the wake of the *Butler* decision. Six weeks after the landmark decision, the Toronto Police brought criminal charges against Glad Day Bookshop, a gay and lesbian bookstore, for selling *Bad Attitude*, an American 'lesbian erotic fiction magazine.' At trial, *Bad Attitude* was found to be obscene, and Glad Day was found guilty under s.163 of the Canadian Criminal Code (C.C.C.). The lesbian s/m representations in the magazine were, in the Court's words, found to 'flash every light and blow every whistle of obscenity.'

The *Bad Attitude* case is illustrative of the new trend in the censorship of sexual representations in the post-*Butler* era. Straight, mainstream pornography appears to be flourishing. But any representations that hint at alternative sexualities continue to be subject to intense scrutiny. Sexual representations that challenge conventional notions of sexuality – gay and lesbian sexuality, s/m sexuality, youth sexuality – are now the focus of the censor's scorn. What is on trial are so-called 'Bad Attitudes': the attitudes of sexual others. In stark contrast to the claims of liberalization, Canadians continue to live in the midst of a broad web of censorship of sexual images. The following are but a few examples of the breadth of post-*Butler* censorship:

• Books, magazines, and videotapes are routinely censored at Canada's borders. The Tariff Code instructs Canada Customs officials to prohibit the importation of 'obscene' materials. Gay and lesbian materials en route to Canada are a frequent target of Canada Customs. Among those books and magazines detained or seized in recent years: *Querelle* by Jean Genet, *The Man Sitting in the Corridor* by Margaret Duras, a Noel Coward biography, and a children's book about body image entitled *Belinda's Bouquet*. The mainstream gay magazine the *Advocate* has been seized, as have a multiplicity of gay and lesbian sex magazines. The U.S. comic *Hothead Paisan: Homicidal Lesbian Terrorist* was seized en route to the Toronto Women's Bookstore. The issue in question contained stories about a cat yoga class, a confrontation with evangelical pro-lifers, and Hothead Paisan masquerading as a straight 'spritzhead.' There is no sex depicted in the issue. According to a communications officer with Canada's Prohibited Importations Directorate: 'It was marked "sexual degradation" but it was even worse than that. It had mutilation and hatred toward men and others' (*X-tra!* December 1992). Even Betty Page trading cards have been detained – Betty Page, the 1950s pin-up model who ruled that decade and returned as icon.[3]

- Metro Toronto Council's cultural funding to lesbian and gay artists has been either threatened or revoked altogether. The Inside/Out Collective, which hosts an annual gay and lesbian film festival, had its funding withdrawn. Buddies in Bad Times Theatre, the largest gay and lesbian theatre in North America, continues to be the focus of political controversy, as Metro Council members, spurred on by Christina Blizzard of the *Toronto Sun*, attack the legitimacy of funding its 'immoral' activities.
- Under the new child-pornography law, Toronto artist Eli Langer and the Mercer Union Gallery were charged with obscenity. After considerable public outcry, the Attorney-General decided to drop the charges against the artist and the gallery, but continued to prosecute Langer's paintings and drawings. If they had been found obscene, the paintings and drawings would have been destroyed.
- Matthew McGowan, a street hustler from Toronto, was charged with making obscene material for two sexually explicit safe-sex videos he made with two young male friends.
- The new child-pornography law has unleashed a police witchhunt for gay men who have sex – often paid – with teenage males. In London, Ontario, where local police have discovered a local 'kiddie porn ring,' in a sixteen-month period, from August 1993 to June 1995, the London police have laid more than four hundred criminal charges against fifty-two men. Only forty are for 'sexual interference' (s.151 C.C.C.), which involves sexual actions with boys under fourteen. (Couture

1995, 16–17). There was only one charge of making 'child' pornography (s.163.1 C.C.C.). Almost half of the criminal arrests have been brought against gay men paying for sex with males under eighteen (s.212(4) C.C.C.). Similar arrests have been made in Vancouver, where once again the police claimed to have uncovered the largest child-pornography ring in Canada. And once again, the target has been gay men who have sex for money with teenage male prostitutes. Virtually no charges have been brought against men who have sex with underage girls.[4]

- In Alberta (1992), Vancouver lesbian visual artists Kiss & Tell's show 'True Inversions' was used to threaten art funding. The show's explicit lesbian sexual imagery and like-minded art was attacked as offending community standards of acceptance. In their book *Her Tongue on My Theory*, the Kiss & Tell collective of Persimmon Blackbridge, Lizard Jones, and Susan Stewart recount the Alberta media/state reaction to their work:

Even though we sorely missed the strong lesbian presence, one straight reviewer in the audience saw many lesbians there. Rick Bell, writing for the *Alberta Report*, talks about an audience full of cheering crewcut lesbians. Where were they all? ... Later ... that review (which contained many more serious inaccuracies than the number of lesbians he saw) ended upon the desk of the Deputy Premier of Alberta. He called a press conference where he referred to 'True Inversions' as 'this abhorrent lesbian show' and asked his fellow cabinet ministers to help put an end to homosexual shows at government-funded institutions ... we became the justification for attacking the Banff Centre's funding ... the review was used as the basis to threaten arm's length funding for Alberta arts groups. (Kiss & Tell 1994, 61)

- Reform Party MPs have recently attacked the National Film Board for spending '$6 million on videos promoting a homosexual and lesbian lifestyle' and for its collection of 'lesbian x-rated films' (Myron Thompson, Reform MP, in a statement entitled 'Too Much for So Little'). The MP's main target was the lesbian film *Forbidden Love*, along with the NFB's collection of ten gay-positive videos, including *Out: Stories of Lesbian and Gay Youth*, and *The Company of Strangers*. Along with Reformer Gerry Breitkreuz, Thompson protested the use of government funds to produce a Canadian AIDS Society safe-sex pamphlet.
- In March 1994, the CRTC warned a Halifax student radio station that

it must stop broadcasting 'sexually explicit' materials, after complaints were brought about the gay and lesbian issues being covered.

- Equally disturbing is the censorship that occurs at another, more subtle, and considerably less public level. Printers, libraries, and school boards routinely make decisions about the availability and circulation of controversial words and pictures. In October 1994, the Hamilton police called a September issue of X-tra! pornographic. Ironically, this claim was in reference to a representation of the art installation *On ne peut pas voir l'image*, which was a collective protest action against the new 'child' pornography law, section 163.1 of the Criminal Code. The representation (words and photograph) can be found in chapter 5, 'On ne peut pas voir l'image,' of this book. Although no charges were laid, the Hamilton Library refused to distribute the issue, and the Library Board subsequently debated whether X-tra! should be banned from the public library altogether. X-tra! West has been banned from libraries in British Columbia's Fraser Valley.

This censorship did not begin with the *Butler* decision. Canada has had a long and illustrious history of regulating and repressing sexual images. But the *Butler* decision has lent legitimacy to this censorial climate. It has given new momentum to the censorship of counter-discursive sexual materials, and has been mobilized to suppress, in particular, gay and lesbian materials. The authoritative pronouncements of the Supreme Court of Canada have given unprecedented credence to the views of anti-pornography feminism and contributed to the further marginalization of those voices who challenge the censorship of sexual representations.

The feminist intervention in the *Butler* decision, and its repressive legal aftermath, has crystallized a divisive and highly complex debate among Canadian feminists on sexuality and sexual representation. It is, however, a debate that has been largely obscured in the media and in legal circles, where *Butler* has been presented as an unequivocal feminist victory. While the pornography question has divided Western feminism like few other issues, this plurality of feminist views on pornography has often been ignored in popular and academic analysis. Most often, an anti-pornography and pro-censorship stance is presented as the singular and universal feminist voice – as 'the' feminist perspective on pornography. A central objective of *Bad Attitude/s on Trial* is to challenge this interpretation. Specifically, this study examines competing feminist claims on pornography to illuminate their assumptions about the nature of sexuality, the forms of its representation, and its place in our lives. Taking a position in opposition to the central contentions of anti-pornography feminism, we argue that consensus on the meanings of pornography is unlikely, if not fantastical: any one sexual image provides dissonant interpretations of disgust, indifference, and arousal. We argue in favour of the decriminalization of obscenity from a range of standpoints intended to problematize the regime of (hetero)sexual rule and the complicity of feminist constituencies in the discourse of moral conservatives. The repressive legal aftermath of *Butler* is analysed to illustrate the perils of feminist support for state censorship. The irreverent strategies of postmodern sex radicals are deployed to foreground vexing, contingent, and sometimes contradictory questions of sexual pleasure, agency, and feminist politics.

In the second chapter, Lise Gotell examines the intervention of the Women's Legal Education Action Fund (LEAF) in the *Butler* decision. LEAF – a Canadian feminist litigation organization – was granted intervenor status in the *Butler* case, where it adopted an anti-pornography position and argued in favour of upholding the obscenity provisions from constitutional challenge. The chapter critically examines the position and arguments adopted by LEAF. It will trace the origins of this position and explore its underlying assumptions. In constructing pornography as the unmediated embodiment of gender domination, antipornography feminist discourse can be seen as an example of feminist foundationalism. Gotell illustrates how LEAF's position in *Butler* is founded on an assertion of certainty, on the claim to speak 'Truth,' and on a rejection of interpretive schemes that admit the complexity and ambiguity of sexual images. By contrasting LEAF's position with arguments advanced by the other parties and intervenors in *Butler*, the chapter provides an overview of socio-legal debates on pornography and censorship. Further, this chapter contextualizes anti-pornography feminism within an extremely complex debate among feminists about sexual representation. The purpose is to set the Supreme Court's historic *Butler* decision in a social and political context.

In the third chapter, Brenda Cossman examines the *Butler* decision itself, and challenges the dominant feminist reading of this case as a feminist victory. Through a detailed analysis of the text of the decision, this chapter provides a very different reading of the test for obscenity established by the Supreme Court of Canada in *Butler*. Contrary to the claims of anti-pornography feminists, and of the Supreme Court, that the law of obscenity is no longer about the prevention of 'dirt for dirt's sake,' Cossman argues that the test for obscenity established in *Butler* remains very much informed by the same conservative sexual morality in which obscenity has traditionally been framed. The sexual subtext of the decision is one in which sex, sexuality, and sexual representation are seen as bad, physical, subhuman, and devoid of artistic or higher intellectual content. In revealing this sexual subtext, this chapter argues that the decision foreshadowed the repressive legal aftermath of the *Butler* decision, in which gay and lesbian sexual representations have been targeted. It reviews several of these cases, including those against Glad Day Bookshop – a gay and lesbian bookstore in Toronto – and demonstrates the extent to which these decisions are informed by the same underlying conservative sexual morality.

In the fourth chapter, Becki Ross examines the efflorescence of Canadian sex-related work produced by lesbians in the 1980s and 1990s, with a particular focus on lesbian sexual representation in the repressive legal aftermath of *Butler* – an era characterized by multiple levels of state, social, and self censorship. It highlights the criminal prosecution of Glad Day Bookshop for selling *Bad Attitude*, an American 'lesbian erotic fiction magazine.' Drawing on court transcripts, this chapter analyses witness testimony, as well as the mainstream media's (non)coverage of the case. Throughout the chapter, links between the moral regulatory discourse devised by turn-of-the-century, first-wave feminists and their second-wave counterparts are revealed. Emerging from this critique, this chapter outlines a feminist anti-censorship 'politics of outrage' as a tool to garner political support for the decriminalization of queer representation.

In the fifth chapter, in keeping with the theme of sexuality as a terrain of struggle and a site of feminist politics of outrage, Shannon Bell advances a conception of pornography that is not distinguishable from philosophy: at the heart of pornography are competing morals, ethics, and value judgments. Bell (ab)uses philosophy to make pornography. She contends that multiple meanings reside in the same image, therefore the image can never be seen; it is and is not. Playing with these meanings can challenge established sexual morality and practice. Building on the theme of the opposition of art/sex, this concluding chapter deploys and deconstructs sexual images to destabilize the distinction between the realms of high theory/culture (philosophy) and low theory/culture (pornography). Bell focuses particular attention on the new child-pornography law and its deployal against gay youth.

We begin with a brief review of the history of obscenity law.[5] We pay particular attention to the role of the courts in articulating and re-articulating the meaning of obscenity. From *Hicklin* (1868) to *Brodie* (1962) to *Butler* (1992), the courts have time and again returned to the test for obscenity, and attempted to provide ever more precise defini-tions to this elusive concept. We argue that this history has been and continues to be a history of moral regulation. State censorship of sexual representations has always operated to establish and reinforce sexual morality. It has drawn lines between legitimate/normal sexuality and illegitimate/abnormal sexuality. Along with a range of other criminal prohibitions on contraception, prostitution, homosexuality, and other forms of 'sexual immorality,' obscenity law has played a central role in moral regulation (Valverde and Weir 1988). Contrary to the claims of anti-pornography feminists, we do not believe that the *Butler* decision represents a radical departure from this history of moral regulation. As we argue throughout *Bad Attitude/s on Trial*, obscenity law in the after-math of *Butler* has as much to do with moral regulation of sexual immo-rality as it did over the last hundred years. While the specific content of sexual immorality may have changed, the object of the law has not.

History of the Legal Regulation of Obscenity

The roots of contemporary obscenity law in Canada lie in nineteenth-century England. Although sexually explicit material was censored well before this period, such material was primarily associated with blas-phemy and sedition. As historians of the emergence of pornography have illustrated, from the sixteenth to eighteenth century, 'pornography was closely linked with political and religious subversion' (Hunt 1990, 35). In the nineteenth century, the discourses within which obscenity was framed and regulated were transformed. Pornography came to be associated specifically with sex, and it was this association with sex that made pornography an evil to be regulated. Sex itself was identified as a dangerous force, and sexual publications as morally corrosive. The regu-lation of pornography in the nineteenth century corresponded with an increase in the production of pornographic materials, as well as a broad-ening of the circulation of these materials through the revolution in printing (Kendrick 1987). It was largely the availability of these materi-als to the masses that caused widespread alarm of the social harm that obscenity could cause.

The common law first recognized the crime of obscene libel in the eighteenth century in the case of *R. v. Curl* (1727). This crime of obscene libel was intended to prohibit conduct that 'tends to corrupt the morals of the King's subjects.' It was only in the late eighteenth century and the early nineteenth century that public attention came to be focused on obscenity, with the emergence of a moral reform movement. The Society for the Suppression of Vice, founded by William Wilberforce in 1802, took upon itself the responsibility for initiating prosecutions against those who published and sold obscene materials. The Society was concerned with the dangerous effect of these materials, particularly on the working classes, who would be led into a downward cycle of immorality through the 'poisonous' influence of obscenity (McLaren 1991, 113).

Efforts to legislate obscenity in England were made in a series of acts in the first half of the nineteenth century: the *Vagrancy Act* of 1824 prohibiting the exposition of obscene books or prints in public places, the *Customs Consolidation Act* of 1853, prohibiting the importation of 'indecent or obscene prints,' and the *Obscene Publications Act* of 1857, which extended the powers of police and magistrates in relation to the common-law offence of obscenity. The *Obscene Publications Act*, introduced by Lord Campbell, and considered the first obscenity legislation, extended the jurisdiction of magistrates and police in relation to warrants for entering premises and seizing materials.[6]

Lord Campbell's bill was not without strenuous opposition. Among its many critics were Lord Lyndhurst, whose comments were perhaps prophetic: 'My noble and learned Friend is to put down the sale of obscene books and prints; but what is the interpretation which is to be put upon the word "obscene"? I can easily conceive that two men will come to entirely different conclusions as to its meaning' (as cited in Kendrick 1987, 116). Lyndhurst raised concerns that the works of great artists such as Correggio, or the poetry of Wycherely and Dryden, could fall within the scope of Lord Campbell's Act.[7] Lord Campbell joined issue with his critics by insisting that 'he had no intention whatever to make Horace, Juvenal, Voltaire or Lord Byron, seizable' (as cited in Kendrick 1987, 117). Rather, he insisted that his bill 'was intended to apply exclusively to works written for the single purpose of corrupting the morals of youth, and of a nature calculated to shock the common feelings of decency in any well-regulated mind' (as quoted in ibid., 1987, 117).

The *Obscene Publications Act* did not contain a definition of obscenity. It was only eleven years after its enactment that the courts provided a definition of obscenity, in the case of *R. v. Hicklin* (1868). The case involved the prosecution of an anti-Catholic tract produced by a militant Protestant group, entitled *The Confessional Unmasked: Shewing the Depravity of the Romaish Priesthood, the Iniquity of the Confessional and the Questions Put to Females in Confession*. Lord Cockburn set out the test for obscenity that was to become the benchmark of obscenity legislation not only in England, but in Canada and the United States as well: 'I think the test of obscenity is this, whether the tendency of the matter charged as obscenity is to deprave and corrupt those whose minds are open to such immoral influences, and into whose hands a publication of this sort may fall' (*Hicklin* 1868, 371). With regard to *The Confessional Unmasked*, Lord Cockburn held: 'This work ... is sold at the corners of streets, and in all directions, and of course it falls into the hands of persons of all classes, young and old, and the minds of those hitherto pure are exposed to the danger of contamination and pollution from the impurity it contains' (*Hicklin* 1868, 372).

Underlying the *Hicklin* test was the nineteenth-century concern with obscene materials: that these materials might fall into the hands of those persons who were particularly vulnerable to its bad influences – namely, the young, the female (often one and the same), and the uneducated, the working-class male. It was not the possession of obscene materials by the educated upper classes that was of concern, but the possibility of the circulation of these materials among those who were morally vulnerable to its poisonous influences. The *Hicklin* test was intended to protect the morals of the lower classes and other vulnerable groups, and thereby promote a public morality that was based on the Victorian discourse of sexuality as a dangerous force to be controlled and repressed.

The *Obscene Publications Act*, and its subsequent interpretation in *Hicklin* must be seen within the context of class and gender relations of nineteenth-century England. Obscenity was only a 'social problem' in so far as it might fall into the hands of women, children, and working-class men, who were seen as irrational by nature and unable to resist the corrosive influences of sexual materials. The gendered moral discourse was part of a more general Victorian discourse on women's sexuality. Criminal regulation of obscenity coincided not only with the extension of laws against prostitution (Shaver 1994), but also with the emergence of the cult of domesticity and the reconstitution of the family (McLaren 1991). Women's sexuality was to be contained within the boundaries of marriage and the family. And the family had to be protected from moral corruption that might permeate it from dangerous external forces.

In Canada, the vagrancy laws represented the only effort to regulate obscenity during most of the nineteenth century. These laws, modelled on the English vagrancy legislation of 1824, provided that 'every Person willfully exposing to view in any Street, Road, Highway or public Place, any obscene Print, Picture or other indecent Exhibition' was to be considered 'a rogue or vagabond' and thereby subject to imprisonment for up to three months. (*Act for the Punishment of idle and disorderly persons and Rogues and Vagabonds, in that part of Great Britain called England*, 1824 (U.K.), Geo. 4, c.83, s.4, as cited in McLaren 1991, 118). After Confederation these vagrancy laws were consolidated; and the *Postal Service Act* (1875) and the *Customs Act* (1879) included provisions prohibiting the use of the mails for the transmission and importation of obscene materials into Canada. It was only in 1892 that Parliament first introduced criminal legislation on obscenity. Section 179 of the *Criminal Code* of 1892 prohibited the public sale or exposure of any obscene book or printed matter.[8]

The law did not provide a definition of 'obscene,' 'disgusting,' or indecent, but rather, like the English legislation, left such definitions to the courts. And the courts obliged by following the *Hicklin* definition. Obscenity law in Canada thereby came to be framed within the same discourse of a conservative sexual morality that presided in England, addressing the protection of public morality through the prohibition of sexual imagery. Until 1949, the *Hicklin* test defined obscenity as that which would 'deprave and corrupt the minds of those whose minds are open to such immoral influences' (*Hicklin* 1868, 371). Sexual representations, in virtually any form, were considered to be immoral.

John McLaren has noted that the similar references to obscenity as a form of moral poison appeared in Canadian case law, underscoring the extent to which the same understanding of the deleterious effects of obscenity was incorporated into our law through the application of the *Hicklin* test. There were, however, during this time, very few prosecutions of obscene materials in Canada. According to McLaren, the absence of a seizure provision similar to that contained in the English *Obscene Publications Act* may help account for what he refers to as the 'unexceptional nature of the reported cases on obscenity in Canada until relatively recent times' (1991, 124). 'Unlike the infamous literary trials in England of the late 19th and early 20th century, their Canadian counterparts are singularly unexciting. Prosecutions were taken against an obscene song performed with indecent gestures in Quebec, the sale of a medicine for stimulating menstrual flow by a Toronto proprietary medicine manufacturer, a series of religious rantings in a pamphlet penned in Windsor, Ontario, a pedlar of obscene books, pictures and photographs up from Buffalo, a New Brunswick satirical newspaper entitled "Free Speech," a movie of a prize fight in Montreal, a religious bulletin put out by a Toronto minister to expose the "obscene" shows put on at a Toronto theatre and a private letter in Saskatchewan' (ibid.). While the cases may have been unexceptional, the Canadian courts closely followed the lead of the English courts in adopting the *Hicklin* test as the definition of obscenity.

As McLaren has further observed, the reported cases of this period do not provide the full picture of efforts to suppress obscenity (ibid., 126). The social-purity movement, from the end of the nineteeth century to the 1920s, included 'the suppression of obscene literature' among its various campaigns to 'raise the moral tone of Canadian society' (Valverde 1991, 17). Between 1892 and 1920, the social-purity movement was strong, and was able to exert considerable pressure on local authorities to take action against those dealing in 'obscene material,' even that contained in serious literature (McLaren 1991, 126). The suppression of obscene literature was part of the more general agenda of policing sexual morality and controlling excessive sexuality. 'The specific sexual activities targeted for control changed over the years: in the mid-nineteenth century, masturbation, especially among boys, was the most talked about vice, ... at the turn of the century prostitution [took] the spotlight, ... replaced in the 1920s by fears about non-commoditized consensual sexual encounters among young people' (Valverde 1991, 29). The social-purity movement was the key actor in shaping national morality over a forty-year period. And much like the societies for the suppression of vice in nineteenth-century England, the social-purity movement had a paternalistic concern for the 'lower class,' which was deemed by the more middle-class 'church people, educators, doctors and community workers' (ibid., 17) to be ripe for moral degeneracy. For middle and lower classes alike, there was an emphasis on domestic virtues – the virtues of home, family, and parenthood – to counter the vices of 'prostitution, divorce, illegitimacy,' and 'obscene literature' (ibid.).

After 1920, with the fading influence of the social-purity movement, there was a waning interest in banning obscene publications, and there were no reported obscenity cases until the 1940s (McLaren 1991, 129). In the late 1940s, a public concern began to emerge as a result of the increasing availability of 'objectionable literature' at news-stands in Canada. Pulp novels and 'girlie magazines' became widely available, at very low costs. In 1952, a Senate Committee on Salacious and Indecent

Literature was established, which held public hearings throughout 1952–3. Although no clear consensus was reached as to the appropriate solution, the committee provided a forum for the discussion of this problem of 'salacious and indecent literature' – voicing concerns, again, that the material could fall into the hands of young persons, who would be vulnerable to its poisonous and corrosive influences.

The committee hearings represented the beginning of a campaign to toughen up Canada's obscenity legislation, spearheaded by D.E. Fulton, who at the time of the hearings was a member of the Opposition, and who later became the minister of justice under the subsequent Conservative government. In 1958, Fulton introduced Bill C-58, which provided a new definition of obscenity. In the words of the minister of justice, 'The object of this clause is to make a statutory extension of the definition of obscenity so as to make it perfectly clear that the law of obscenity does apply to a certain type of objectionable material that now appears on the newsstands of Canada and is being sold to young people of our country with impugnity' (as quoted in Charles 1966, 253). In Fulton's view, this definition would capture 'the kind of muck on the newsstands against which our efforts in this definition are directed' and would 'exclude books otherwise meritorious but containing the occasional passage, which if torn from the context might be considered objectionable' (ibid., 254).

The campaign to toughen up Canada's obscenity laws in the 1950s bore more than a passing similarity to the campaigns in the nineteenth century. The proponents of the law were concerned with the spread of cheap and widely accessible 'pulp' books and magazines, which could easily fall into the hands of young persons. As in the nineteenth century, it was the mass distribution of inexpensive materials that were easily accessible to a broad range of readers that created concern. Further, as in the nineteenth century, it was the potential for moral corruption of vulnerable groups – most specifically, young persons – that was the major cause for concern. Finally, the 1950s witnessed a return of gendered moral discourses circulating around the purity signifiers of wife, mother, and family. In the postwar period, the family was rearticulated as the most basic and sacred of social units, and familial ideology was firmly reinscribed. As in the earlier purity movement the family was shored up against all that was outside it, all that condoned and portrayed sex outside its borders – pornography, prostitution, and homosexuality.

The new 1959 legislation, section 150(8) of the Criminal Code, defined obscenity as follows: 'For the purposes of the Act, any publication a *dominant characteristic* of which is the *undue exploitation of sex*, or of sex and any one or more of the following subjects, namely, crime, horror, cruelty and violence shall be deemed to be obscene' (emphasis added). Under this definition, which remains unchanged in the current s.163(8) of the Code, the legal question came to focus on the interpretation of 'dominant characteristic' and 'undue exploitation of sex.' The first judicial interpretation of this new definition of obscenity came in 1962, with the criminal prosecution of D.H. Lawrence's novel *Lady Chatterley's Lover*, in *R. v. Brodie* (1962). Judson J., writing for the majority of the Supreme Court of Canada, held that the test for obscenity enacted in 1959 was exclusive of all other tests, and that the *Hicklin* test was no longer to be applied (*Brodie* 1962, 701). Judson J. held that the sole test for obscenity was whether a dominant characteristic of the material in question is the undue exploitation of sex. In order to make such a determination, the book must be read as a whole. The undue exploitation must be a dominant characteristic of the whole work and not merely a dominant characteristic of particular parts or aspects of the work taken in isolation or out of context (ibid., 702). Judson J. held that the search for a dominant characteristic of the work must also consider the purpose of the author: 'Had he a serious literary purpose or was his purpose one of base exploitation?' (ibid.). In Judson J's view, a dominant characteristic of the book could not be determined 'without an examination of its literary or artistic merit' (ibid.).

On the question of whether the exploitation of sex was undue, Judson J. held: 'I do not think that there is undue exploitation if there is no more emphasis on the theme than is required in the serious treatment of a novel with honesty and uprightness' (ibid., 704). Judson J. was of the view that it was beyond question that *Lady Chatterley's Lover* was such a serious work. 'It has none of the characteristics that are often described in judgments dealing with obscenity – dirt for dirt's sake, the leer of the sensualist, depravity in the mind of an author with an obsession for dirt, pornography, an appeal to the prurient interest, etc. The section recognizes that the serious-minded author must have freedom in the production of a work of genuine artistic and literary merit and the quality of the work, as the witnesses point out and common sense indicates, must have real relevance in determining not only a dominant characteristic but also whether there is undue exploitation' (ibid., 704–5). Judson J. further held that prevailing community standards are relevant in determining whether the publication in question constitutes an undue exploitation of sex, and adopted the test set out by a New Zealand court in *R. v. Close*, which held: 'There does exist in any community at all times – a general instinctive sense of what is decent and what is indecent, of what is clean and what is dirty' (as cited in *Brodie* 1962, 705). On the facts, the Court concluded that *Lady Chatterley's Lover* was of serious literary merit, and did not offend prevailing community-standards.

The community-standards test, which came to dominate as the test for obscenity, was further developed in *R. v. Dominion News and Gifts* (1964). The Supreme Court of Canada fully adopted the reasons for the dissenting opinion of Freeman J. of the Manitoba Court of Appeal. Freeman J. was of the view that community standards fall somewhere in between 'those of lowest taste' and 'those with rigid, austere, conservative, or puritan taste.' Community standards should be 'something approaching a general average of community thinking and feeling' (*Dominion News* 1963, 116). They should also be 'contemporary' and 'local' – that is – 'Canadian' (ibid., 117).

While the 1959 law and the community-standards test developed by the courts in *Brodie* (1962) and *Dominion News* (1964) were intended to establish an objective standard for obscenity, the results were less than successful. The idea of a national community standard was illusory. Since the courts decided that neither empirical proof nor expert evidence was required to establish this community standard, the determination came to be made according to the judiciary's 'general instinctive sense' of the sexual morality of Canadians (Busby 1994, 167). Far from establishing an objective standard, the 1959 obscenity law, as interpreted and applied by the courts, came to represent little more than an exercise in judicial discretion and subjectivity, which produced inconsistent and unpredictable results (Campbell and Pal 1989, 118–19).

The 1960s witnessed a rethinking of the role of the state in moral regulation, and a liberalization of criminal and other laws that had sought to uphold standards of sexual propriety. Divorce laws and criminal prohibitions on contraception, abortion, and homosexuality were all reformed. While civil libertarians called for a similar liberalization of the obscenity laws, no such reform was introduced in Canada. However, the terms of debate began to shift during this period. Civil libertarians drew upon the 1954 *Wolfenden Report* in England, which held that there exists 'a realm of private morality and immorality which is ... not the law's business' (*Wolfenden Report* 1964, s.61, cited in Kinsman 1987, 139). According to the *Wolfenden Report*, this realm of private morality should be beyond legal intervention (Kinsman 1987, 139).

The distinction between private and public morality set the discursive framework for the pornography debates in the 1960s between the religious (moral) conservatives and the civil libertarians.[9] The religious conservatives portrayed pornography as a sin because it promoted sexual pleasure and the satisfaction of desire without any procreative purpose; and they held that pornography was an offence to decency and public morality. The civil libertarians argued that obscenity legislation should be repealed on the grounds that interest in sex is normal, healthy, and good; they contended 'that not all material that is offensive to public morality need ... be harmful.' (Lacombe 1994, 24).[10] Drawing on John Stuart Mill's essay On Liberty, the libertarians argued that 'the only purpose for which power can rightfully be exercised over any member of a civilized community against his will is to prevent harm to others' (cited in Lacombe 1994, 24). The right to free speech could be restricted only if this speech causes harm to others.

The terms of the debate shifted again in the 1970s with the emergence of the feminist anti-pornography movement. In this period, some Canadian feminists began to draw attention to violent and degrading images of women in pornography, and to make connections between violent and degrading representations and the systemic subordination of women. Some North American anti-pornography feminists argued that pornography was a factor in sexual violence, based on the contention that pornography eroticizes the real violence that men perpetrate on women; others contended that pornography was the very cause of women's oppression. The key theorists and spokeswomen included Catharine MacKinnon, Andrea Dworkin, Susan Brownmiller, and later Susan Cole in the Canadian context. The feminist anti-pornography theorists put forth a comprehensive and totalizing theory: acts of sexual violence against women are instrumental in maintaining the patriarchal system; pornography is the propaganda of these acts and this system. Anti-pornography feminism began to reconstitute the meaning and harm of pornography. Harm towards women replaced sexual immorality as the problem in need of redress. Pornography itself was redefined as 'a systemic practice of exploitation and subordination based on sex that differentially harms women' (LEAF 1991a, 7).

Anti-pornography feminism provided the basis for a fundamental shift in the discursive framework of the pornography debate. Social harm, that is, 'the harm that pornography inflicts on women's right to equality, was the new ground on which to criminalize pornography' (Lacombe 1994, 33). The religious and conservative opposition to pornography – that it offended decency and public morality – gave way in the 1980s to a discourse that located pornography in the context of women's oppression. Radical feminist anti-pornography discourse was incorporated into conservative religious discourse. This reasoning 'that pornography, by glorifying the sexual subordination of women, assaults women's dignity, humanity, and equality ... brought together feminist and conservative organizations into a precarious alliance of anti-pornography, pro-censorship forces' (ibid., 47).

By the 1980s, this discursive shift in the harm of pornography, from decency and public morality to the exploitation of women, and the precarious alliance it produced, began to bring legislative efforts to again reform the obscenity provisions. The pornography debate intensified with the *Report of the Special Committee on Pornography and Prostitution* (Fraser Report) in 1985 and subsequent efforts by the Conservative government to once again toughen up Canada's obscenity laws. The Fraser Report recommended the criminalization of violent and degrading sexually explicit material; it did so on the grounds that the material harmed women's right to equality. The report reflected the pro-censorship alliance of conservatives, fundamentalists, and radical feminists (Lacombe 1994, chap. 4). The discourse was feminist: 'the philosophical rationale for criminalization' was the radical feminist argument that 'the detrimental effect of pornography' was 'on women's right to equality, rather than its immoral content' (ibid., 81). The Conservatives came into government while the report was still in progress. They rejected its recommendations as too liberal and proposed a new bill, C-114 (1986), and then, when it failed, C-54 (1987). These bills were much more restrictive. Lacombe argues that the Conservatives' traditional orientation to pornography as offending decency and public morality resulted in the construction of pornography as a threat to family values rather than to liberal-democratic principles, as the Fraser Report had viewed it. Bill C-114 was contested, for different reasons, by feminist, religious, and family organizations; it died on the order paper without debate (Lacombe 1994, chap. 5). Bill C-54 represented an attempt to rewrite the bill to please opposing groups. This time, the feminist language of degradation and dehumanization appeared in the proposed law. But an alliance of librarians, civil libertarians, and feminists against censorship[11] defeated Bill C-54, primarily on the libertarian grounds that the bill restricted intellectual freedom and that it was anti-democratic; feminists argued that it was also anti-sex (Lacombe 1994, chap. 6).

Despite the failed efforts of legislative reform, the 1980s represented an important transformation in the discourse of anti-pornography. Anti-pornography feminists, losing in the legislative round, regrouped and shifted their attention to the courts. And beginning in the mid-1980s, the feminist anti-pornography critique began to find its way into the law, as a new test was introduced into the law of obscenity.[12] This test picked up on the language of anti-pornography feminists, which described pornography as degrading and dehumanizing to women. In *R. v. Towne Cinema* (1985), this test was adopted by the Supreme Court of Canada. Considerable confusion ensued, however, as to the relationship between this degrading and dehumanizing test and the previous community-standards test.

In *R. v. Butler*, the Supreme Court of Canada, facing a constitutional challenge of s.163 of the Criminal Code, was given yet another opportunity to reshape the test for obscenity. Now, according to the Supreme Court, the question of morality was to be settled once and for all. The law of obscenity was no longer to be seen as regulating public morality or imposing a uniform standard of sexual morals. Rather, the law of obscenity must be seen as based on preventing harm, particularly harm towards women. The test for determining whether material is obscene is now based on the classification of pornography into three categories: (1) representations of explicit sex with violence which will almost always be found to be obscene; (2) representations of explicit sex without violence that are degrading and dehumanizing – these representations will be obscene if they are found to cause harm; and (3) representations of explicit sex, without violence, that are not degrading and dehumanizing, and do not involve children in their production, these will generally not be found to be obscene. The three classifications are to be made according to the community-standards test as set out in *Brodie* – that is, what Canadians will tolerate other people being exposed to. The artistic defence would remain the final step in a determination of whether a representation constituted the 'undue' exploitation of sex.

Anti-pornography feminists have claimed the *Butler* decision as an unequivocal feminist victory, representing a decisive and important break in the history of obscenity law as a form of moral regulation. We take issue with this and various other claims of anti-pornography feminism. We do not believe that the *Butler* decision is an unequivocal victory for feminism – indeed, we do not see it as a victory at all. Nor do we see the *Butler* decision as representing a fundamental transformation in the law of obscenity. The language has changed, but the moral regulation has not.

The history of obscenity law in Canada reveals that intensified campaigns to regulate obscenity have emerged within periods of tremendous social change. The uncertainty and anxiety produced during these periods of social upheaval are met with calls to protect the moral fabric of society from decay. As Lise Gotell argues in her chapter, the contemporary anti-pornography campaigns must be seen in this light. While the harms of pornography are now cast within feminist discourse, the underlying concerns of contemporary campaigns are all too consistent with the anti-pornography campaigns of the past (protecting vulnerable individuals – women, children, and working-class men – from the corrosive influences of pornography; shoring up the family; and protecting vulnerable sexualities – women, children, and youth – within the family).

Sexuality, Representation, Sexual/Moral Panic, Law

While each of the following chapters examines different aspects of the *Butler* decision, and its aftermath, from our different disciplinary locations, we share a theoretical framework that weaves these different strands together. Our study takes as its point of departure the theoretical insights of postmodern feminism on the questions of knowledge, power and the discourses of sexuality (Smart 1993, 1994). We deploy these insights to challenge the assumptions about sexuality, representation, and law that have informed anti-pornography feminism.

Sexuality

Sexuality has become an intensely contested site within feminism. As discussed above, some feminists in the 1970s began to develop a critique of pornography that identified a harm quite distinct from that targeted by the conservative critique. The focus of the harm of pornography shifted from the representation of sex per se to the representation of sexism. These feminists began to see pornography not as simply about explicit sexual representations, but as the eroticization of the sexual subordination of women. Pornography came to be seen as a form of sexual violence – as the eroticization of this violence – and, in turn, as contributing to the perpetration of this violence (MacKinnon 1987; Dworkin 1981; Cole 1989). These feminists attempted to redefine pornography as 'a practice of sexual subordination' for the sexual pleasure of men. This critique of pornography was closely associated with, and formed a basis for, the development of the radicial feminist critique of sexuality. Sexuality was identified as a major cause, if not the cause, of women's oppression (Brownmiller 1975; MacKinnon 1982, 1983). It was in and through sexuality that women were constructed as passive, submissive, and subordinate. And pornography was identified as a central component of this system of sexual subordination.

Other feminists resisted this classification of pornography, as well as the identification of sexuality as exclusively a source of danger and subordination. Many argued that sexuality must be recognized as a more complex force in women's lives. Carol Vance, for example, has argued, since the beginnings of the sex wars in the 1980s, that feminists need to be attentive to not only the danger of sexuality, but also to the pleasure of sexuality (Vance 1984). She argued that anti-pornography feminism, in its exclusive focus on the danger that sexuality has presented in women's lives, has all but forgotten the creative, disruptive, empowering force of sexual pleasure in women's lives (ibid.).

In contrast to the thrust of anti-porn feminism, we take the position that sexuality cannot be viewed solely as sexual domination. At the same time, we argue that sexuality is not as unproblematically a site of unmodified pleasure and agency as early sex radicals may have asserted. Postmodern insights on power, sexuality, and social-constructionist theory allow us to break the binarism of constructing female sexuality as either a site of domination or a process of freedom. Postmodern feminism holds that there are many feminisms (both named and unnamed); that there is no one reality and no one site of transgression and resistance; and that bringing reality down to one truth, as anti-pornography feminists do in their construction of pornography as 'sexual reality' (MacKinnon 1987, 149), absents more than it encompasses. The feminist view à la MacKinnon is that 'pornography is a form of forced sex' (ibid., 148). In our view, pornography and sexuality must be understood as a terrain of struggle and contradiction – a site of ambiguity. This means that one can acknowledge that the danger aspect of female sexuality has increased and at the same time recognize that the pleasure aspect has intensified. To take this further, we argue that at the very same time as the state (law, courts, and police) are targeting the sexuality of others, there is simultaneously occurring knowledge production by these others or so-called deviant sexualities, as Becki Ross documents in terms of lesbian representations in chapter 4, and Shannon Bell produces in her work on sexual representation in chapter 5.

We agree with Michel Foucault's well-known and by now clichéd insight that power is productive; the fact that it has become an academic cliché in social history, postmodern theory, and feminist scholarship does not in our view diminish the crucial importance of this insight. Power produces knowledges, institutions, bodies, pleasures, desires, and truths. Power operates through the construction of particular knowledges that become accepted as truth and reality. At the same time, power produces resistances. The body is central to Foucault's analysis; at the bottom of his theorizing is the discursive constitution of the body. The human body is the site at which all forms of domination are ultimately inflicted and registered, and it is the site of resistance. The human body is simultaneously a biophysical given and a cultural construct. What has come to be recognized as female is a cultural construct right down to the biosocial level of the body. The body is contextualized and given meaning in discourse, in the verbal, visual, fictive, historical, and speculative attempts to document existence. The body is given different meanings in different discourses, and the meanings of the body in discourse shape the materiality of the lived body.

In the modern period, sex became and remains a focal point for the exercise of power through the discursive production of the body. Sex has no essential nature or meaning and never exists outside discourses of sexuality. Sexuality is, for Foucault, historically and socially constructed: 'Sexuality must not be thought of as a ... natural given which power tries to uncover. It is the name that can be given to a historical construct' (Foucault 1980, 105). What we 'know' about sexuality, the history of sexuality, is 'a history of our discourses about sexuality' (Weeks 1991, 33).

Foucault distinguishes between sexual practices that have always been with the human body and 'sexuality,' which names them, constructs them, and assigns them values, meaning, and positions in the sexual hierarchy. Although different sexual populations have existed in all historical periods, it was not until the Victorian period that they were systematically marked and identified: mapped like a geographical terrain. According to Foucault, it was the codification of sex that distinguished Victorian sexuality from that of earlier epochs; it is this drive to classify, codify, and punish, the driving force of the Victorian discourses of sexuality, that constructs the official discourses of sexuality and some of the not-so-official discourses, such as radical feminism (to an extent), in the late twentieth century. As Bell argues in chapter 5, this paranoic drive to self-construction is contingent on the surveillance and punishment of otherness in the self and others.

Foucault has shown that the codification of sexuality was governed by the endeavour to expel from reality the forms of sex that were not amenable to the economy of reproduction, placing sex in a binary system of licit/illicit used to define sexual activities and produce sexualities. The codification of sexuality is a state political/legal strategy at points of recurrent and recombinant sexual/moral panic: a sexual/moral paranoia over 'illicit' sexual activities and sexualities.

Knowledge produced sexual social identities through regulation, surveillance, and the labelling of human activity. That is to say, power is exercised in the very naming of sexual acts: it categorizes and codifies bodies, pleasures, and desires, producing official knowledge of the other. Power, however, also produces resistance; power operates according to what Foucault has identified as a 'reflux movement' (Foucault 1978, 39). The other, those who have been identified and classified, speak, enter, and disrupt the dominant social/political/legal discourse, producing a counter-discourse to map their own territory and create their own positive identity.

For Foucault, Foucauldians, and postmodern feminists, sexuality itself is a terrain of struggle: sexuality is never completely determined by power or completely outside power; sexuality is never simply a site of domination or of resistance; there are no inherently liberatory sexual practices or repressive sexual practices. As any sexual practice is co-optable and any is capable of becoming a site of resistance (yes, even monogamous heterosexuality), context and sexual ethics are all. Not surprisingly, it is the sexual outsiders who have concretized what constitutes ethical sexuality. Gayle Rubin advocates a pluralist sexual ethics based on a democratic morality that does not privilege one type of sexuality and disprivilege other sexualities; sexual acts should be assessed by 'the way partners treat one another, the level of mutual consideration, the presence or absence of coercion, and the quantity and quality of the pleasure they provide' (Rubin 1984, 283). According to this definition, 'a prostitute and client, engaging in commercial sex, who treat one another with respect and dignity, are just as ethical as a monogamous lesbian couple, engaging in noncommercial sex, who treat one another with respect and dignity' (Bell 1994, 94–5).

Pornography, like prostitution and homosexuality, has and continues to have a discursive significance in the constitution of our sexualities. Pornography is one of the dominant terrains on which the meanings of female sexuality are currently contested by feminist authors and activists. This book represents an attempt to reconceive feminist debates on pornography in light of postmodern insights on power and sexuality. In the past, the debate has been polarized between sexuality as domination (radical feminists) and sexuality as freedom (libertarian feminists). We believe the debate can be rendered more complex with the insights of postmodern feminism: that sexuality is at once a terrain of power and agency, and a site of gender/race/class inequalities.

While anti-pornography feminists have 'elevated the pornographic sign to ... epistemic status' (Merck 1993, 59) in female subordination, feminist sex radicals have become overzealous in their insistence on sexuality as exlusively a site of pleasure and agency. Sexuality, in the sex wars, became polarized in an either/or opposition – it was a site either of oppression and danger or of pleasure and agency. The point initially made by Vance, which has been lost sight of in the ensuing years of feminist debate, is that sexuality is both/and: both a site of pleasure/power/agency and a site of danger/inequality/restriction. Our sexualities are complex and contradictory, always in the process of being constituted and reconstituted through a multiplicity of discourses, one of which is pornography.

Representation

The insights of postmodern feminism are also useful in challenging the understanding of representation that has informed anti-pornography feminism. Both anti-pornography feminism and the judicial approach to the regulation of obscenity share a literalist approach to representation, within which images are understood to have a clear and unequivocal meaning that can be interpreted objectively. As Dany Lacombe has argued, anti-pornography feminism is based on 'a traditional understanding of language as transparent, as a direct expression of meaning' (Lacombe 1994, 38). It is within this understanding of language and representation that anti-pornography feminists can stake their claim that pornography has a clear and unequivocal meaning – the eroticization of male domination and female subordination.

Building on the insights of postmodernism that meaning is historically and contextually specific and contingent, *Bad Attitude/s on Trial* challenges this unidimensional approach to representation and meaning. We challenge the idea that pornography has only one meaning, the idea that the *Butler* decision has only one feminist interpretation, the idea that the meaning of lesbian and other sexual representations can be determined objectively without reference to the specific communities within which these representations are produced, exchanged, and consumed. We attempt to build on the insights of feminists such as Rosalind Coward, who argued from the early 1980s that the meaning of pornography as a form of representation was contextually specific. Meanings 'arise from how various elements are combined, how the picture is framed, what lighting it is given, what is connoted by dress and expression, the way these elements are articulated together ... In other words, just like language, there is no intrinsic meaning in a visual image, the meaning of an image is decided by the way it is articulated, how the various elements are combined together' (Coward 1982, 11).

The chapters that follow are united in this insistence that subjectivity and context matter in the interpretation of sexual imagery, and that images can be simultaneously subject to multiple interpretations. We believe that anti-pornography feminism's approach to representation is flawed in its denial of the multiplicity of meaning and the relevance of context in the production of meaning. An image may be offensive to some, challenging to others, and sexually arousing to yet others. 'Sexually explicit representations, images and texts are neither reactionary nor liberating in and of themselves' (Wilson 1993, 26). The meaning of any particular image will depend on the location of the viewer, in a broad range of intersecting discourses that constitute her subjectivity. Rather than being clear and unequivocal, the meaning of sexual representations is a site of political and discursive struggle.

As postmodern feminists, we see pornography not as a singular reality but as a discourse[13] of sexual representation composed of many genres: mainstream heterosexual, couples from a feminist point of view à la Candida Royalle (the New York producer and director of Femme Productions),[14] lesbian, gay, s/m, lesbian s/m, and on and on. Lacombe and many of the authors in the recent collections Sex Exposed (1993) and Dirty Looks (1993) argue for a politics of subversion in which sexual others, those deemed obscene and thus off/scene, come on/scene (Williams 1993a, 234) and produce images of their sexualities, or as an act of guerilla warfare deconstruct the codes of the dominant pornography genre, and in so doing upset the sexism often present in mainstream sexual imagery. This politics of subversion is precisely the intent of Bell's transgressive acts in the final two sections of chapter 4, 'Making Pornography' and 'On ne peut pas voir l'image.' As Mary McIntosh contends: 'Making feminist "pornography" and declaring ourselves as sexual beings is not simply something that we do for our own pleasure; ... it is also a way of undermining all the oppressive things that sexuality has meant for women in the past' (McIntosh 1993, 167).

Sexual/Moral Panic

The discourses of sexuality and pornography have been rendered all the more complex in what Linda Singer refers to as 'the age of epidemic' (Singer 1993). A sexual panic, brought on by the AIDS crisis, has deeply pervaded political and cultural life, producing a 'logic of contagion.' The further one is away from what Cossman, in chapter 3, has identified as the law's construction of 'good sex,' the lower one is located on the downward spiral of contagion. An associational link has historically been made and remains, in varying degrees of intactness, between non-monogamous sex, lesbian and gay sex, sadomasochism, commercial sex, intergenerational sex (if the younger person is under eighteen), and disease. In Jeffery Weeks's words: 'Moral panic occurs in complex societies when deep rooted and difficult to resolve social anxieties become focused on symbolic agents which can be easily targeted. Over the past century sexuality has been a potent focus of such moral panics – prostitutes have been blamed for syphillis, homosexuals for the Cold War and pornography for child abuse and violence' (Weeks 1991, 118). While this concept of sexual/moral panic informs the book's problematization of the *Butler* decision, Gotell, in chapter 2, specifically connects sexual/moral panic to periods of perceived social instability. Arguing that our current life world is characterized by instability comparable in magnitude to that of the Industrial Revolution, Gotell documents and critiques how sex and sexuality are increasingly represented as out of control and dangerous and how the current language and practice of law and order feeds into the broader societal desire for stability. Bell, in chapter 5, juxtaposes the official media story of the Child Porn Panic in London and Toronto, Ontario, with the narratives of those talked about – hustlers and johns – in order to deconstruct the meaning of 'child' porn and paid sex with teenage boys.

Law

Anti-pornography feminists have been unrelenting in their efforts to use law against the harms that they claim flow from pornography. In the 1970s and 1980s, they campaigned for law reform (see Lacombe 1994). When those efforts failed, anti-pornography feminists turned their attention to interventions in the courts, in an effort to reshape existing obscenity legislation. Convinced of the clear and pressing danger of pornography, anti-pornography feminists have seen law as a central tool in addressing this harm. Further, Canadian anti-pornography feminists have placed their faith in a particular form of law – they have advocated state censorship, within the framework of the criminal law, of sexually explicit images that degrade and dehumanize women. In contrast, anti-censorship feminists have vigorously opposed state censorship. Cana-dian socialist feminist anti-censorship activists in the early 1980s, although sharing concerns about the sexist nature of much mainstream pornography, attempted to locate these sexist images within the broader context of sexist cultural images (Burstyn 1985a; Valverde 1985). These feminists were particularly concerned with the potential abuse of state censorship. They argued that lesbian, gay, feminist, and other marginal-ized groups are most likely to suffer at the hands of such state power (Burstyn 1985a). The answer to the sexist nature of pornographic repre-sentations, then, was not seen to lie in state censorship, which would decontextualize pornography, but rather in the production of alternative images and representations. These socialist feminists have since been joined by feminist sex radicals in opposing the censorship of sexual rep-resentations, and in condemning the efforts of anti-pornography femi-nists to strengthen Canada's obscenity laws.

In *Bad Attitude/s on Trial*, we continue to build on this critique of state censorship. We share the concerns of the anti-censorship feminists who feared the abuse of this power. And we share the concerns of the sex radicals, who saw in the censorship laws the denial of women's sexual agency and pleasure. Using the insights of feminist legal theory and of postmodern feminism, we also wish to push forward the under-standing of the role of law in social change. Early anti-censorship femi-nists did not, by and large, develop their analyses of the role of law, but rather tended to adopt a more instrumentalist conception of the state as serving capitalist and patriarchal interests. This has lead some anti-pornography feminists to suggest that anti-censorship feminists abandon law altogether as a site of feminist engagement. We believe that this view not only misrepresents the position of anti-censorship femi-nists, but moreover unduly simplifies the role of law in social change.

In defending LEAF's intervention in the *Butler* case, and the role of equality-rights litigation in the area of obscenity, Karen Busby has argued, 'we do not accept that women should abandon law while strug-gling to transform other institutions which contribute to the subordina-tion of women, principally because law is so implicated in shaping and rationalizing these institutions. Furthermore, this forum has the poten-tial to disrupt established social and political norms' (Busby 1994). We do not dispute Busby's defence of law as a site of feminist struggle and engagement. We do, however, believe that there is a considerable divergence between rejecting the feminist potential of criminal obscenity legislation and the abandonment of law. The alternative is not, as Busby suggests, 'an unregulated pornography industry' (ibid.). The potential role of law and legal discourse cannot be understood in such simple dichotomies. In between advocating censorship and allowing an unregulated pornography industry lie a multiplicity of legal alternatives. Legal regulation need not be criminal in nature, but rather could take the same form of regulation of other industries. Existing employment laws, designed to provide some level of protection to employees, could be applied to the sex trade. Such alternative forms of regulation are obscured in the arguments of anti-pornography feminists, who endeavour to defend their faith in the power of the criminal law of censorship. Criticizing obscenity law and rejecting the legitimacy of the censorship of sexual speech is not synonymous with abandoning law as a site of feminist struggle. We do not eschew law's role in social change – we simply reject its role in bringing about such change through the repression of representations.

We are of the view that law and legal discourse is a far more complex and contradictory site of engagement than envisioned by anti-pornography feminism, which assumes that law is a simple instrument of social change. New legal tests do not simply displace older legal discourse, but interact in complex and unanticipated ways. Law is not an instrument, but a site of contradiction, where new discourses are superimposed on old, and where legal victories are rarely unequivocal. Each chapter here explores different dimensions of law's role in regulating pornography, and illustrates the ways in which complexities of sexual identity are lost within legal discourse. The chapters examine different aspects of law's resistance to feminist claims in relation to obscenity. Lise Gotell explores the nature of the legal arguments made in the *Butler* case, and illustrates the co-optability of anti-pornography feminist arguments by the legal system in what she has termed 'the new politics of anti-pornography.' Gotell argues that the growing legal and political salience of anti-pornography feminism lies in the specific character of its discourse. In particular, its claim to represent the 'Truth' of pornography as seen from the perspective of 'victims,' lends it moral force. Similarly, its rejection of interpretive schemes that admit the complexity of sexual images constitutes anti-pornography feminism as a discourse of certainty. It is, Gotell contends, the foundationalist character of anti-pornography feminism as a discourse that empowers it in the legal and political domains. Brenda Cossman examines the way in which the old legal discourse of sexual morality continues to inform the *Butler* decision, notwithstanding the superimposition of a new legal discourse. The law, dressed up in the feminist discourse of preventing harm towards women is, according to Cossman, just sexual morality in drag. Becki Ross demonstrates the difficulty of telling more complicated stories about sexuality in specifically legal discourse. Complexities of identity and subjectivity are displaced and distorted. As an expert witness in the *Bad Attitude* case, she experienced the challenge and frustration of trying to convey the complex construction of lesbian sexuality. Shannon Bell challenges *Butler* and the 'child' porn law with pornosophy: a strategy of conscious porn resistance through representation (words and images) of lesbian, sadomasochistic, and youth sexualities.

The recognition that law is often resistant to feminist claims need not result in an abandonment of legal strategies. We believe that law is a site of contest over the social, political, and cultural meaning of sexual representations. While legal discourse is often resistant to feminist claims, it is a site of contradiction within which feminist claims do make gains. And in this contest over the social, political, and cultural meaning of sexual representations, it is the claims of anti-pornography feminism that have made significant inroads. We do not believe, however, that these inroads are positive ones. Our position on sexuality and representation leads us to a fundamental disagreement on the identification of the harm of pornography. In addition, the history of state censorship leads us to a very different conclusion as to the merits and feminist potential of obscenity legislation and the censorship of sexual speech. The history of obscenity law is a history of moral regulation – regulation that has intensified in periods of rapid social change. And despite claims by anti-pornography feminism that *Butler* has transcended this moral regulation, we argue throughout *Bad Attitude/s on Trial* that the 'new and improved' obscenity law remains thoroughly embued with sexual morality. Each of the chapters attempts, in its own way, to resist the inroads of anti-pornography feminism by articulating a strong feminist voice against the claims of anti-pornography feminism and challenging the view of *Butler*.

In *Bad Attitude/s on Trial*, law, sexuality, and representation are all treated as sites of contradictions, contradictions that are denied in the efforts to regulate and repress sexual representation in s.163 of the Criminal Code. We share a concern about the understandings of representation and sexuality that inform obscenity law, and that will invariably inform any effort to repress sexual images. We believe that state censorship of pornography stifles women's own search for ways of expressing the complexities of our sexual lives and serves to inhibit women's sexual agency and power. Within this shared theoretical framework, each chapter, in its own way, challenges the view that *Butler* represents an unequivocal feminist victory.

While early anti-censorship feminists may have failed to develop a more subtle and nuanced theory of the state and of the role of law in social change, it is nevertheless evident that their analysis of the effects of obscenity law and censorship has been all too accurate. The power to censor at our borders, in our courts, and more informally in our schools, libraries, and galleries, has time and time again been used against gay, lesbian, feminist, and other marginalized groups. Nor is there any evidence emerging that this targeting of alternative sexualities is now a thing of the past. The post-*Butler* era, while signalling the beginning of a period of liberalization for mainstream, heterosexual pornography, is proving to be just as hostile to alternative sexual representations as the pre-*Butler* era. Linda Williams has argued in the context of American obscenity law that the liberalization of sexual representations has had contradictory results. On the one hand, the shift away from mere sexual explicitness as the criterion for obscenity has resulted in a proliferation of sexual representation – 'a remarkable on/scenity of sexuality which has become an important means of representing a wide range of sexual identities once labeled deviant – gay, lesbian, bisexual, sadomasochist, not to mention ... female sexuality' (Williams 1993b, 47). But Williams points out that at the same time 'this new on/scenity' has, paradoxically, become 'the means to a new form of scapegoating' (ibid.). The increasing visibility of diverse sexualities, Williams argues, has been accompanied by 'a tendency to blame sex and especially sexual deviants for such diverse societal ills as AIDS, child molestation, rape, and sexual harassment' (ibid.). New sexual villains are emerging in the wake of this liberalization – the 'homosexual sadomasochist stalking defenceless children' (ibid., 53).

We believe that a similar trend is beginning to emerge in the post-*Butler* era in Canada. Sexual explicitness is no longer the litmus test for the obscene. Now, something more is required – something violent, something degrading, something involving children. And as the new obscenity test is being deployed, gay and lesbian sexualities, sadomasochist sexualities, and youth sexualities are attracting its attention. The new sexual villain, epitomized by Canada's new child-pornography law, is the homosexual pedophile, stalking innocent children. Yet, when we look beneath this vilified image at the way in which this law is being enforced, and at its real targets, something rather different emerges. As we discuss below, it is primarily gay men, engaged in commercial sex with teenage male hustlers, who are being targeted by this law. It is an image which many may still find disturbing – yet, it is a rather different image from that of the homosexual pedophile coercing young children into sex. The pedophile, while perhaps epitomizing the new sexual villain, is not the only sexual deviant that is being targeted and scapegoated within the era of obscenity. As we discuss in the section that follows, and throughout *Bad Attitude/s on Trial*, gay and lesbian sexuality, sadomasochistic sexuality, and other alternative sexualities all continue to be a major target of obscenity law.

Post-*Butler* Porn and the Sites of Censorship

The struggles over the legal regulation of pornography have not ended with the *Butler* decision. While the Supreme Court has resolved the issue of the constitutionality of the existing obscenity law for the time being, the application of the *Butler* test continues to be a site of contestation. Conflicts over the meaning of degrading and dehumanizing sexual representations are unlikely to be resolved in the foreseeable future. Further, Canada Customs continues on its search-and-destroy mission against obscene materials at Canada's borders. And in the immediate aftermath of the *Butler* decision, the federal government moved to introduce a new child-pornography law. While these sites of censorship and conflict are examined and analysed in different ways in the chapters that follow, we turn here to provide a brief overview of these areas of ongoing censorship. A brief look at the practices of customs censorship and the early enforcement of the new child-pornography law provides a glimpse into the intensification of moral regulation over 'sexual deviants' – as gay and lesbian sexualities, s/m sexualities, and youth sexualities all continue to attract the attention and scorn of the censor.

Customs Censorship of Sexual Representations

Since the nineteenth century, customs officials have routinely scrutinized, seized, and destroyed printed materials at Canada's borders. The first Customs Tariff in 1867 empowered officials to prohibit the importation of 'representations of any kind of a treasonable, seditious, immoral or indecent character.' The targets of Canada Customs have changed over the years. At the turn of the century, the novels of Zola, de Maupassant, Daudet, and Balzac were prohibited. In the 1920s, the novels of Joyce and Lawrence joined the list of prohibited materials. In the 1930s, communist literature was a popular target; in the 1950s, it was pulp novels (Ryder 1995). By the 1970s, pornography had become the major target of customs censorship. While massive amounts of material were detained at the border, with some 35,000 titles on Canada Customs's index of prohibited materials by 1980 (Campbell and Pal 1989, 136), the practice of customs officials increasingly came to target non-dominant sexual representations. It was during this period that gay and lesbian material came to be heavily scrutinized (Bearchell 1993).

The law under which all of these materials were scruntinized, seized, and destroyed remained substantially unaltered for over one hundred years, until 1985, when the Federal Court of Appeal found it to be unconstitutional. The Court declared that the words 'immoral or indecent' were an overly vague restriction on freedom of expression as guaranteed by s.2(b) of the Charter (*Lushner* 1985). Within days of the decision, the federal government enacted an amendment to the Tariff Code, prohibiting the importation of material that would constitute obscenity, hate propaganda, treason, or sedition under the Canadian Criminal Code (R.S.C. 1985, C-46).

In order to assist customs officials, Revenue Canada subsequently issued guidelines of interpretative policy and procedures. These guidelines, set out in Memorandum D9-1-1, were intended to assist customs officials at ports of entry determine whether particular materials fell within the prohibited grounds.[15] The most notorious of the provisions was s.6(a)(8): 'Goods which depict or describe sexual acts that appear to degrade or dehumanize any of the participants, including ... Depictions or descriptions of anal penetration including depictions or descriptions involving implements of all kinds.' The prohibition on descriptions of anal sex was qualified in section 9 of Memorandum D9-1-1, a section that rather vividly illustrates the obsession with anal sex that animated the guidelines. Section 9(a) provided that materials 'intended primarily to provide advice on how the risk of AIDS or other sexually transmitted infections can be minimized' were not prohibited. Section 9(b) provided: 'Goods which communicate in a rational and unsensational manner information about a sexual activity that is not unlawful and in which the illustrations are not prurient in nature are not to be prohibited. For example, goods which communicate in such a manner information about anal penetration committed in private between a husband and wife or between two consenting adults will be released.' Section 9(c) provided that sex toys and sex aids should not be considered to be obscene, and that goods are not to be prohibited on the basis of advertisements, 'including implements specified as "anal" or specific products such as "Anal Lube."' Section 9(d) provided that representations which 'merely suggest that anal penetration is being performed are not to be prohibited.' The comprehensive and almost obsessive prohibition of descriptions or depictions of anal sex was specifically directed at gay materials, and has been the provision most extensively used to prohibit the importation of gay material into Canada.

Memorandum D9-1-1 contained many other provisions specifying the type of sexually explicit materials that would be considered to be obscene, and thereby prohibited from import. Section 6 also includes the following:

(1) Depictions or descriptions of sex with violence, submission, coercion, ridicule, degradation, exploitation or humiliation of any human being, whether sexually explicit or not, and which appear to condone or otherwise endorse such behaviour for the purposes of sexual stimulation or pleasure;

(2) Depictions or descriptions of sexual assault. Any goods that depict or describe a sexual activity between male/female, male/male or female/female which appears to be without his/her consent and which appear to be achieved chiefly by force or deception;

(3) Depictions or descriptions of bondage, involuntary servitude and the state of human beings subjected to external control, in a sexual context;

(4) Depictions or descriptions which appear to be associating sexual pleasure or gratification with pain and suffering, and with the mutilation of or letting of blood from any part of the human body, involving violence, coercion, and lack of basic dignity and respect for a human being;

(5) Depictions or descriptions of sexual gratification gained through causing physical pain or humiliation or, the getting of sexual pleasure from dominating, mistreating or hurting a human being. This includes depictions and descriptions of physical force which appear to be used so as to injure, damage or destroy; of extreme roughness of action; of unjust or callous use of force or power; of spanking, beating or violent shoving in a sexual context.

Under these guidelines, virtually any sexually explicit representation that even hints at bondage or sado-maschocism would be deemed to be obscene, and prohibited from import.

Memorandum D9-1-1 was drafted four years before the Supreme Court of Canada's decision in *Butler*. At least some of these guidelines were quite clearly inconsistent with the post-*Butler* law of obscenity. The prohibition on descriptions of anal sex was the most obvious violation of the *Butler* standard. According to the law of obscenity following the *Butler* decision, sexually explicit representations without violence that are not degrading or dehumanizing and that do not involve children are, according to the Supreme Court of Canada, 'generally tolerated in our society.' This standard applies to all sexually explicit depictions and descriptions. There was no basis in the decision of the Supreme Court to suggest that different rules ought to be applied in the context of anal penetration. The provision in Memorandum D9-1-1 singling out depictions of 'anal penetration' for broader prohibitions than vaginal or oral penetration was a clear departure from the decision of the Supreme Court of Canada. Yet, materials depicting anal penetration continued to be seized at our borders by Canada Customs as a matter of course. And, under this provision, gay materials continued to be particularly favourite targets of Canada Customs. Even lesbian sex magazines *Quim* and *Bad Attitude*, on route to the Toronto Women's Bookstore, have been seized by Canada Customs on the basis of the depiction of anal sex. Appeals of the seizures have been unsuccessful. In September 1994, Revenue Canada finally issued new guidelines for scrutinizing materials at Canada's borders. Under the new Memorandum D9-1-1, the importation of material that depicts or describes anal penetration is no longer ground for prohibition; the guidelines on obscenity are otherwise unchanged. 'Canada Customs had revised Memorandum D9-1-1 so that anal penetration – box (g) on Customs' notice of detention – was no longer listed as grounds for prohibited entry' (Fuller and Blackley 1995, 117). Janine Fuller and Stuart Blackley, authors of *Restricted Entry*, suggest that the timing, a mere two weeks before the Little Sister's Art and Book Emporium's (Vancouver) scheduled trial date for their challenge against the practices of Canada Customs, 'was hardly coincidental' (ibid.).

Little Sister's first attempted to challenge the targeting of gay and lesbian materials by Canada Customs following the seizure of the *Advocate*, a gay news magazine, in 1987. In appealing the seizure, Little Sister's would also challenge the constitutionality of customs censorship. The case was scheduled to be heard in 1988, but two weeks before the trial, Canada Customs decided that the two magazines were not obscene. When Little Sister's requested that the magazines be returned, they found out it was too late: Customs had already destroyed them. And Little Sister's lost its opportunity to challenge the constitutionality of customs practices. In 1990, Little Sister's, this time joined by the British Columbia Civil Liberties Association, decided to try again, and filed a constitutional challenge to Canada Customs's right to censor materials at our borders. First, they claimed that in prohibiting the importation of materials into the country solely on the basis of obscenity, the Customs Tariff violated freedom of expression under s.2(b) of the Charter. Second, they argued that it was unconstitutional to detain materials without a proper determination as to whether the material in question was obscene. Third, they claimed that the administration of the Customs Tariff by Canada Customs discriminated against gay and lesbian authors, readers, and distributors, and thereby violated the right to equality guaranteed by s.15 of the Charter. The trial was initially set for 1991, but was delayed pending the Supreme Court of Canada decision in *Butler*.

In February 1992, after the Supreme Court of Canada upheld the constitutionality of Canada's obscenity laws, Little Sister's and the BCCLA revised their case, dropping the first challenge to the censorship itself. The case was again delayed, when government lawyers unsuccessfully attempted to have the case dismissed. In 1993, when the trial was finally scheduled to be heard, the government asked to have the case rescheduled, since in its view there was insufficient time allotted to deal with the complexities presented by the case. The trial was again postponed. In the fall of 1994, Little Sister's, alongside the BCCLA, finally had its day in court.

Little Sister's and the BCCLA have focused on two constitutional issues: the violation of freedom-of-expression and the violation of equality. The freedom of expression argument is based on the way in which customs decisions are made. Canada Customs bans material on the basis of obscenity without having made a proper determination of whether the material is obscene. 'Commodity specialists' review the materials, and if, in their view, the material falls within Memorandum D9-1-1, the materials are detained. This kind of censorship, known as 'prior restraint,' is considered to be particularly invidious, since the decision to ban the materials is made behind closed doors, and long before the materials have an opportunity to make their way to the shelves of Canada's bookstores. There is no opportunity for public debate, there is no public hearing, and by and large the materials are censored with no public knowledge. Customs remains publicly unaccountable for its decisions.

The focus of Little Sister's equality arguments is not that there are more gay and lesbian materials detained, but that shipments on route to gay and lesbian bookstores are subject to much heavier scrutiny than shipments to other bookstores in Canada. And Little Sister's had some interesting evidence. Books that are routinely stopped on route to Little Sister's seem to have had little problem making their way onto the shelves of Canada's more mainstream bookstores. As a case in point, the manager of one of Vancouver's biggest bookstore chains, in preparation for the trial, ordered a shipment identical to one that was detained on its way to Little Sister's. And the shipment arrived – untouched.

Just as the trial date was repeatedly postponed, Smith J.'s ruling was falsely rumoured to be forthcoming more than a few times over the thirteen months following the final day of court, 20 December 1994.[16] The decision, announced 19 January 1996, was simultaneously a victory for anti-censorship forces and a loss. The British Columbia Supreme Court ruled that the Customs Tariff does not violate the Charter. First, the Court held that there was no violation of s.15 equality rights. Despite the fact that the legislation had an unequal effect on 'homosexuals,' the Court was of the view that 'homosexual obscenity is proscribed because it is obscene, not because it is homosexual,' and thus the unequal impact of the law is not discriminatory within the meaning of section 15 of the Charter (*Little Sisters* 1996, para. 136). On the question of freedom of expression, the Court held that although the violation of s.2(b) of the Charter was appropriately conceded, this violation was a reasonable limit under section 1 of the Charter. In so ruling, the Court relied heavily on the reasoning in the *Butler* decision. Smith J. specifically rejected the argument that the *Butler* decision should be distinguished because it dealt primarily with heterosexual sexual representations. In the Court's view, the material in *Butler* did include homosexual sexual representations; and, moreover, 'there is a body of social science evidence that would support Parliament's reasoned apprehension that obscene pornography produced for homosexual audiences causes harm to society' (ibid., para. 195).

Despite its conclusions that the Customs Tariff was constitutional, the Court went on to hold that the practices of Canada Customs did in fact discriminate against gay Canadians and violated the Charter by blocking some gay publications at the border. Smith J. ruled that the plaintiffs, Little Sister's and the B.C. Civil Liberties Association, 'have succeeded in showing that the administration and application of the material sections of the legislation have frequently contravened those sections of the Charter' (ibid., para. 278). The result of the decision is thus mixed. Although the ruling is a clear signal to Customs to clean up its act, and to stop harrassing gay bookstores and publications, it nevertheless upheld the constitutionality of Canada Customs's broad censorship powers. Little Sister's and the B.C. Civil Liberties Association have announced that they are filing an appeal to have the Customs Tariff ruled unconstitutional.

Child Pornography

The new child-pornography law is also becoming the site of considerable social, cultural, and legal controversy. The law added a section to the Canadian Criminal Code – s.163.1 – that prohibits the production, distribution, and possession of child pornography. Both visual and written materials are covered by this law. The penalty for an offence is up to five years in prison for possession, and up to ten years for production, distribution, importation, or sale. A similar section has been added to the Tariff Code – the law under which Canada Customs seizes materials at the borders that are considered to be obscene. Child pornography has been added to the list of materials prohibited from entering Canada.

Section 163.1 defines child pornography as: '(a) a photo, film or other visual representation that (1) shows a person who is or who is depicted as being under the age of 18 years and is engaged in explicit sexual activity or (ii) the dominant characteristic of which is the depiction for a sexual purpose, of a sexual organ or the genital region of a person under the age of 18; or (b) any written material or visual representation that advocates or counsels sexual activity wtih a person under the age of eighteen years that would be under this Act.' There are many disturbing aspects to this broad definition. For example, young persons between the ages of fourteen and seventeen cannot produce sexual representations of themselves even though they can legally engage in such sexual activities. Also, the definition of child pornography not only includes individuals who are under eighteen, but also anyone *pretending* to be under eighteen. The explicit representation of sexual activity between two consenting adults, in which one person pretends to be under eighteen becomes, by definition, child pornography. Under this definition, actors may be prohibited from playing the roles of the persons under the age of eighteen in scenes with explicit sexual activity. Under this definition, even the representation of sexual fantasies, in which one person acts out the role of a person under age, is prohibited. Representations of sexualized dominance and submissiveness are, within this law, linked with child pornography. In the law's view, child pornography is bad not only because it sexually abuses children in its production, but also because its consumption causes the sexual abuse of children. Once again, we see the increasingly pervasive, but unsubstantiated, idea that pornography causes abuse and violence. Fantasy and reality become two sides of the same coin – and this new law goes after both (Cossman 1993, 17).

Section 163.1 of the Criminal Code prohibits the production, distribution, and sale of obscene materials, as well as their possession for the purposes of distribution or sale. In the *Butler* decision, the Supreme Court of Canada stated that sexually explicit materials involving children would be considered as obscene within the meaning of s.163 of the Criminal Code. Therefore, under the existing law, the production, distribution, and sale of sexually explicit representations of children were prohibited, as was their possession for the purposes of distribution or sale. The *only* aspect that the law did not cover was simple possession of child pornography. If the government wanted to make possession of child pornography an offence, it could have made a small amendment to s.163. But that was unlikely to attract much public attention. Instead, the minister of justice introduced a new law specifically directed to child pornography, and specifically intended to capture headlines, showing that the government was serious about cracking down on the producers, distributors, and consumers of kiddie porn. Gayle Rubin, in her discussion of the American late-1970s child-porn panic, states: 'For over a century, no tactic for stirring up erotic hysteria has been as reliable as the appeal to protect children. The current wave of erotic terror has reached deepest into those areas bordered in some way, if only symbolically, by the sexuality of the young' (Rubin 1984, 271).

The issue of child pornography is a difficult one for many people – its mere mention conjures up images of the sexual abuse of young girls and boys. It is an issue clouded in what Rubin describes as erotic hysteria, which operates to preclude any serious consideration of the legal efforts to regulate and criminalize sexual representations of anyone under the age of eighteen. Yet, it is an issue that must be subject to serious inquiry. The law as it is currently framed is not simply designed to prevent the sexual abuse of children. It is, first and foremost, a law that is aimed at controlling the sexuality of youth – and as it is playing out, particularly, the sexuality of gay youth.

Within six months of the passage of the child-pornography law, Toronto police had laid charges against Eli Langer, a Toronto artist, and Sharon Brooks, the director of Mercer Union Gallery, where Langer's paintings and drawings were being exhibited. Although the new child-pornography law includes an artistic defence, in the view of the Metro police: 'It's a firm belief at this end [that] artistic merit is no excuse, no defence ... It's our feeling that [the exhibit] is simply not art and falls under the category of child pornography' (Detective John Ferguson, as quoted in Taylor 1993c, A7). After considerable public outcry, the attorney general decided not to proceed with the charges, but to proceed instead by way of s.164 of the Criminal Code for forfeiture to the Crown of all paintings and drawings initially seized at the Mercer Union Gallery. On 23 February 1994 Langer's paintings and drawings were thus seized by the Toronto police. In effect, it was Langer's paintings and drawings that were on trial, as opposed to Langer himself. If the paintings and drawings had been found 'guilty' – that is, if the court had been satisfied that they were child-pornography, within the meaning of s.163.1, then they would have been forfeited to the Crown, and destroyed.

Langer brought a constitutional challenge to the child-pornography law in s.163.1 and the forfeiture provisions in s.164, on the grounds that these provisions violate freedom of expression, as guaranteed by s.2(b) of the Charter. The Canadian Civil Liberties Association, the Canadian Conference for the Arts, and PEN Canada all intervened in the case, in support of Langer's position that the child-pornography law is unconstitutional. Although McCombs J. ruled that Langer's images did not pose a 'realistic risk' of harm to children, finding that they met the test of 'artistic merit' under the law, McCombs J. did not declare the child-pornography law unconstitutional. He was of the view that the child-pornography provisions did violate section 2(b) of the Charter, but that these violations were reasonable limits under section 1. The legislative objective of protecting children from sexual abuse and from the harmful effects that the Court believed was caused by child pornography were sufficiently important to warrant overriding freedom of expression. The Court was unmoved by the arguments that the definition of child pornography was overbroad; rather, in its view, this broad reach of the legislation was necessary to carry out the objectives of protecting children.

Significantly, however, McCombs J. did state that although the potential harm to children should always be taken into account, a work must not be dismissed as child pornography simply because it is disturbing. 'For artistic merit to flourish,' he said, 'artists must be free to set limits, to provoke and to challenge, and of course, to fail' (*Langer* 1995, 29). On the question of determining whether a work has artistic merit, the Court held that the views of the artistic community ought to be taken into account. Yet, the Court qualified this respect to be accorded to the view of the artistic community by stating that courts must also take 'community standards' and the potential risk of harm to children into account in determining whether a work has artistic merit. In the Court's words, 'society's interest in protecting children is paramount, and where the safety of children is concerned, community standards of tolerance based on the risk of harm are more important than freedom of expression, no matter how fundamental ...' (ibid., 315).

Langer, in June 1995, requested permission at the Supreme Court of Canada to appeal McCombs's decision upholding the constitutionality of s.163.1 and s.164. Leave to appeal to the Supreme Court was denied, and, as is often the case, no reasons were given.

Notwithstanding the acquittal, the prosecution of Eli Langer's paintings and drawings has raised serious issues of where the lines are to be drawn between pornography and art. This theme of drawing the line between sex and art is further explored by Brenda Cossman in her deconstruction of the *Butler* obscenity doctrine, and by Shannon Bell in her representation of lesbian, sadomasochistic, and youth sexualities as a philosophical/pornographic/political gesture.

In the meantime, arrests under s.163.1 are intensifying, as police across the country claim to be discovering major child-pornography rings. In London, Ontario, some fifty-two men have been charged in relation to what the police have alleged to be a child-pornography ring. As Shannon Bell discusses in chapter 5, almost none of the men has actually been charged under section 163.1 of the Criminal Code. The so-called child pornography ring is really about teenage male hustlers.

Police claim to have discovered similar child-pornography rings in other Canadian cities. In Vancouver, the vice squad has shut down what it claims to be the largest source of child pornography in Canada. While police insist that children 'well under the age of 18' are involved, media coverage has suggested that, once again, the videos largely involve teenage street hustlers. Shannon Bell examines aspects of this new moral panic on child pornography in her chapter, and the extent to which the law is being deployed primarily against gay men and teenage street hustlers. The discourse of 'child pornography' is being deployed to police the boundaries of legitimate and illegitimate sexual activity, a boundary that places gay teen sexuality firmly outside the realm of 'good sex.'

Sex Speech and Sex Laws

It is important to emphasize that the focus of *Bad Attitude/s on Trial* is on the legal regulation of sexual speech. We do not believe that our arguments can be abstracted and applied to other legal interventions in the regulation of speech. Our study does not address the issue of hate speech, nor do we believe that the arguments that we raise are directly applicable to the legal regulation of hate speech. Contrary to the claim of some anti-pornography feminists, the legal regulation of pornography is not the same as the legal regulation of hate speech. Our analytical points of departure include our insistence on the specificity of forms of legal regulation and the need to historically and socially contextualize sexual representations. Sexual representations cannot and should not be conflated with representations of racism and anti-Semitism. Nor should these areas of legal regulation be analogized. While some arguments around the efficacy of censorship may be applicable to both obscenity and hate speech, we are of the view that the objectives underlying obscenity law and hate-speech law differ in important ways. The prohibition of hate speech is intended to repress speech specifically intended to promote hatred towards racialized and otherwise disadvantaged groups. The objective of obscenity law, by contrast, has historically been the repression of sexual speech and the imposition of a sexual morality. As we argue throughout this volume, this objective remains substantially unaltered in the aftermath of the *Butler* decision. The point, however, is that these two areas of legal intervention are different, and the focus of our analysis and critique is the legal regulation of obscenity.

In our view, if any analogy is to be made between the legal regulation of obscenity and other interventions of the criminal law, it is with other sex laws, rather than with other speech laws. Obscenity legislation has more in common with the regulation of other forms of consensual sexual activity such as prostitution. The legal regulation of pornography and prostitution share a similar history, dating back to nineteenth-century efforts to protect public morality.

There are many provisions still contained in the Criminal Code that prohibit sexual activity between consenting adults. For example, although the sale of sexual services is no longer criminalized, many aspects of prostitution remain within the purview of criminal law. While prostitution itelf is not criminalized, communicating for the purposes of prostitution is prohibited by s.213(c). Further, s.212 prohibits procuring or soliciting for another person, s.210 keeping a common bawdy house and s.211 taking a person to a common bawdy house, and s.212(1)(j) living on the avails of prostitution. What these latter three prohibitions mean is that if one person is setting up appointments for others she or he can be charged with procuring or pimping, if two or more sex workers are working together in their home they can be charged with keeping a common bawdy house, and a person who lives or is habitually in the company of a prostitute (friends and companions) can be charged with living off the avails of prostitution.

The section of the Criminal Code entitled 'Offenses Tending to Corrupt Morals' under which the obscenity provisions are found includes the following offences:

- immoral theatrical performances ('an immoral, indecent or obscene performance, entertainment, or representation in a theater') (s.167)
- mailing obscene matter (s.168)
- anal intercourse, unless it is in private, and between husband and wife or two consenting adults over the age of eighteen years (s.159)[17]
- corrupting the morals of a child, which prohibits 'adultery or sexual immorality' in the home of a child, and thereby 'renders the home an unfit place for the child' (for the purposes of this section, a child is defined as a person under the age of eighteen years) (s.172)
- a householder permitting certain sexual activity ('an owner, occupier or manager of a premise' may not knowingly permit a person under the age of 18 to be in the premises 'for the purposes of engaging in any sexual activity prohibited' by the C.C.C.) (s.171)

A very similar conservative sexual morality, with its roots in nineteenth-century Victorian moralism, can be seen to underlie all of these sex laws that criminalize sexual activity between consenting adults. At the same time, it is important to continue to emphasize the specificity of the legal regulation of sexual speech and the specificity of sexual representations. The analogy with other sex laws runs the risk of conflating sexual representations with sexual acts. For the purposes of obscenity, this distinction between sex acts and sexual representations is a significant one. Obscenity legislation is distinct in its efforts to criminalize the sexual representations themselves, rather than the sex acts that are depicted. Sex acts that are themselves not illegal (sex between two sixteen-year-olds, for example) may, according to the obscenity laws, become illegal if they are depicted. Ironically, obscenity law at the same time assumes a direct correspondence between sexual representation and sexual acts. While the production of sexual representations obviously includes its models engaging in sexual acts, the acts and their representation cannot be collapsed as one and the same. The complex relationship between sexual representations and sexual acts is obscured in the legal discourse of obscenity, as well as in the discourse of anti-pornography feminism that has informed the law, in the assumption that the representation is a literal and objective depiction of the underlying sexual act.

The complex relationship between sexual representations and sexual acts is further obscured in the argument that obscenity law is intended to address the coercive conditions under which women in the mainstream pornography industry may work. Although we may have reason to be concerned about the conditions under which sexual images are produced, these conditions are not the appropriate focus of obscenity law. Repressing the representation does nothing to address the underlying material conditions under which these representations may have been produced. Employment conditions should be the focus of employment laws. Women in the sex industry – be it prostitution or the production of pornography – should be entitled to the same kind of employment protection that other workers are afforded. They should not have to work in conditions that are hazardous. They should not have to work in conditions against their will. Taking prostitution and pornography out of the criminal code would be the first step towards a restructuring of the legal regulation of sex work. A second step would then be to enforce the range of laws that otherwise apply to employment. Employment-standards law, human-rights law, occupational-health-and-safety law, all workers-compensation law could all substantially improve the conditions under which sex work occurs.[18] Such legal regulation could directly address the coercive conditions under which some women in the mainstream pornography industry may work. Obscenity legislation cannot.

NOTES

1 Section 1 states: 'The Canadian Charter of Rights and Freedoms guarantees the rights and freedoms set out in it subject only to such reasonable limits prescribed by law as can be demonstrably justified in a free and democratic society.' (Government of Canada, *Constitution Act*, 1982)

2 Sections 15 and 28 of the *Canadian Charter of Rights and Freedoms* state:

15. (1) Every individual is equal before and under the law and has the right to equal protection and equal benefit of the law without discrimination and, in particular, without discrimination based on race, national or ethnic origin, colour, religion, sex, age or mental or physical disability.

(2) Subsection (1) does not preclude any law, program or activity that has as its object the amelioration of conditions of disadvantaged individuals or groups including those that are disadvantaged because of race, national or ethnic origin, colour, religion, sex, age or mental or physical disability.

28. Notwithstanding anything in this Charter, the rights and freedoms referred to in it are guaranteed equally to male and female persons.

3 Betty Page's enduring fame is documented in *The Betty Pages Annual*, vol. 2 (New York: Pure Imagination 1993) and *Betty Page Confidential*, ed. Greg Theakston (1994). The latter discloses: 'Known as the Queen of Curves, Miss Pinup of the World, the Queen of Hearts, the Dark Angel, the Queen of Bondage ... An estimated half million pictures were taken of her by almost every professional and amateur photographer in New York' (Theakston 1994, 11).

4 This is perhaps not surprising, given that the age requirement for consensual heterosexual intercourse is 14 years.

5 For a more comprehensive discussion of this history, see Kendrick 1987. In the Canadian context, see McLaren 1991. For an excellent and detailed discussion of the more recent legislative history, see Lacombe 1994.

6 Lord Campbell's motive was to establish an effective machinery for the legal destruction of obscene publications under the provisions for the existing common-law offence of obscene libel. This new machinery was to work largely through summary procedures administered by magistrates and justices of the peace as part of a routine policing of the streets. See Hunter, Saunders, and Williamson 1993, 60.

7 Lord Lyndhurst was not alone in his opposition to the bill. Lord Cranworth, the Lord Chancellor, and Lord Wensleydale also expressed opposition, as did several commentators in legal periodicals. *The Jurist* was of the view that the Bill conferred 'very dangerous powers.' *The Justice of the Peace* and *The Law Times* expressed similar concerns (Manchester 1988, 223).

8 In 1903, the Code was amended to include 'any immoral, indecent or obscene play, opera, concert, acrobatic, variety or vaudeville performance' (*Act to Amend the Criminal Code*, S.C. 1903, s.2).

9 See Lacombe 1994 for a discussion of the debate between Canadian moral conservatives and civil libertarians, and of the impact of the Canadian feminist discourse on these two discourses. Lacombe provides a documentation and theorization of blue politics – the politics around pornography and cen-

sorship – up to and including the *Butler* decision. In this book, we are theorizing post-*Butler* politics.

10 See Lacombe 1994, chap. 2.

11 The new grouping *feminists against censorship* separated pornography and sexism from censorship on the grounds that the law has not been particularly fair to other sexualities. The feminist argument against censorship criticized the anti-pornography movement for its bias against sexuality and its contention that pornography reveals men's true sexuality (Lacombe 1994, 55–63). Feminists against censorship put forth what has become known as a postmodern understanding of representation. There is no intrinsic meaning in a visual or written text: the meaning of an image is determined by the way it is articulated. Their proposed strategy 'was to make public, through art, the sexism and heterosexism in cultural representations and to challenge this (hetero)sexism by producing alternative sex-positive images' (ibid., 59).

12 *R. v. Doug Rankine* (1983), 9 C.C.C. (3d) 53 (Ont.Co.Ct); *R. v. Ramsingh* (1984), 14 C.C.C. (3d) 230 (Man.Q.B.); *R. v. Wagner* (1985), 36 Alta. L.R. (2d) 301 (Q.B.); *R. v. Red Hot Video* (1985), 18 C.C.C. (3d) 1 (B.C.C.A.).

13 A discourse combines and is a combination of social practices, forms of subjectivity, and power relations. Discourse is a way of constituting knowledge and identity. In the case of pornography, this knowledge is of the body; the identity of pornographic/non-pornographic pivots on the axis of what is marked licit and illicit, normal and obscene.

14 For an exploration of Royalle's philosophy and work see Bell 1995, 17–31.

15 The guidelines were drafted to closely mirror the reforms that were being proposed to the obscenity legislation by Bill C-54.

16 For a thorough discussion of Little Sister's case against Canada Customs, a documentation of the two-and-a-half month trial, and the testimony of many of Little Sister's witnesses and Canada Customs officials, see Fuller and Blackley 1995. See also the introductions by Pat Califia and Janine Fuller to *Forbidden Passages: Writings Banned in Canada* (Pittsburgh: Cleis Press 1995). *Forbidden Passages* is a compilation of 'excerpts from some of the most significant publications seized at the Canadian border as sexually "degrading," "obscene" or politically suspect' (note from the publisher, Cleis Press). It is published as a fundraiser to help Little Sister's with its legal costs of over two hundred thousand dollars.

17 Section 159 of the Criminal Code has been held by the Ontario Court of Appeal to be unconstitutional. In *R. v. M.(C.)* (1995) 23 O.R.(3d) 629, the Court held that section 159 preventing anal intercourse unless the parties were 18 years of age or married violated the Charter of Rights. In the Court's

view, s.159 was discrimination on the basis of age, and was not a reasonable limit on this equality right.

18 For a contemporary discussion of prostitution from a feminist prostitute point of view, see the following works on prostitution: Bell 1994 and 1995; Laurie Bell, ed., *Good Girls / Bad Girls: Sex Trade Workers and Feminists Face to Face* (Toronto: Women's Press 1987); Frederique Delacoste and Priscilla Alexander, eds, *Sex Work: Writings by Women in the Sex Industry* (Pittsburgh: Cleis Press 1987); Gail Peterson, ed., *A Vindication of the Rights of Whores* (Seattle: Seal Press 1989); and Anne McClintock, 'Sex Workers and Sex Work,' *Social Text* 37 (Winter 1993): 1–10.

2

Shaping *Butler*: The New Politics of Anti-Pornography

LISE GOTELL

LEAF, like many other feminist organizations who view violence against women as a measure and agent of women's inequality, count[s] the court's decision in *Butler* as a feminist breakthrough. It marks an extraordinary shift in the traditional rationale for obscenity laws from a community standard based on a general instinctive sense of what is ... indecent ... to an obscenity law premised on sex inequality and harms towards women ... LEAF believes that this law, if appropriately applied, will prohibit pornography's most harmful forms, that is those that combine sex with violence, degradation or the depiction of children.[1]

In our neighbor nation to the north, Canada's Supreme Court has determined that racist hate expression is unconstitutional (*Keegstra*) and that society's interest in promoting equality outweighs a pornographer's speech rights (*Butler*). Taken together, these two rulings are a breakthrough in equality jurisprudence, representing major victories for women and all people targeted for race hate. (MacKinnon and Dworkin 1994, 3)

I was very happy when the *Butler* decision came down. I thought that it was a significant advance in the law. But I'm disappointed in the failure of the police and state agents to understand what *Butler* really means. (Busby as quoted in Toobin 1994, 71)

In a context marked by repressive legal interpretations of 'obscenity,' the continued targeting of marginal sexual voices by police, courts, and customs officials, and an ongoing debate about the 'true' meaning of the *Butler* case, interpretations and reinterpretations of this so-called landmark legal ruling proliferate. This book as a whole represents an intervention in this debate, an attempt to disentangle the complexities of the post-*Butler* legal and political landscape. This chapter, however, takes a step backwards into the pre-*Butler* context, the necessary beginning point in any effort to tell the emerging story of pornography, law, feminism, and censorship in Canada in the 1990s. It is, of course, well understood by contemporary scholars that legal decisions do not simply fall from the clouds. A powerful legitimating myth of law is that it stands outside the social context and operates as a neutral and 'objective' set of rules capable of authoritatively resolving social conflicts. Yet, as Bartholomew, among others, has emphasized, judicial decisions are 'forged by a multiplicity of agents, strategies, contexts and events' (Bartholomew 1992, 10–11). Social and political actors struggle in the courts to advance contending claims. These actors, in turn, are shaped by and emerge from within a set of specific social relations. The judiciary, for its part, is also thoroughly inscribed within a broader social context, making assertions of the separability of law and politics little more than an illusion. Judges do not simply make decisions based upon legal precedent and the relative merits of contending legal arguments. Instead, dominant discourses filter and privilege certain legal claims and depictions of reality, just as they marginalize and exclude others (Smart 1989, 162).

It is the purpose of this chapter to dissect the context from which the *Butler* decision emerged. In the effort to answer the question 'What shaped the Supreme Court's interpretation in this case?' perhaps the most obvious and tangible focus is on the contending legal arguments put forward by the various participants in the case. In many ways, the positions advanced in this case – including those of the Appellant, government actors, and civil-libertarian, feminist anti-pornography, and conservative anti-pornography intervenors – represent a distillation of the extra-legal pornography debate that had evolved in Canada since the late 1970s. In attempting to understand the *Butler* decision, an approach located at this level would seek to find the legal argument that appears most clearly reflected in the decision itself. Indeed, it is an approach such as this that has become the 'official' story of *Butler*.

According to the Women's Legal Education and Action Fund (LEAF), a feminist litigation organization that intervened in this case to advance an anti-pornography and pro-censorship position, the *Butler* decision constitutes an important victory. In its *Butler* intervention, as LEAF has since repeatedly asserted, it sought to disrupt the dominant, moral-conservative underpinnings of obscenity regulation in favour of an approach emphasizing sexual equality and the 'harmful' effects of pornography for women. In turn, as LEAF contends, the Supreme Court accepted the essence of its position, thus ushering in a new and feminist-inspired revolution in the legal regulation of obscenity (LEAF 1991a, 14; Busby 1994, 176). As then litigation director Helena Orton remarked immediately following the release of the Supreme Court decision, 'This is an important legal ruling for women. This decision says very clearly what pornography is, what pornography does and the danger pornography poses to women's equality. It is a unique court ruling' (as quoted in LEAF 1992, 14).

'Unique' is an adjective that could be invoked repetitively in describing the underlying threads of LEAF's interpretation of 'what shaped *Butler.*' It is LEAF's contention that its position on pornography and obscenity law represented a unique contribution to legal argumentation in this case. This position is asserted as being unique because, unlike the arguments of other participants supporting the constitutionality of obscenity law, the LEAF position claimed to reject traditional 'moralistic' justifications for the regulation of sexual representation. As LEAF asserts, its critique of pornography and support for legal regulation are inscribed within a power-based framework sensitive to the harms that flow from sexual representation. In short, these arguments for retaining obscenity law are represented as unique because they are 'not moral' (see Busby 1994). If its own arguments are asserted as unique, so too is the Supreme Court's ruling in this case and for the same reason – that is, because, according to LEAF, this decision reflected a distinctly 'not moral' and feminist-influenced justification of obscenity regulation (ibid., 7).

Of course, as Cossman argues in chapter 3 of this book, the assertion that the *Butler* ruling represented a rejection of the moral-conservative foundations of obscenity law rests on a very superficial reading of this decision. Instead, as she demonstrates, the Supreme Court's reasoning must be understood as a subtle and careful grafting of anti-pornography feminist claims onto more traditional moral-conservative discourses about sexual representation. In a similar vein, I will argue in this chapter that LEAF's claims about the uniqueness of its position in *Butler* are derived from a very narrow conception of what constitutes a moral claim. As Smart has pointed out, much feminist discourse on sexuality has tended to equate or conflate 'morality' with one specific manifestation of morality, that is with a narrow, Judeo-Christian or Victorian version of sexual morality (Smart 1993, 185–6). At the same time, however, feminists have often ignored the manner in which moral ideas and rhetoric have grounded feminist speech. While purporting to embrace a politics *sans* morality, anti-pornography feminism has imbued its own assertions of feminist politics with a moral superiority, constituting its own claims about sexual representation as 'true,' as 'good,' and as the expression of the best interests of the 'disempowered.'

On the whole, LEAF's assertions about the uniqueness of its contribution to *Butler* are overstated. The distinctions between LEAF's position and the positions of the other supporters of obscenity regulation as expressed in legal arguments in this case are much narrower than they first appear. LEAF's arguments, the positions of government actors, including the attorneys-general of Manitoba and of Canada, and the arguments advanced by the conservative anti-pornography organization Group Against Pornography[2] in fact rest upon a number of strikingly similar assertions about law, sex, and sexual expression. All rely upon moral claims; all share a conception of sexuality as being dangerous and out of control; all emphasize women's passivity and powerlessness in the face of sexual danger; all view sexual expression as devoid of positive meaning; all embrace an understanding of law as capable of objective determination; and all unequivocally support the necessity of continued criminal regulation of sexual imagery.

If one purpose of this chapter is to challenge LEAF's claims to have singularly influenced and shaped the Supreme Court's decision, another objective is to challenge an approach that places primary emphasis on contending legal argument as the main determinant of legal rulings. Legal arguments do not spring forth onto the judicial arena unshaped by the broader social context from which they emerge. Rather, these arguments are given meaning in a social context that renders certain claims meaningful and others unintelligible. In this chapter, I contend that we must place anti-pornography discourse, including feminist anti-pornography discourse, conservative anti-pornography discourse, and state support for the criminal regulation of pornography, within the broader context of these postmodern, post-Keynesian times. In the context of these times, sexual danger is increasingly configured as the most intelligible construction of sexuality. By contrast, assertions of sexual power, pleasure, and agency are rendered both unintelligible and undesirable, as images of an out-of-control sexuality that threatens to break apart the social structure come to dominate cultural meanings. Anti-pornography discourse, in all of its diverse variations, represents the assertion of foundations, of certainty, and of 'Truth' against the instabilities and 'dangers' of this postmodern era. This is a discourse entirely in sync with the dominant cultural context. Its promise of stability reaffirmed constitutes its appeal and serves to explain the increasing political purchase of anti-pornography politics.

In this chapter, I suggest that foundational forms of discourse,[3] including anti-pornography discourse, must be viewed as a reaction to the uncertainties that mark the political current era. Critically, however, foundational discourses are also highly compatible with, and are in fact privileged within, the domain of law. As theorists such as Smart, Eisenstein, and others have asserted, law is a ruling discourse, akin to science. Law's power rests on its claim to 'Truth.'[4] Law is a metanarrative that professes to be objective, to be able to distinguish true from false, and in this way legal knowledge, like scientific knowledge, is set apart from and above other forms of knowledge (Smart 1990, 197; Eisenstein 1988, 43). Because of the centrality of 'Truth' within legal discourse, law tends to conjure up legal subjects who speak in similarly forceful tones (Smart 1989, 71; Williams 1990, 759). An assertion of 'Truth,' as I will illustrate, is indeed the key and defining feature of the feminist litigation organization LEAF's anti-pornography position in *Butler* (LEAF 1991a). What grounds LEAF's factum in *Butler*, as we will see, is indeed a preference for incontestable legal 'Truth' over unstable politics, for discoveries over decisions, and for stable subjects armed with established rights over unwieldy pluralities adjudicating for themselves on the basis of argument and persuasion. This form of feminist discourse, which I will refer to as feminist foundationalism, has the effect of silencing feminist politics, when feminist politics are understood as a site of normative contestation.[5] The *Butler* case, in effect, exemplifies the strategic compatibility of feminist foundationalism and law; at the same time, it demonstrates the manner in which foundational forms of discourse operate to inhibit feminist politics.

This chapter will elaborate on these arguments as it attempts to situate the *Butler* decision, moving from a discussion of broad, sociocultural conditions towards an examination of contending legal arguments in this case. The first part of the chapter will lay out the context of *Butler* as broadly as possible. It will examine how the creation of 'sexual panics' has tended to accompany periods of perceived social instability. Through this discussion, I will make the claim that in the current period sex and sexuality are increasingly represented as being out of control; this representation, in turn, must be seen in relation to the unsettled contours of our recent political life. The second part of the chapter will illustrate how this particular representation – sex as danger – has been articulated in

Canada through the elaboration of a 'new politics of anti-pornography.' Particular attention will be devoted to shifts in anti-pornography feminist, moral-conservative, and state discourses on pornography and obscenity that have together constructed this 'new politics.' The final part of the chapter will contrast contending legal arguments in the *Butler* case. It will contend that these arguments can only be properly understood within the framework of the 'new politics of anti-pornography,' a politics that privileges certain understandings of sexual representation whilst marginalizing others. The articulation of the new politics of anti-pornography on the terrain of law can be observed in the legal claims of those defending Canadian obscenity law. This discussion will illustrate how dominant cultural constructs and the constraints of legal discourse both rhetorically empowered and reinforced the similarity of feminist, conservative, and government anti-pornography discourses in the Court. At the same time, through an analysis of the arguments of those challenging the constitutionality of obscenity law and through a critical probe of the defenders' positions, this chapter will highlight the repressive character of the new politics of anti-pornography – that is, its intolerance of diversity, both sexual and political.

Situating *Butler*: Uncertain Times, Sexual Panic, and the Asserted 'Imperatives' of Regulation

The complex intermingling of some very real changes has ... caused a crisis of values and meanings, a climate of uncertainty and for some, confusion. In such a climate deep currents of feeling come to the surface and find expression in what are called moral panics. Moral panics are flurries of social anxiety, usually focusing on a condition or person, or a group of persons, who have become defined as a threat to accepted social values and assumptions. They arise generally in situations of confusion and ambiguity, in periods when the boundaries between legitimate and illegitimate behaviours seem in need of redefining or classification. (Weeks 1986, 96)

To say that we live in uncertain times may seem somewhat clichéd. We do, however, exist in times of great instabilities, similar to the Industrial Revolution and to the era of postwar reconstruction, and yet perhaps more fundamental in magnitude and form. Social theorists have labelled the current period 'postmodernity,' a time not only of profound social change but also of theoretical and political disorientation (Brown 1991; Lyotard 1993, 49). The Cold War is over; the nuclear family form is in decline; national economies are being globalized; and cradle-to-grave employment is being replaced by 'flexible' and precarious work. We are caught within, as Lyotard writes, an 'involuntary destination towards a condition that is increasingly complex' (ibid., 49). Just as all of the familiar foundations that served to ground the citizens of the postwar order have been thrust into disarray, so too have we witnessed the erosion of the metanarratives that once organized our lives. Our ability to map and navigate social change and dislocation has been thwarted by the academically eroded foundations of Truth, facticity, and the modernist subject (Brown 1991, 65). Precipitated by earth-shattering events such as the Holocaust and Hiroshima, modernist notions of development have been increasingly discredited and faith in the possibility of progress has been eclipsed (Lyotard 1993, 49). Postmodernity is a time of fundamental rupture, a time when everything seems up for grabs, a time marked by uncertainties perhaps even more profound than in previous eras. As Brown describes postmodernity, it is 'fragmentation without corresponding wholes, heterogeny without unity ..., deterritorialization of production and peoples, social surfaces without depths' (Brown 1991, 64). Those of us forced to inhabit this era and wishing to act politically within it often feel a sense of free fall, as if the earth has suddenly fallen away. For some this may create feelings of endless possibilities; many others, however, experience these formless times as both uncertain and unstable.

Critically, the era of the Keynesian state is also ending (McBride and Shields 1993; Gamble 1988). The idea that the state can manage the economy to create growth and maintain employment, as well as a social safety net, has been challenged from many sides. The Keynesian state has been attacked by the Right as the cause of burgeoning deficits and declining competitiveness. Its defenders on the Left seem to give in to the new logic of neoconservatism as soon as they manage to gain electoral power. In this new era of post-Keynesian, neoconservatism, state actors have thus surrendered certain policy instruments. They have also lost their ability to justify their actions through the now outdated Keynesian rhetoric of state interventionism. Policy-makers face an extremely anxious electorate; but at the same time, the old Keynesian notion that the governments must spend to create stability has now been discredited. This context of instability, anxiety, and the decline of the Keynesian state frames what I have referred to elsewhere as the 'new politics of anti-pornography' (Gotell 1996). In turn, it is within the 'new politics of anti-pornography' that we must situate positions advanced by the participants in *Butler*.

As we have argued in the introduction to this book, historically, campaigns for the regulation of obscenity have tended to intensify during periods of social disorder and perceived moral decline. As anyone familiar with the literature on sexual politics will know, the conceptual framework of 'moral panic' has become a well-established lens for situating the escalation of anti-obscenity politics (see Rubin 1993a; Arcand 1991, 142; Weeks 1986 and 1991). As Weeks explains the significance of the concept, 'Moral panic occurs in complex societies when deep rooted and difficult to resolve social anxieties become focused on symbolic agents which can be easily targeted. Over the past century sexuality has become a potent focus of such moral panics ... Whilst the concept of a moral panic does not explain why transfers of anxiety like these occur – this has to be a matter of historical analyses – it nevertheless offers a valuable framework for describing the course of events' (Weeks 1991, 118). Those who have employed this conceptual framework to analyse obscenity conflicts are, like Weeks, emphatic in their insistence that social disruptions do not, in themselves, simply translate into moral panics around sexuality (sexual panics). The occurrence, discursive character, and content of a moral panic must be analysed specifically and historically. At the same time, however, the moral-panic framework suggests the need for contextualization, highlighting the importance of viewing struggles over the regulation of sexual representations beyond their most apparent and immediate manifestations and in relation to wider social changes.

The recurrence of moral panics around obscenity at times of rapid and fundamental social change has been explored by a wide variety of analysts. Arcand, for example, locates the first great anti-pornography campaign – the Victorian social-purity movement – within the disruptions of the Industrial Revolution, a period of the disordering of established things. As he contends, the social-purity movement played a key role in the nineteenth-century effort to reconstruct order in the world through the consolidation of a Victorian sexual morality (Arcand 1991, 142). It was during this period that the first criminal prohibitions on obscenity emerged in Canada, Britain, and the United States. A second period of intensified pressures for the re-regulation of sexual representation occurred in the immediate post-Second World War period (Rubin 1993b, 5). During this period as well, the contours of the social order were unsettled as states sought to construct what would come to be known as the postwar compromise. Ultimately expressed through the creation of a welfare state and the promise of full (male) employment, the underpinnings of the postwar social order rested upon the affirmation of the nuclear family as the building block of society. Once again, a political concern about unconstrained sexuality and the unsettling power of 'obscenity' accompanied these political efforts to re-construct society; and it was within this context that Canadian obscenity law was reformed and 'toughened up' (Lacombe 1988, 37; Campbell and Pal 1989, 116).

The current era, like the latter part of the nineteenth century and the 1950s, represents yet another period when sexuality is more sharply contested and more overtly politicized (Rubin 1993b, 4; Vance 1984). As Rubin writes, 'It is precisely in times such as these, when we live with the possibility of unthinkable destruction, that people are likely to become dangerously crazy about sexuality ... [Contemporary conflicts about sexuality] acquire immense symbolic weight. Disputes about sexual behaviours often become vehicles for displacing social anxieties and discharging their attendant emotional intensity' (ibid., 3–4). In addition to other signifiers of social and political uncertainty and instability, sex and sexuality have increasingly been represented as 'out of control' and 'dangerous.' Pidduck has observed the recurrent contemporary tendency to represent sexuality through the metaphor of war – from government reports, with titles such as *The War against Women*, to feminist texts on sexuality, with titles such as *The War Zone* – as something innately violent that threatens to undermine the social order and that evokes an apocalyptic fearscape (Pidduck 1994, 5). In a similar vein, Singer contends that the contemporary discourse of the erotic has become suffused with fear. Sexual 'violence,' sexual 'abuse,' 'unsafe' sex – all of these elements combine to form the new discourse of sexuality (Singer 1993). As in earlier periods, the line that appears to stand between sexual order and social chaos is presented as dangerously permeable; fears abound that this barrier 'will crumble and something unspeakable will skitter across' (Rubin 1993b, 14).

If sexual panics have tended to occur during times of social upheaval, it is at least in part because of the dominant understanding of sexuality in Western society – an understanding that has had a longevity outlasting the specific occurrence of these panics. In dominant medical, psychological, and popular discourses, sexuality has been understood as a force of nature that exists prior to social life (what has been termed sexual essentialism); sex has been understood negatively, as innately destructive and dangerous, unredeemed unless it can be associated with some higher purpose (what has been termed sexual negativity); behaviours have been judged according to a single standard, in which a line between acceptable 'good' sex and unacceptable 'bad' sex is rigorously maintained (what has been termed the hierarchical system of sexual value); finally, practices that transgress this line have been understood as threats to the social order (what has been termed the domino model of sexual peril) (Rubin 1993b). In effect, sexuality has been seen as a nat- ural and barely constrainable force, which by its very essence requires regulation or else frightening instabilities may follow. Consequently, as Rubin points out, sexuality has been 'burdened with an excess of signifi- cance' in Western society (ibid., 11).

That sexuality should come to be represented as 'out of control' in times of broader instabilities does indeed have something to do with its dominant construction in Western society as an explosive libidinal force, threatening at every turn to disrupt the social order. Yet, the notion of sexuality as a force of nature, barely controllable, is itself a social con- struction. For Foucault and a whole range of other theorists (many inspired by his work), sexuality is constituted in society and history. It is the outcome of cultural, psychic, and political environments (Weeks 1991; Rubin 1993b; Singer 1993; Foucault 1978). It is not 'natural'; it has no existence separable from its construction in discourse. And while its dominant construction in Western society has been within an extremely punitive and repressive social framework, this does not mean that repression is the essence of sexuality. Instead, as Foucault has empha- sized, dominant discourses limit but also produce sexualities. The insight that sexuality is the result of social organization, that it is pro- duced, alerts us to the role of social actors in helping to constitute mean- ing systems. For sexuality to be seen as 'out of control,' it must be constructed as such. There is, in other words, no inevitable relation between periods of social anxiety and sexual panics; the creation and character of a sexual panic depend upon its context, as well as upon its articulation by a wide variety of social and political actors.

The character of the contemporary sexual panic must be understood as both like and unlike its predecessors. It is true that, in content, the construction of sexuality as an intense, threatening force that must be strictly regulated remains a constant defining feature of the current era. But the context that frames this panic has certain specific features. First, the contemporary panic follows a time of unprecedented sexual explo- ration and politicization – what some have referred to as the sexual rev- olution beginning in the 1960s (Rubin 1993b; Singer 1993, 115–16). Central to the sexual revolution were confrontation with and transgression of forms of sexual authority; the emergence of conspicuous and proliferating sexualities that sought to violate and expose forms of sexual repression; and the politicization of new sexual identities – including gays, lesbians, and women – who sought affirmation and enfranchisement of their needs and desires. Occurring alongside and intimately related to the sexual revolution, the 1960s and 1970s witnessed some liberalization of laws regulating such previously defined 'moral' issues as homosexuality, divorce, contraception, and abortion (Weeks 1986, 106–7; Durham 1991, 8). In the present atmosphere of social anxiety, the optimism of the sexual revolution has been undermined and its proliferative logic and liberalizing impetus identified by many actors as a cause of social decline. This is because the new sexual politics thrown open by the sexual revolution were profoundly unsettling, disrupting many taken-for-granted beliefs and causing confusion 'in the mental universe of many people, especially those already threatened by other changes' (Weeks 1986, 106). As Gamble notes, for example, sexual freedom has been condemned by many critics for a creating a 'general questioning of authority and the undermining of the moral community represented by the traditional family' (Gamble 1988, 198). Similarly, Singer has emphasized how the construct 'epidemic,' generated initially as a discursive response to AIDS, has become the contemporary discourse of the erotic. Treated as a retributive consequence of past transgressions, the discourse of sexual epidemic provides the occasion for heightened surveillance and repression of marginalized sexual communities. Epidemics are by their very nature represented as something 'out of control,' a threat to the very order of things, precipitating a form of panic logic that seeks dramatic managerial and regulatory responses. Not confined simply to AIDS, as Singer stresses, sexual politics are being reconfigured by their mediation through the construct of epidemic (Singer 1993, 28–30).

A second contextualizing feature of the contemporary sexual panic is its insertion within and alongside what I have referred to as postmodern, post-Keynesianism. Previous moral panics also occurred within contexts of social uncertainty. Nevertheless, during both the Industrial Revolution and the era of postwar reconstruction, anxieties over social dislocation could be allayed by still dominant modernist notions of progress, emancipation, technology, and discovery and, ultimately, the promise of a better life. These were periods of economic change and growth and of expanding state activities. In the current period, by contrast, the modernist faith in a better future has been disrupted and now, more than ever, we are caught within a kind of free-fall anxiety. If the social instabilities of the past precipitated moral panics, the anxieties of the present, uncushioned by the hope of progress, may create the conditions for an even more profound sexual 'repression.' Ours is a time when the 'excesses' of the past have been highlighted as the cause of social decline and the solutions posed take the form not of expansion or discovery, but instead of restraint, constraint, and caution. In economics, discourses of neoconservatism urge political restraint as the answer to economic crisis and locate the cause of economic decline in 'excessive' and interventionist state policy. Contemporary discourses of sexual danger echo and parallel the cries of neoconservative voices. The 'excesses' of the sexual revolution are decried and sexual prudence, control, and constraint are recommended as responses. In short, what Singer refers to as a 'recessionary erotic economy' replaces the transgressive logic of the sexual revolution (Singer 1993, 116).

The constitution of a 'recessionary erotic economy,' however, is not simply an automatic consequence of present social instabilities. Its specific discursive character and political force are the result of a wide variety of social, political, and legal struggles. It is the purpose of much of the remainder of this chapter, and indeed of this book as a whole, to explore and describe a particular and significant site of current sexual contestation – that is, legal conflicts over sexual representation. But it is also critical to understand that such struggles do not take place in a vacuum. Legal conflicts over obscenity are inseparable from wider social conflicts, and current social conflicts about the meaning of sexuality and about pornography, in turn, must be situated within the present context of postmodern anxiety.

Against the disorienting free fall of this postmodern world, as Brown argues, foundational forms of politics become attractive to many social and political actors; in periods of grave uncertainty, actors who can present and identify sites of instability and who promise a return to certainty are very likely to be highly influential. Foundational discourses are those in which primary premises (for example, reason, experience, morality) function as authorizing grounds (Butler 1992, 7). These times of postmodern uncertainty and anxiety produce a disposition towards something Brown calls 'reactionary foundationalism.' As she describes it, reactionary foundationalism is one 'strategy for coping with our lost condition in post-modernity.' It is 'both a symptom and an act of resistance' to the complex political terrain that postmodernity forces us to inhabit (Brown 1991, 67–8). Critically, it is a strategy that is not inherently right-wing, but is instead deployed across the political spectrum, by both the Left and the Right. Reactionary foundationalism presents itself as the indispensable thread for preserving some variously defined common good – be it 'Western civilization,' or 'authority,' or the 'family,' or 'feminism.' This form of politics promises stability in the face of instability. It is a strategy characterized by an intolerance of ambiguity, freedom, and contradiction; it asserts foundations, primary premises that are constituted as unquestionable – as 'Truth.' As I will demonstrate in this chapter, those who precipitate the current moral panic around pornography all embrace foundational discourse.

The constitution of the contemporary sexual panic must be seen within the imperatives and seductions of foundational forms of politics. In many ways, the assertion of sexuality as a site of danger, a cause of social disorder, brings with it the justification of radical and repressive policies and is broadly consistent with the unsettled configurations of the current era. And yet, as we shall see in our consideration of the 'new politics of anti-pornography,' the seductions offered by foundational discourses and their specific articulation by social and political actors differ. While the major voices calling for the intensified state regulation of obscenity all express foundational discourse, these voices and their objectives vary. Together, however, they produce a panic around pornography that renders the expression of sexual power, pleasure, and agency increasingly unintelligible.

Framing *Butler*: The New Politics of Anti-pornography

By the end of the 1980s, in the period immediately before the *Butler* case, a new politics of anti-pornography had emerged in Canada. The constraining norms of the pornography debate as mediated through this new politics were as follows: sexual representation was viewed as harmful; sexuality was defined as inherently violent and dangerous; pornography was increasingly subsumed within the social problem 'violence against women'; and the necessity of new forms of legal regulation became widely accepted. The emergence of this new politics must be seen as an effect of discursive mobilization by diverse social and political actors. Specifically, we can link the establishment of a new anti-pornography politics to the evolution of feminist and conservative anti-pornography discourses. In addition, the emergence of neoconservativism as a new governing rhetoric during this period made government actors increasingly open to coercive governing instruments, of which efforts to restrict pornography assumed some place of importance. In turn, however, these developments must themselves be situated within broader political and social uncertainties – conditions that, as I have suggested, privilege foundational forms of politics offering the promise of stability.

The evolution of feminist anti-pornography campaigns during the 1980s constitutes the first significant factor in the changing matrix of pornography politics. As several analysts have asserted, anti-pornography feminism has developed into a political movement with significant rhetorical force (Smart 1993, 184; Frug 1992, 149; Lacombe 1994, 6). Lacombe, for example, contends that, in Canada, the feminist case against pornography had become almost hegemonic by the 1980s; as a strong indication of the rhetorical power of feminist anti-pornography discourse, other social actors had altered their positions to encompass some discussion of the impact of pornography for women's oppression (Lacombe 1994, 6). The force of feminist anti-pornography discourses seems quite remarkable in light of the declining overall influence and distressing political fortunes of the women's movement during this same period. But, ironically, it is in relation to a political climate increasingly hostile to feminism that we can ultimately understand shifts in anti-pornography feminism, as well as its emergent power.

During the 1980s, there occurred an escalation of feminist anti-pornography struggles in the United States, in Britain, and in Canada (Lacombe 1994, 29; Vance 1993a and 1993b; Frug 1992, 145–53; Wilson 1993, 18). As feminist anti-pornography campaigns have intensified, they have also become more focused and more fundamentalist in their claims about pornography and women's oppression. Feminist political activism around pornography began in North America in the late 1970s. Mobilizing around a newly asserted relationship between pornography and women's subordination, a number of anti-pornography feminist groups sprang up. In Canada, these included organizations such as Women Against Violence Against Women, Canadians Against Pornography, the Canadian Coalition Against Media Pornography, and numerous provincial and local organizations. Initially, the focus of many of these groups was 'consciousness raising': touring pornography districts; viewing and discussing pornography; demonstrating in front of sex shops and theatres (Lacombe 1994, 29). Over the 1980s, however, both the strategies and orientation of anti-pornography feminism have undergone a change. Specifically, there has been a shift away from an effort to understand women's sexuality and how we internalize oppressive notions of femininity towards a simpler view that squarely blames pornography for creating a climate of sexual violence (Wilson 1993, 18; Rubin 1993b, 19). As Lacombe notes, the feminist campaign against pornography 'increasingly neglected to address the complexity of social relations organizing sexism, thus betraying its original premise that pornography is a product of sexism' (Lacombe 1994, 29). Instead, pornography has been deemed the ultimate foundation of women's oppression, and based upon this discovery, new and sweeping forms of state regulation have been demanded.

In attempting to account for this shift to a more fundamentalist discourse, Merck and Wilson both suggest that the recent trends within anti-pornography feminism may represent a response to current uncertainties (Merck 1993, 60; Wilson 1993, 28). The newer orientation of feminist anti-pornography politics can be understood as a reaction to instability – specifically, to the political splits and reversals that have beset the feminist movement over the last fifteen years. As many have noted, feminism occupies a highly tenuous position within the current political context. The rise of neoconservatism as a new governing consensus has meant the wearing down of many of the women's movement's early political gains. Furthermore, the dismantling of the welfare state both ideologically and structurally, has eroded the mechanisms through which future gains can be achieved (Brodie 1994; Smart 1994, 23). In addition, conflicts within feminism have escalated. Both feminist theory and feminist strategy have been exposed as representing a narrow set of concerns, reflecting most closely the experiences of white, middle-class, Western, heterosexual, and able-bodied women (Flax 1990, 50; Smart 1994, 23). In other words, the presumption that there was a feminist 'We' being properly represented came under sharp attack by those who asserted that 'such representation was spurious and that gender should not obliterate race, ethnicity, sexuality and so on' (Smart 1994, 23). In short, struggles around differences among women and the exclusive character of much feminist politics have made it increasingly difficult to speak of feminism in singular or universal terms (Flax 1990, 50). One reaction to these current conflicts is to embrace diversity and to try to craft a feminist politics that is more attentive to differences and necessarily more complex. Another reaction is to retreat to the safety of universal claims and fundamentalist approaches in the attempt to recreate some principle of feminist unity (Brown 1991, 64; Smart 1994, 24).

The new feminist politics of anti-pornography may be understood as exemplifying the latter strategy. It reflects a politics of simplified certainty in which the complexities of sexuality are reduced to an assertion of male domination and pornography is constructed as both the ideological support and the expression of male sexual power. Pornography is a particularly good site for demonstrating the practice of feminist theoretical insight, as Frug has astutely argued (Frug 1992, 151). The selective visual presentation of certain pornographic images provides a graphic and seemingly self-evident means of illustrating women's subordination. It remains exceedingly difficult to demonstrate, for example, the complex nature of women's positions in the economy and in the labour force. By contrast, anti-pornography feminism's claim that sexuality is the linchpin of male domination can be graphically illustrated through the ritualistic showing of pornographic slides with women being tortured and beaten (Kaminer 1992, 116; Rubin 1993b, 22). The narrative underlying such rhetorical strategies is as follows: 'In pornography, women get fucked' (Frug 1992, 151). This is asserted as the 'Truth' of pornography, and any feminist position that challenges this 'Truth' is presented as being not really feminist at all (see MacKinnon 1987). In short, Wilson describes the new feminist politics of anti-pornography as a form of secular fundamentalism, 'a way of life, or a world-view ... which insists that the individual lives by narrowly prescribed rules ... a faith that offers certainty.' As she explains, '[although] the search for a new life can be exhilarating, ... it can also lead to anxiety' (Wilson 1993, 28–9).

If anxieties over the current state of feminist politics can be seen as a key factor in the emergence of feminist anti-pornography politics during the 1980s, so too must anxiety, albeit differently located, be understood as a fundamental underlying cause of renewed conservative anti-pornography mobilization. The emergence of a grass-roots and conservative movement against pornography (based in the churches and in conservative and anti-feminist groups, such as the Coalition for Family Values, Canadians for Decency, and R.E.A.L. Women) can be viewed as a reaction to anxieties about the 'epidemic' of pornography and the perceived liberalization of obscenity case law (Lacombe 1994, 45–53; Vance 1993a). As a central voice within 1980s pornography debates, the New Right's position did not necessarily represent a discursive shift from previous eras. The concerns of this movement were, in fact, similar in thrust to concerns that had prompted state legislators to enact and tighten obscenity laws during earlier periods. Nevertheless, unlike the 1950s, when concerns about obscenity remained primarily confined to the legal and legislative arenas, by the 1980s, moral-conservative anti-pornography discourse was being articulated through a social movement with a significant grass-roots base (Gotell 1996, 284).

This contemporary mobilization behind conservative anti-pornography politics can be linked to two factors. First, given the newly politicized and plural character of the pornography debate, there existed, for the first time, a perceived imperative to defend the moral-regulatory basis of obscenity law against a wide range of challenges. Second, as analysts of the New Right have contended, the origins of this social movement must be understood in the context of social change, including the decline of the nuclear family form and the successes of feminist and other progressive movements in challenging traditional structures and attitudes (Petchesky 1984, 247; Erwin 1988, 147–8). The New Right's anxiety about change and the decline of traditional authority structures, such as patriarchy, grounds its critique of pornography. Conservative groups contend that pornography offends public decency and promotes moral decline. While incorporating some elements of anti-pornography feminist rhetoric, such as arguments about sexual violence, the axis of New Right pornography discourse is the claim that pornography poses a threat to the family (Vance 1993a, 35; Lacombe 1994, 48; Currie 1992, 195). By endorsing 'extramarital' sex, pornography is seen to unleash sex from the bounds of heterosexual marriage and to undermine traditional gender roles within the family (Berger, Searles, and Cottle 1991, 18). And because the family is constituted as the foundation of society, pornography thereby threatens social stability. For this reason, the Right, like anti-pornography feminism, has repeatedly called for tougher laws on pornography.

It is important to recognize that while anti-pornography feminists have condemned the moral-conservative foundations of Canadian obscenity law, they do not reject the notion that law should be used to ensure some form of moral order. The feminist campaign against pornography seeks to reform and recast the moral foundations of law to incorporate a normative concern for sexual harm. In accepting the moral-regulatory function of law, and in other significant respects, anti-pornography feminism thus enters into an uneasy rhetorical and political alliance with the moral right.[6] This alliance has been expressed in joint mobilization for new legislation to counteract pornography (Lacombe 1994, 103–4), and, as important, in a shared discursive terrain. Anti-pornography feminists and conservative voices over the 1980s were harmonious in their claims, even if they were not quite singing the same tune. Together they defined pornography as a grave social problem, harmful to women and a cause of social decline, and together they pressured political actors for new regulatory responses.

Changing political agendas on pornography constitute the final major ingredient in the construction of a new politics of anti-pornography over the 1980s. Just as feminist and conservative campaigns against pornography have evolved in response to uncertainties and anxieties, the character of political responses has also shifted in reaction to a fundamentally altered political context. When pornography re-emerged on the political agenda, it was largely because of heightened mobilization around this issue. By the 1970s, there were increasing calls for the amendment of Canada's 1959 obscenity law coming from a variety of perspectives. Civil libertarians, the arts community, gay and lesbian activists, and indeed some feminists argued for liberalization, criticizing the exceedingly subjective and repressive character of the existing legal regime. Emergent feminist and conservative anti-pornography groups, by contrast, stressed the necessity of new managerial responses to deal with an asserted explosion of violent and degrading pornography.[7] On the whole, these diverse voices threatened the legitimacy of the existing legal regime, but posed conflicting, if not irreconcilable, solutions for obscenity-law reform. The character of early Liberal government responses to these conflicting pressures, however, differed markedly from those of Progressive Conservative federal governments of the late 1980s. The ascendance of neoconservatism as a new approach to governing and the elaboration of a new politics of anti-pornography by social actors altered both the nature of legislative proposals as well as the discourse within which pornography was constructed as a policy problem. On the whole, we can observe the increasing political equation of sexuality and 'danger' and a related intensification of proposed regulatory responses.

It was within the context of heightened social conflicts over pornography that Liberal governments first sought to amend the 1959 obscenity law. Between 1977 and 1984, the Liberals introduced three anti-pornography bills and established two commissions concerned with obscenity reform. Each attempt to pass new legislation, however, met with criticism from all sides. In particular, these exercises illustrated the difficulties of establishing a legislative definition for pornography (Campbell and Pal 1989, 119–27). It is ironic that as the emergence of pornography as a social problem acted to push obscenity law onto the political agenda, it simultaneously made authoritative policy response increasingly difficult. While Liberal governments were unable to construct a new policy consensus on pornography, it is possible to identify certain underlying themes of their reform initiatives and proposals:

- first, Liberal efforts emphasized the 'urgency of the problem of sexually explicit material' (Canada, House of Commons, Standing Committee on Justice and Legal Affairs 1978, 18:3);
- second, the Liberals accepted that the problem of pornography should continue to be addressed primarily through criminalization;
- third, these efforts recognized the principle of sexual equality and proposed to introduce the concept of 'undue degradation of the human person' into the Criminal Code provision on obscenity (Campbell and Pal 1989, 122);
- fourth, child pornography was identified as a central concern, and specific and harsh prohibitions were proposed (ibid.).

In sum, the Liberal approach to pornography accepted the existing criminal obscenity framework and sought to insert emergent concerns about sexual inequality and child abuse into this framework. These legislative efforts certainly indicate, as Lacombe contends, 'the extent to which the anti-pornography movement had made itself gradually heard in Ottawa' (1994, 79). And yet, despite the growing influence of anti-pornography discourse and its evident assimilation by political actors, it remains true that considerations of freedom of expression as well as the desire to liberalize some forms of sexual expression also informed the Liberal law-reform efforts (Campbell and Pal 1989, 122).

With the election of the Mulroney Conservatives, however, the creation of a new and coherent pornography policy took on new urgency and the discourse within which this political issue was framed shifted markedly.[8] Immediately after their election in 1984, the Conservatives embraced a 'family values' platform, promising measures to control pornography. While adopting certain elements of anti-pornography feminist rhetoric, especially regarding the connection between pornography and sexual violence, the government justified tougher criminal restrictions on pornography as necessary for the preservation of the 'family.' As expressed by the prime minister: 'Our Canadian family is the cornerstone of all decent social initiatives. The Canadian family will be defended in this Parliament by this government, at all times and in all circumstances ... With more threats to the fabric of our family life, it is the government's duty to act in response. That is why we will be moving in this session against pornography, child abuse and drug abuse'

(Campbell and Pal 1989, 128). The Conservative government's express commitment to pornography reform resulted in the introduction of two extremely tough anti-pornography bills. Both Conservative bills sought to move away from an approach based upon broadly worded provisions to be interpreted by the courts, and instead provided a set of quite specific statutory definitions of pornography.[9] These initiatives embraced the view that pornography was amenable to categorization and clear definition.

The Mulroney government's second pornography bill (Bill C-54), for example, proposed to allow for limited access to 'erotica,' but prohibited the following sweeping categories of pornography: sexually violent conduct; a degrading act in a sexual context; lactation or menstruation in a sexual context; masturbation or ejaculation; and vaginal, anal, or oral intercourse. Reflecting a repressive intent, the legislation also proposed to criminalize 'any matter that incites' or 'advocates' any of these acts (Scheier 1988, 61–2). In effect, this bill represented an attempt to instil an almost Victorian sexual Puritanism. It ambitiously sought to cordon off pornography into a discrete and broad realm of representations. Pornography was defined through a literalist interpretive framework (the 'I know it when I see it' approach to pornography),[10] and the breadth of the legislation's categories encompassed, if not nudity, then virtually all depictions of sexual activity.

Within the Conservative government's pornography initiatives, we can observe a rearticulation of moral-conservative discourse on sexual representation. Reflecting most closely the claims of New Right rhetoric, this recasting of official obscenity discourse also relied on anti-pornography feminist arguments. Conservative law-reform efforts were justified as reflecting the government's commitment to addressing both violence against women and 'degradation in a sexual context' (Minister of Justice, as quoted in Lacombe 1994, 118). As Vance notes, it is now no longer acceptable to cast the dangers of sexual imagery as a threat to morality alone. In this context, the incorporation of anti-pornography feminist rhetoric provides an opportunity to modernize what is at heart an older conservative agenda (Vance 1993a, 39). The assimilation of feminist rhetoric, which began with the Liberals, was raised to an art form under the Tories. Through this exercise in discursive blending, the Conservative government, especially with Bill C-54, sought to create a 'compromise' on pornography that appealed both to its conservative constituency and to feminist anti-pornography activists. But as with earlier law-reform efforts, this compromise proved difficult to construct, and, ultimately, the government allowed this very controversial bill to die on the parliamentary order paper (Lacombe 1994, 120–32; Pal and Campbell 1989, 142–50).

It is tempting to interpret shifting legislative discourses on pornography and failed efforts at law reform to the push and pull of social pressures and to the difficulties involved in creating a social and legislative consensus on this issue. It is indeed this kind of interpretive framework that has dominated efforts to understand Liberal and Tory law-reform initiatives and their demise (see Lacombe 1994; Campbell and Pal 1989). Yet it is also important to situate these developments within a wider context. The evolution of state responses to pornography and the emergence of a new politics of anti-pornography under the Tories must be seen in the context of the decline of the Keynesian state and the elaboration of a new state form – the neoconservative state. This state form seeks legitimation through its ability to constrain itself: to retreat from the economy; to reduce social spending; and to decrease budgetary deficits. At the same time that the neoconservative state represents a 'rolling back,' however, it simultaneously has meant a 'rolling forward' (Gamble 1988, 28). The instantiation of the neoconservative state has involved a radical redrawing of political boundaries – not so much a retraction of state authority as its reconstitution.

The reduction in state size and spending that has characterized neoconservative governments of the 1980s has coincided with an enhancement in state power and authority – the leaner, yet meaner, state (Gamble 1988, 30, 36; McBride and Shields 1993, 37, 88; Whitaker 1987, 2). As the components of the postwar order are dismantled, including the Keynesian welfare state, the need for strong government to maintain social authority correspondingly increases. In this conjuncture, then, a law-and-order agenda becomes enormously popular with neoconservative politicians and policy-makers. As Keane argues, neoconservatism works to 'increase the effectiveness of state policies by downgrading the instrumental dimensions of the state (as provider of goods and services to civil society) in favour of its role as a powerful, prestigious and enduring guardian of the Nation ... and as a guarantor of domestic law and order [and] social stability ... This is neoconservatism's recipe for simultaneously restricting the scope of the state and increasing its power' (Keane 1988, 8–9). The ascendance of neoconservatism in both Britain and the United States has been accompanied by an erosion of civil liberties and an increase in state coercion. In Canada, under Progressive Conservative governments, law-and-order policy also took on new urgency (Whitaker 1987; McBride and Shields 1993, 37). Significantly, one central expression of this embrace of law-and-order politics lies in evolving political responses to 'violence against women.' In fact, Tory efforts to appear responsive to 'women's' issues were framed almost entirely within a law-and-order agenda. While the former federal government came to loggerheads with the organized feminist movement because of its steady assault on social policy, it simultaneously began a series of initiatives designed to combat the problem of 'violence against women.' These included new sexual-assault legislation; new gun-control legislation; a new anti-stalking law; a parliamentary inquiry on violence entitled 'The War Against Women'; the commission of a Panel on Violence Against Women; new research funding on family violence; and, importantly, two failed attempts to pass tough pornography laws (Levan, 1995; Pidduck 1994).

It is crucial to understand the reconfiguration of political responses to pornography within this wider context. Increasingly over the 1980s, government actors have promoted the view that pornography is a serious social problem, a threat to the Canadian family and to women. Increasingly, pornography as a issue has been subsumed within the social problem of violence against women, such that the two are most often understood as inseparable in policy discourse. In the 1991 parliamentary-committee report, 'The War Against Women,' for example, pornography is simply collapsed into the policy category 'violence against women' (Canada, Standing Committee on Health, Welfare, Social Affairs, Seniors and the Status of Women 1991). Similarly, in the 1993 final report of the government-appointed Canadian Panel on Violence Against Women, pornography is considered under the heading 'Underacknowledged Forms of Violence.' As this report states, 'Strict causal relationships between pornography and violence against women may be difficult to determine, but there is growing evidence that makes the link ... Whether or not pornography leads directly to real acts of violence, it still degrades women, atomizes them into pieces of a sexual puzzle and depicts them in subservient and demeaning poses and positions' (Canadian Panel on Violence Against Women 1993, 50–1). With this discursive swallowing of sexual representation into violence, the 'problem of pornography,' like the 'problem of violence against women,' has been used to justify the expansion of the criminal-justice system.[11] In turn, criminalization becomes a preferred policy response to social anxiety – preferred because it promises to contain social disorder, preferred because it enhances the authority of the state, preferred because it can promise these things without, at the same time, detracting from the neo-conservative objective of constraining social spending. As Snider writes, 'Criminalization is politically appealing because it simplifies conflicts by stressing moral indignation over reason, offering a "concrete terrain of struggle, a reachable result"' (Snider 1994, 81).

In the end, of course, Conservative efforts to pass tough new laws against pornography were not successful. But this should not blind us to the critical discursive shift that has taken place. By subsuming pornography into violence and by inserting it into a broader law-and-order agenda, government actors have contributed to the construction of a sexual panic. Much like the moral-purity discourse of the last century, new state discourses on pornography rely on an image of women as silent and passive victims of male violence and idealize the state as protector. The creation of a sexual danger zone circulates in state discourses, as the opening words of the government-appointed Canadian Panel on Violence Against Women attest: 'Every day in this country, women are maligned, humiliated, shunned, screamed at, pushed, kicked, punched, assaulted, beaten, raped, physically disfigured, tortured, threatened with weapons and murdered' (Canadian Panel on Violence Against Women 1993, 1). Criminal-justice responses to the problem of sexual violence depend upon the creation of a climate of sexual fear. Anxieties about sexual violence are very real; but they are, at the same time, created through government efforts to mobilize support for criminalization.[12] Indeed, as Singer has noted, 'The logic of [a sexual] epidemic depends upon the perpetual revival of the anxiety it seeks to control' (Singer 1993, 28; Pidduck 1994, 7–8, 10–12). At the level of symbolism, these new discourses imply that women are unsafe and can only be made safe through the protectionist activities of the state. In this way, a fearful, protected feminine object is created.

It is within this discursive context that the *Butler* case took shape. The combined effects of feminist and conservative anti-pornography discourses, together with law-and-order responses by political actors, have been to produce an almost hegemonic construction of sex and sexual representation. Through this construction, pornography has been increasingly understood as a force that threatens to unleash an uncontrolled and uncontrollable sexuality. Pornography has been seen as a cause of sexual violence and social disorder. And, critically, within this 'new politics of anti-pornography,' those voices emphasizing sexual pleasure, free sexual expression, and/or the rights of sexual minorities are more and more marginalized. In the *Butler* case, as we will observe, litigants supporting the constitutionality of obscenity law, including the feminist litigation organization LEAF, were able to draw upon this cultural common sense. And it is in relation to 'the new politics of anti-pornography' that these apparently diverse arguments must be seen. Those challenging the legal regulation of obscenity, by contrast, were placed on the defensive – outside the dominant contemporary construction of sexuality, seemingly asking the judiciary to open up a sexual danger zone.

Shift to the Courts: The Legal Arguments in *Butler*

Legislative decisions to set aside obscenity-law reform did not mean a de-escalation of pornography struggles nor an end to what I have termed the new politics of anti-pornography. Conflicts over pornography continued unabated in the wake of defeated bills and altered political agendas. And despite legislative stalements on this issue, political commitments to obscenity regulation did not subside. In the absence of a definitive political response, however, pornography struggles moved into the courts. As we have argued in the introduction, the legal arena has always been a key site for the elaboration and development of obscenity policy. In many ways, then, this shift to the courts represented a continuation of long-established patterns. Yet the entrenchment of the Charter of Rights in the Canadian Constitution signalled a new and more authoritative role for the judiciary in the realm of obscenity policy. Given the Charter's protection of expression rights (s.2(b)), it was inevitable that obscenity legislation would become the object of a constitutional challenge. In addition, however, the Charter also offers constitutional guarantees of sexual equality (ss. 15 and 28) and it recognizes that rights may be reasonably limited in a 'free and democratic society' (s.1). Consequently, constitutional support for most sides of the pornography debate could be found in the text of the Charter.

The first constitutional challenge to obscenity law to reach the Supreme Court was *R. v. Butler*. What was perhaps most significant about the *Butler* challenge was the threat that it posed to the very legitimacy of the criminal regulation of obscenity in Canada. As I have argued, a central point of convergence in all variants of anti-pornography discourse has been the claim that pornography is a grave social problem that demands criminal regulation. For government actors, the abandoning of legislative-reform agendas did not mean a waning commitment to this principle. In fact, the federal government's decision not to act after the defeat of Bill C-54 can be understood as an implicit endorsement of the existing criminal obscenity regime. This endorsement was made explicit in comments of former Conservative Justice Minister John Crosbie, who argued in 1990 that 'Canada is just as well off without a [new law on pornography]' (Lacombe 1994, 133). If, for governmental actors, *Butler* posed a threat to existing policy and to state control over the legal regulation of obscenity, for conservative anti-pornography activists, this challenge called into question the principle that criminal law should be used to maintain moral order – a central tenet of the conservative position. For anti-pornography feminists, as well, this constitutional challenge was seen to be serious. While feminist support for the existing obscenity law was perhaps weaker than that of either governmental or conservative actors, the alternative – that is, no criminal regulation of pornography – was seen as a much greater danger. Justifying its decision to intervene in *Butler*, LEAF stated that '[we] could not support a position that would have eliminated the criminal regulation of pornography, given the pervasive and direct effects of pornography on women's lives' (Busby 1994, 174).

The Supreme Court decision to hear the appeal in *Butler* thus provided a forum for the rearticulation of pornography struggles. Significantly, within this new forum, those defending the constitutionality of obscenity law could draw upon the dominant construction of sexuality established through the 'new politics of anti-pornography.' In other words, the equation of sexuality with danger, and the understanding of sexual representation as harmful, could be deployed in order to bolster arguments about the necessity of the criminal regulation of obscenity. If extralegal constructions of sexuality established one set of parameters for this legal debate, the articulation of pornography struggles on the terrain of law brought additional constraints. As pornography struggles shift to the courts, those who wish to influence judicial responses must couch their claims in a language and structure that is compatible with law. As some legal theorists have emphasized, law's power rests on its promise to determine the 'Truth' of social events. Law claims to be 'objective,' to be able to distinguish what is 'True' from what is 'false.' For this reason, legal arguments that can assert 'Truth' and can present simple, certain, and authoritative pictures of social reality are likely to be privileged within legal discourse (Smart 1989, 71). Anti-pornography discourses, as I have suggested, rely heavily on such authoritative claims (pornography has one meaning, pornography is harmful, the harms of pornography have been scientifically established, criminalizing pornography reduces harm). By contrast, those advocating the deregulation of pornography are forced to rely on a set of hypothetical, potential, and contingent claims (pornography has many meanings, sexual expression promotes self-fulfilment and democracy, pornography produces alternative sexualities). Furthermore, in challenging the constitutionality of obscenity law, one is necessarily forced into questioning law's own image of itself as 'objective.' For if this challenge is to be successful, it must establish that the legal regulation of obscenity has been subjective, arbitrary, or discriminatory.

The dominant extralegal construction of sexuality, together with the specific constraints imposed by legal discourse, produced a remarkable overlap among those advocating the constitutionality of obscenity law. Quite in contrast to LEAF's claims, the slippage between government and conservative rhetoric and its own position is readily observable. Moreover, LEAF's arguments in *Butler* represent a clear expression of the new feminist politics of anti-pornography. Within its factum in *Butler*, all complexity is denied. LEAF's legal claims are represented as if articulating a unified, authoritative, and universal feminist position on pornography.

The Challenges: Civil Libertarians and Sex Radicals

In the extralegal context, those voices challenging the legitimacy of the criminal regulation of obscenity have increasingly been placed on the outside of dominant constructions of sexuality. Yet, although claims about a sexual danger zone have come to dominate social and political meanings, their hegemony has not been absolute. Instead, as Foucault has asserted, the power deployed in the construction of a sexual panic functions not as a movement of repression, but rather as a force of production (Foucault 1979, 15). While now dominant discourses of sexual danger provide the occasion for the enhanced regulation and surveillance of sexuality, so too do they produce sites of resistance. In particular, sexual communities and identities empowered through the sexual revolution have been forced to struggle within and against the new recessionary erotic economy. Social struggles for the decriminalization of obscenity have taken on a heightened significance within this context and have continued with renewed force in the wake of the establishment of a 'new politics of anti-pornography.' Nevertheless, because political actors have been increasingly unresponsive to demands for freedom of sexual expression, advocates have been pushed into the courts to articulate their claims. In the *Butler* case, the basis of the Appellant's challenge rested on the assertion that section 163 of the Criminal Code restricted freedom of expression, that these obscenity provisions were, in addition, vague and overbroad, and, finally, that the restriction of obscenity has a purpose grounded in morality, a purpose discordant with the principles of a free and democratic society (Butler 1991). The Appellant's challenge was supported by and elaborated upon in the joint intervention of the Canadian Civil Liberties Association/Manitoba Association for Rights and Liberties (CCLA/MARL 1991), and in the intervention of the British Columbia Civil Liberties Association (BCCLA 1991). These two interventions articulated distinct constitutional claims against obscenity regulation. The arguments of the CCLA/MARL reflected a classic civil-libertarian position against the criminal regulation of obscenity. The BCCLA factum, by contrast, while emphasizing the importance of expression rights in a free and democratic society, drew significantly on anti-censorship feminist and sex-radical claims about the 'destabilizing' power of sexual speech. Each of these positions in its own way, however, was located outside the dominant discourse of sexuality and issued a fundamental challenge to the myth of legal objectivity. The ability to draw on dominant social constructions or to appeal to the central legitimating myth of law – rhetorical strategies that would reinforce the claims of those opposing the *Butler* challenge – were thus unavailable to the CCLA/MARL and to the BCCLA. And, in their place, these intervenors could offer only abstract principles or hypothetical assertions about the value of sexual expression.

The essence of the CCLA/MARL intervention is straightforward, representing a thoroughly liberal condemnation of censorship and of criminal obscenity law on the basis of a principled and abstract defence of freedom of expression. The first and most critical underlying thread in the CCLA/MARL position was to stress the fundamental importance of free expression in a democratic society. As it stated, this freedom is the 'indispensable condition of nearly every other form of freedom,' ensuring a 'diversity of thoughts, opinions and beliefs' and erecting a defence against 'tyranny and conformity' (CCLA/MARL 1991, 2). Next, the CCLA/MARL sought to establish that s.163 of the Criminal Code clearly infringes upon the expression guarantee of the Charter; as it elaborated, the purpose of s.163 is to prohibit 'with penal sanctions' the expression of particular meanings – specifically, the 'creation, publication, and distribution of meanings which unduly exploit sex or sex and any one or more of crime, horror, cruelty and violence' (ibid., 5–6). The factum then went on to make the argument that s.163 cannot be justified under section 1 of the Charter as a reasonable limit prescribed by law because it lacks a pressing and substantial objective. In making this claim, the CCLA/MARL asserted the inconclusiveness of research concerning the relationship between pornography and social harms (ibid., 11–12). Finally, the CCLA/MARL contended that s.163 represents an unjustifiable limit on freedom of expression because it is vague and overbroad.

In this manner, the intervention issued a powerful condemnation of judicial interpretation of section 163 of the Criminal Code. According to the CCLA/MARL, the limits on expression imposed by this section have been 'vague, ambiguous, uncertain' and 'subject to discretionary determination' (CCLA/MARL 1991, 7). The wording of the provision itself does not specify what is to be considered 'undue exploitation of sex' (ibid., 9), and the community-standards test applied by the courts to define criminal obscenity has relied on subjective judicial perceptions of what constitutes a national standard of tolerance (ibid., 9). At the same time, the law imposes criminal sanctions when individuals are not able to know with certainty that they have committed an offence (ibid., 13). As the CCLA/MARL concluded, the main consequence of the uncertain application of this law is that it 'does not allow an individual citizen to predict the legal consequences of his or her actions' (ibid., 10). This, in turn, has a 'chilling effect on legitimate expression' (ibid.).

In sum, the factum constructed a liberal attack on state censorship, a position that the CCLA had advanced and defended in diverse contexts since the 1960s in Canada (Lacombe 1994, 25, 55). For civil libertarians, central to the pornography debate has been the issue of freedom, that is, freedom from state censorship and invasion of privacy. Within this perspective, sexuality is constructed as a terrain of individual freedom and privacy, devoid of power relations. State intervention in this sphere, without empirically proven evidence of social harm, is, therefore, seen as an illegitimate exercise of legal authority (Berger, Searles, and Cottle 1991, 22). This is the perspective that grounded the CCLA/MARL intervention in *Butler*. Significantly, this intervention relied upon abstracted principles such as 'expression,' 'liberty,' and 'privacy,' and it failed to articulate any explicit defence of sexual expression. Implicit in the CCLA/MARL factum is the claim that sexual expression is valuable because it is just like any other form of expression. Obscenity regulation, by consequence, is wrong because it arbitrarily restricts expression, because it censors without compelling evidence of social harm.

Against the powerful narrative 'sexuality as danger' and 'pornography as harm,' the CCLA/MARL factum offered mere emptiness – that is, a conception of sexuality as devoid of content and of pornography as simply another form of expression. Furthermore, its most persuasive argument for striking down section 163 was constructed on the basis of a sweeping attack on the central legitimating myth of law, legal 'objectivity.' And in the place of criminal law's pledge to regulate, to contain, to protect, and to preserve the social order, the CCLA/MARL could offer only the highly uncertain and contingent promise that the free marketplace of ideas, combined with education, would provide a defence against sexism and misogyny (CCLA/MARL 1991, 3, 18).

While in agreement that s.163 constituted an unjustifiable limitation on freedom of expression, the BCCLA intervention offered a much more specific defence of sexual expression and a more contextualized critique of obscenity law, grounded in a careful analysis of its historical objectives and impact. Significantly, this intervention is alone among the participants in this case in articulating a positive theory of sexual expression. But the position advanced by the BCCLA, like that of the CCLA/MARL, was characterized by its contingency; it defended the deregulation of sexual expression with promises of destabilization and the erosion of dominant sexual norms.

Informing the BCCLA factum is a strong assertion of the value of sexual expression in a democratic political community. Sexual expression is valuable because sexuality itself is important to community life. Drawing on the feminist insight that the 'personal is political,' the BCCLA factum made the claim that sexuality is not something that is properly confined to the 'private' sphere, outside political and community life (BCCLA 1991, 4). On the contrary, sexual norms, behaviours, and identities have a bearing on the structure of political life. Challenging the dominant equation of sexuality with nature in Western society, the BCCLA advanced a conception of sexuality as socially constructed. In turn, sexual expression, according to this intervenor, plays a fundamental role in creating and constituting sexual norms. Sexual speech is, in other words, important precisely because it is political. As the factum states, sexual expression 'tells us something about ourselves that some of us, at least, prefer not to know. It threatens to explode the uneasy accommodation between sexual impulse and social custom – to destroy the carefully spun web holding sexuality in place' (ibid., 6). If sexual expression is important at a general level because it is the realm of debate and contestation about sexual norms, the BCCLA also emphasized that this form of expression is of particular significance to certain groups within the community. For sexual minorities, sexual speech constitutes a 'means of self affirmation in a generally hostile world' (ibid.). For women, as well, the development of sexual imagery can be a means of finding voice and creating a sexuality that challenges how women have hitherto been constructed (ibid., 15).

In stressing the potentially disruptive power of sexual expression, however, the BCCLA was not advancing the position that pornography is uniformly liberatory. Instead, the second thrust of this factum is to assert that the meaning of pornography is neither singular nor apparent. According to the BCCLA, pornography holds conflictual meanings – it can reaffirm male power and misogyny and it can also 'flout conventional sexual mores,' 'ridicule sexual hypocrisy,' 'underscore the importance of sexual needs,' and affirm 'sex for no other reason than for pleasure' (BCCLA 1991, 5). Against the widespread claim that the 'Truth' of pornography is 'harm,' the BCCLA thus emphasized the contradictory character of pornography. As the factum states, the impact of pornography is not linear or straightforward; it is instead 'multiple, ... layered and highly contextual' (ibid., 11).

Added to its assertions about the destabilizing power of sexual expression and the irreducible complexity of pornography is the BCCLA's critique of the objectives and application of section 163 of the Criminal Code. By canvassing the history of Canadian obscenity law, the factum demonstrates that the express objective of s.163, when first enacted, was to enforce a 'particular standard of morality, or perhaps that which is regarded as politically correct' (BCCLA 1991, 8). Further, as interpreted by the courts through the community-standards test, the effect of this law has been to impose judicial 'views of correct sexuality on a diverse community' (ibid., 15). Quoting an American feminist anti-censorship brief, the BCCLA maintained that the impact of the community-standards test has been to 'disapprove of those images that are least conventional, and privilege those that are closest to majoritarian beliefs about proper sexuality' (ibid.). The moral-conservative objectives of Canadian obscenity law are especially evident, according to this factum, in relation to sexual minorities. In particular, the interpretation of this law has often systematically discriminated against 'homosexuals,' because they are by definition located outside majoritarian sexual norms (ibid.).

In effect, the BCCLA constructed a normative argument[13] against Canadian obscenity law on the basis that it enforces uniformity and suppresses sexual diversity and plurality. But combined with this normative assertion, the BCCLA contended that the moral basis of obscenity regulation renders it unconstitutional. It is unconstitutional because enforcing a particular standard of morality, that is, 'asserting the possession of an insight into the moral universe that is intrinsically superior' cannot be viewed as a pressing and substantial concern that would justify the restriction of freedom of expression (BCCLA 1991, 8–9). The BCCLA conceded that a morally based law might be constitutionally justified when there is a close connection between immoral conduct and social harm (ibid., 8). But it argued, echoing the claims of the CCLA/ MARL, that there is no reliable evidence to demonstrate a causal connection between pornography and acts of violence (ibid., 11). Furthermore, following from its assertions regarding the complexity and ambiguity of pornography, it maintained that it is impossible to make conclusive statements about the relationship between sexual imagery and attitudinal changes; this relationship is tenuous and complex (ibid.). Finally, and again concurring with the CCLA/MARL, the BCCLA emphasized the overbreadth of obscenity law. This law has not merely targeted material that is 'violent or subjugating to women'; instead, as noted in the factum, the obscenity provision has applied to material that consists of 'nothing but exploitations of sex by explicit portrayals of sexual acts' (ibid., 9).

In sum, the BCCLA issued a powerful challenge to the legal regulation of obscenity grounded in a set of claims that represented a firm rejection of the dominant understanding of sexuality in Western society. Against the understanding of sexuality as a force of nature, the BCCLA asserted that sexuality has no essence; it is instead a site of conflict and the result of social construction. Against sex negativity, that is, the idea of sex as innately dangerous, the BCCLA asserted that sexuality can sometimes constitute a force of change, liberation, and pleasure. Against the rigid division of sex into 'good sex' and 'bad sex,' the BCCLA asserted respect for sexual plurality and diversity. And against the understanding of sex as a threat to the social order, the BCCLA highlighted the importance of the erosion of dominant sexual norms and emphasized the role that pornography could play in such a project.

In these ways, the BCCLA issued a powerful critique of commonsense understandings of sexuality. At the same time, however, the force of its critique placed its arguments on the outside – outside of dominant understandings of sexuality and outside the kinds of rhetorical strategies privileged in the arena of law. In the context of a social space suffused with images of sexual violence – women tortured, beaten, and murdered – the BCCLA's call for 'destabilization,' exploration, and deregulation becomes understood as a plea for anarchy (Smart 1994, 24). Indeed, as Vance has emphasized, the net effect of the cultural construction of sexuality as danger has been to suggest that we are 'less sexually safe than ever and that discussions and explorations of pleasure are better left to a safer time' (Vance 1984, 4). In this context, the promises offered by decriminalization, plurality, and diversity seem too little when weighed against the assumed dangers of unregulated sexuality. In effect, the normative emphasis that the BCCLA places on uncertainty and instability seems incongruent with the anxiety-ridden and stability-craving character of these times. More than this, however, the assertion that pornography has no essence, no 'Truth' to be discerned by the judiciary, represented a firm denial of law's power. In effect, the BCCLA factum can be seen as a firm rejection of foundationalist claims. The factum challenges an essentialist view of sexuality and insists that sexuality has no essence. It refuses law's 'Truth' and asserts that pornography has no 'Truth' amenable to legal regulation. Despite the compelling nature of the BCCLA critique, its embrace of anti-foundational discourse thus placed it in a position of strategic disadvantage on the terrain of law.

Defending the Status Quo: Government Actors and Moral Conservatives

If dominant meanings, systems, and the strategic imperatives of legal discourse functioned to marginalize the positions advanced by CCLA/ MARL and by the BCCLA, they simultaneously reinforced the claims of those seeking to uphold section 163 of the Criminal Code. In particular, those who sought to defend the status quo operation of obscenity law were placed in a position of strategic advantage. Key among the defenders of obscenity regulation in this case were the Respondent – the Attorney General of Manitoba (A.G. of Manitoba 1991), the Attorney General of Canada (A.G. of Canada 1991), and the organization the Group Against Pornography (GAP). In some respects, the functions of these participants were distinct. Government actors were placed in a position of defending the existing law as a result of Butler's constitutional challenge. GAP, by contrast, is a conservative, Manitoba-based anti-pornography organization that intervened in this case to advance an essentially conservative moral defence of s.163. Nevertheless, the positions put forward in these three factums were remarkably similar. Each of these participants appealed to dominant notions of sexuality as a force of nature, as dangerous and out of control. Each denied the value of sexual expression as expression. Each sought to justify the constitutionality of obscenity regulation by appealing to legal objectivity and to law's power to determine 'Truth.' And each attempted to defend the imperatives of criminalization through moral-conservative discourses shrouded in feminist rhetoric. Together, the positions taken by the A.G. of Manitoba, the A.G. of Canada, and GAP represented a legal expression of the new politics of anti-pornography.

In this case, the common motivating objective for government actors and for GAP was to preserve the power of the state to control and censor sexual representations. As elaborated by GAP, '[it is critical to] prevent obscene activities from being elevated to a constitutional status that would impair the process of future regulation of such activities by law makers' (GAP 1991, 11). In fact, a strong defence of the supremacy of Parliament underlies all three factums. The A.G. of Manitoba and the A.G. of Canada, for example, emphasized (using precisely the same words) that it is 'not the task of the court to substitute its judgment for the legislature' (A.G. of Manitoba 1991, 4; A.G. of Canada 1991, 15; GAP 1991, 2–3). Where Parliament has made an assessment about competing claims, they argued, the judiciary should not second-guess. Through the appeal to judicial deference, then, these three participants sought to affirm the legitimacy of obscenity policy and to insulate this policy from constitutional review.

In defending obscenity law against this constitutional challenge, however, these litigants would be forced to respond to the claims made by the Appellant and by the interventions of the CCLA/MARL and the BCCLA. The first question raised through this constitutional challenge was whether or not s.163 infringes upon the expression guarantee of the Charter. While GAP sought to demonstrate that this legislation does not conflict with s.2(b), the factums of both government actors conceded that obscenity law does restrict freedom of expression. Despite this apparent difference, however, all three of the defenders adopted a similar position on sexual expression – that is, if sexual expression can be understood as expression at all, it constitutes a lesser form of expression.

The claim that sexual expression lies far away from the intent of the expression guarantee of the Charter represents a dominant and resounding theme in the arguments of the A.G. of Manitoba, the A.G. of Canada, and GAP. In making this claim, these factums rely heavily on the idea that sexuality is something that is purely physical, distinct from and less valuable than the pursuits of the 'spirit' and the 'intellect' (see

Cossman, this volume). The factums draw upon, and in turn reinforce, a distinction between mind and body that has underpinned the dominate construction of sexuality in Western society. Sexual expression is considered of the 'body'; when not combined with some other redeeming purpose, it is seen to be without any meaningful content. As the factums state,

It is human thought/spirit alone or combined with physical activity that encompasses 'meaning' and therefore, 'expression' ... [t]he depiction of sexual acts ... solely to titillate and shock an audience, does not convey meaning. It is submitted that a line must be drawn so as to preserve the true intent of freedom of expression, and obscenity crosses that line. (GAP 1991, 9)

Purveyors of obscene material have demonstrated little concern for the conveyance of meaningful content, and it is difficult to conceive how their appeal to prurient interests promotes in any way values such as the pursuit of truth, individual self-fulfillment and participation in the political process. (A.G. of Canada 1991, 22)

[T]o equate the robust exchange of ideas and political debate with commercial exploitation of obscene material demeans the grand conception of [freedom of expression] and its high purposes in the historic struggle for freedom. (A.G. of Manitoba 1991, 13)

Implicit in these quotes is the idea that sexuality is a force of nature outside intellect. Within this view, sexual expression is something directed at the body. Sexual expression represents mere 'titillation' and seeks to 'appeal to prurient interests'; it is further diminished by the fact that it is within the realm of commerce and thus outside of 'the robust exchange of ideas and political debate.' According to this perspective, sexuality alone cannot be the domain of speech because it is base. To be considered expression, sexual speech must be combined with some higher purpose, be it 'artistic, social or scientific' (A.G. of Canada 1991, 21). The body must, in essence, connect with the mind; the body must be transcended. Drawing upon this dualistic construction 'mind/body,' the claim that sexual expression is a lesser form of expression is cemented. This claim, in turn, becomes used for a similar purpose in all three factums. While GAP deploys this argument to contend that s.163 does not violate freedom of expression, all three defenders of the status quo suggest that the restriction of sexual speech is subject to a lesser standard of justification than other infringements of s.2(b) (GAP 1991, 12; A.G. of

Manitoba 1991, 12–13; A.G. of Canada 1991, 22). And all, in the end, reach the conclusion that s.163 of the Criminal Code represents a reasonable limit on freedom of expression under s.1 of the Charter.

In attempting to demonstrate that criminal obscenity legislation is constitutionally justified, GAP, the A.G. of Manitoba, and the A.G. of Canada make a series of similar and interlinked arguments. Their first step is to assert that s.163 is neither vague nor overbroad. All three factums rely heavily upon appeals to the 'power of law' in order to support this contention. According to these litigants, the tests developed by the courts to determine 'undue exploitation of sex' constitute clear and objective standards for the determination of criminal obscenity. Despite the fact that the community-standards test, for example, explicitly relies on the 'judiciary's general instinctive sense' of what constitutes a national standard of tolerance, the A.G. of Canada asserts that this test has been 'refined through repeated judicial determination and has become a reasonably certain tool' (A.G. of Canada 1991, 6; see Busby 1994, 167). Furthermore, this factum claimed that there does indeed exist a societal understanding of what constitutes a national standard, such that 'it may be reasonably argued that distributors of sexually exploitative material are well aware of the point beyond which they face the fear of prosecution' (A.G. of Canada 1991, 9).

As for other legal tests that have been applied to determine 'obscenity,' the defenders argue that they too are capable of 'certain' application (see Cossman, chapter 3, for an elaboration of these tests). The internal-necessities test, by which the judiciary has sought to distinguish materials with a 'purely' sexual content from materials that possess 'artistic merit or serious purpose,' has, according to the A.G. of Canada, been 'enunciated with reasonable precision by the Appellate Courts' (A.G. of Canada 1991, 10). The degradation test, elaborated fairly recently by the courts to further 'clarify' the meaning of obscenity, is also claimed to constitute a clear legal standard. As the A.G. of Canada states, 'Degradation, in context, is a word of common usage, requiring no additional qualifiers. It refers to the debasement of individuals deprived of their dignity and treated as less than equal' (ibid., 12). For the A.G. of Manitoba, as well, the meaning of 'degradation' is presented as if readily apparent, referring to 'material, that although not violent, depicts people, usually women, in decidedly subordinate roles in their sexual relations with others or that depicts people engaged in sexual practices that would to most people be considered humiliating' (A.G. of Manitoba 1991, 9).

It is ironic that while both government factums are intent upon demonstrating the clarity of degradation as a legal standard, there are, nevertheless, clear differences within their understandings of what constitutes 'degrading.' For both, it means the depiction of inequality in sexual relations; although what constitutes inequality is, of course, always a highly subjective question. For the A.G. of Manitoba, however, degradation also means 'sexual practices that most people would consider humiliating.' The A.G. of Manitoba thus imports a majoritarian standard of acceptable sexual behaviour into the meaning of 'degradation.' Degrading is that which falls outside of the sexual norms of the community as defined by the majority. In their attempts to constitute degradation as a stable legal category, then, the A.G. of Canada and the A.G. of Manitoba reinforce the very instability of this term. Indeed, as Vance has noted, within the pornography debate 'degradation' is a cross-over term, used by feminists and conservatives alike and implying a range of conflictual meanings depending on the context within which this term is used (Vance 1993a, 36).

The contextual and subjective quality of terms such as 'community standards,' 'artistic or other serious purpose,' and 'degradation' is, nevertheless, emphatically denied in the factums of the A.G. of Canada, the A.G. of Manitoba, and GAP. The factums rely on a literalist interpretive framework, assuming that the category 'obscene' is capable of clear legal demarcation. According to such an approach, neither context nor subjectivity is seen to influence the 'meaning' of sexual imagery. Instead, the 'meaning' of sexual material is assumed to be readily observable on its face and apparent to all those who observe (see Vance 1993a, 40). Furthermore, invoking law's own image of itself as 'objective,' the factums construct the task of determining criminal obscenity as if it were a purely formulaic exercise. It is strongly asserted that established judicial tests, together with the rigorous application of legal method, will always produce 'correct' legal answers to the question 'What is obscene?' As both the A.G. of Canada and the A.G. of Manitoba claim, this law is not vague because the courts have applied it 'without insurmountable difficulty' (A.G. of Manitoba 1991, 18–19; A.G. of Canada 1991, 12). While almost surprising in its logical leaps, the claim that obscenity law is objective and certain because the courts have had no problems in applying it is significantly reinforced through its underlying appeal to legal objectivity and 'Truth.' The powerful assumption that law is a sphere of logic and rationality, divorced from politics and bias, informs and bolsters the arguments of these litigants.

Following from the assertion that the application of Canadian obscenity law is objective, the A.G. of Manitoba, the A.G. of Canada, and GAP move on to construct a defence of the objectives of s.163. While framing their defence within a older conservative moral narrative about 'indecency and immorality,' the litigants seek to modernize this narrative through couching it in more contemporary arguments, arguments drawn mainly from anti-pornography feminism and social science. Nevertheless, none of the defenders of the status quo shies away from justifying the specifically 'moral' objectives of s.163. As these factums state,

... morality has long been recognized as one of the purposes in respect of which the criminal law may be enacted. (A.G. of Manitoba 1991, 10; GAP states that it concurs with this section of the Respondent's factum, GAP 1991, 18)

Public morality is unquestionably a valid basis for the exercise of the criminal law power and the protection of the community's moral consensus constitutes itself as a pressing and substantial concern even in the absence of evidence that concrete harm would otherwise result ... an example of this is the fact that anal intercourse is prohibited wherever more than two persons take part or are present. (A.G. of Canada 1991, 18)

The role of law as guardian of the moral universe is clearly defended and applauded in each of these factums. Implicit here is the assumption that the depiction of sexual practices that lie outside of majoritarian norms constitutes a threat to the community itself. Unconfined sexuality, in other words, is represented as thoroughly and innately dangerous. Sexual minorities, in particular, are singled out as a jeopardy to society. Furthermore, as the GAP factum contends, pornography also poses a threat to the 'family.' As GAP asserts, the consumption of soft-core pornography leads to 'an appetite for more deviant, bizarre or violent types of pornography ... *normal sex no longer seem[s] to do the job*' (my emphasis). Pornography is thus claimed to produce a 'devaluation and depreciation of the importance of monogamy and a lack of confidence in marriage as a viable ... institution' (GAP 1991, 16). The A.G. of Manitoba's factum is similar in thrust when it argues that 'a sensitive, key relationship of human existence, central to family life ... can be debased and distorted' by obscenity (A.G. of Manitoba 1991, 7). In effect, the defenders of the status quo rigorously erect a line between 'good sex' and 'bad sex,' where good sex is sex in 'marriage,' sex that is not 'bizarre,' sex that is not 'homosexual' (see Cossman chapter). In turn, obscenity law is presented as a force of stability and order – as the barrier standing between 'indecency,' 'disorder,' and the 'depraving and corrupting aspects of obscenity,' on the one hand, and 'public safety' and 'the quality of life of a community,' on the other (see A.G. of Canada 1991, 14; GAP 1991, 19; A.G. of Manitoba 1991, 11).

Grafting onto arguments about the role of obscenity law in sustaining the moral order, these litigants also emphasize that s.163 plays an important role in protecting women from harm. Anti-pornography feminist rhetoric about sexual harms was, in this way, merged with and overlaid upon conservative and moral discourses. But, significantly, none of these factums argues that this more contemporary 'feminist' objective has supplanted the older moral-conservative rationale of obscenity law. Instead, the objective of 'preventing harm' is placed alongside the legislation's specifically moral purposes and constructed as if thoroughly consistent with these purposes.

In making the argument that obscenity law protects women from harm, the A.G. of Canada, the A.G. of Manitoba, and GAP make use of both anti-pornography feminist discourse and social-science research. The A.G. of Manitoba and GAP are especially emphatic in their deployment of social science 'evidence' on sexual violence. In these factums, the 'evidence' of the links between 'violent' pornography and violence against women is presented as if clear and absolutely persuasive (A.G. of Manitoba 1991, 8; GAP 1991, 14). Moreover, both factums go to some lengths to assert that 'non-violent, degrading material bears a causal relationship to antisocial acts of sexual violence' and to negative attitudinal changes such as 'less serious view[s] of rape'[14] (A.G. of Manitoba 1991, 9; GAP 1991, 16). The A.G. of Canada, for its part, acknowledges that the social-scientific 'evidence' is not conclusive; but, at the same time, its factum emphasizes that 'some findings go so far as to establish a link between certain material and violence against women' (A.G. of Canada 1991, 15). For the A.G. of Canada, scientific evidence is not necessary to establish the relation between pornography and gendered harms. As it claims, in the absence of proof of a causative link, it is nevertheless 'reasonable to conclude' that significant harms follow from obscenity and that 'it is unquestionable that women are the group most likely to suffer the deleterious effects of its dissemination' (A.G. of Canada 1991, 16–17).

In effect, in articulating the specific dangers of obscenity, these factums reflect the new politics of anti-pornography as it had been constituted over the 1980s by moral-conservatives and by neoconservative government actors. Much like the Tories in their law-reform efforts, those defending the status quo in the *Butler* case engaged in a carefully executed effort in discursive blending. Moral concerns about decency, immorality, abnormal sex, and family decline are here combined with newer concerns about sexual violence, the degradation of women, and gender harm. These factums happily assimilated anti-pornography feminist discourse; in this way, pornography becomes subsumed within 'sexual violence' at the same time as it gets constructed as a threat to the moral consensus. Significantly, pornography and obscenity are viewed through an unremittingly negative lens by these litigants. The only acceptable forms of sexual representation that are acknowledged are those that transcend a purely sexual content. Sexual expression per se is represented as a force of instability, disorder, and violence. In a similar rhetorical move, the possibilities that women may possess sexual agency and find pleasures in sexuality and sexual representation are emphatically denied. Women are constructed as passive victims of violence who are victimized, in turn, through sexual representation. The necessity of criminal regulation of pornography is thus presented as both a moral and a social imperative. Criminalization is safety and certainty against social instability and harm.

Discourses of sexual panic are both deployed and reinforced by these litigants in order to justify the imperatives of criminalization. And, in the end, the arguments that they construct are empowered through their rhetorical appeals to certainty and stability. Indeed, as Singer has argued, part of the attraction of this kind of position is that 'it offers totalizing forms of explanatory closure.' Social instability is presented as a symptom of an erosion of authority – '[t]he failure to heed authority, in the name of 'liberalization,' 'tolerance,' lies at the root of the crisis as we suffer the consequences of sexual proliferation' (Singer 1993, 31–2). Law, in turn, is represented as a return to authority, a form of authority that is at once certain and objective.

LEAF's Intervention: Anti-pornography Feminism in the Courts

In *Butler*, the feminist litigation organization LEAF intervened to advance an unequivocally anti-pornography and pro-censorship position. If the 1980s witnessed the dawn of a new politics of anti-pornography, so too did LEAF's position in *Butler* express a new feminist politics of anti-pornography. This politics was at once more intractable and highly sweeping in its assertions. A central thrust of LEAF's intervention was to reject the moral-conservative foundations of s.163 and, therefore, many of the specific claims that had been made by government actors and by the organization GAP. Nevertheless, if LEAF's position must be set apart from the defenders of the status quo, so too must it be seen in relation to the claims of these litigants. While rejecting moral conservatism, LEAF simultaneously embraced many specific elements of these positions. LEAF's argument, for example, relies on an appeal to the potential objectivity of law. Its intervention also draws heavily upon discourses of sexual danger, on an entirely negative view of sexual expression, and, much like the defenders of the status quo, propels an image of women as passive 'victims.' Moreover, echoing the rhetorical style of the 'status quo' litigants, this factum systematically erases all diversity and complexity, substituting instead its own authoritative monologue. In keeping with the strategic imperatives of legal discourse, LEAF presents its arguments as if it were articulating a singular and unified feminist voice on pornography. Although not embracing conservative moral discourse, it adopts moral rhetoric nonetheless, locating its particular position upon the moral high ground of the feminist pornography debate (Smart 1993, 196).

It is extremely important to examine the specific threads of this position in *Butler*, for as we emphasize in this book, LEAF's own story of this case has become the 'official' interpretation. Careful attention to this factum is also demanded because, as LEAF has complained, '[s]ince *Butler's* release our position has been simplified, even caricatured, and criticized, sometimes vociferously by the media, civil libertarians and gay men' (Busby 1994, 1). In addition, however, a thorough deconstruction of what was argued in *Butler* is also critical in light of LEAF's own representative claims in the courts. Since its formation in 1985, this organization has consistently claimed to speak for and represent the concerns of Canadian women in constitutional litigation. LEAF's claim to speak as the singular constitutional voice of the Canadian women's movement pervades its early literature (Gotell 1995, 114). As restated more recently in a defence of its *Butler* intervention, 'LEAF's *mandate is to promote women's equality* through legal action' (my emphasis; Busby 1994, 172).

In fact, LEAF has been quite successful in representing itself as the 'Chartered' voice of Canadian feminism; so successful indeed that in the courts, the media, and many academic analyses, it is unquestioningly viewed as the litigation arm of the women's movement.[15] Despite this image, it is true that for much of its history, LEAF's links of accountability with other feminist organizations have been not well established (Gotell 1995, 114). While consultation has begun to emerge as a more integral part of LEAF's procedures,[16] it remains true that such outreach activities occur on an ad-hoc basis and are not a prerequisite for engaging in litigation (LEAF 1993; LEAF 1990, 14). In view of the extremely contentious debates that have taken place within Canadian feminism on pornography and censorship (Currie 1992, 195–6; Lacombe 1994), it is, of course, highly significant that LEAF made the decision to intervene in *Butler* without the benefit of outside consultations.[17]

If there are not formal relationships of accountability between LEAF and other feminist actors, on what basis can this litigation organization claim legitimacy and voice? On what basis could LEAF intervene in *Butler* to advance a coherent 'feminist' position on the complex question of pornography and obscenity law? In the absence of established mechanisms of accountability to extralegal feminist actors, LEAF's 'authority' has rested first on an assertion of legal expertise. Legal expertise empowers feminist legal actors because it allows them to speak from within the rules of legal discourse, vesting in them the ability to determine the 'relevancy' of complex lived experiences. Always this process involves a distillation that lends legitimacy to feminist legal actors, just as it marginalizes other feminist voices who speak from outside the boundaries of legal discourse.[18]

If LEAF's authority has rested on the assertion of expertise, so too has it rested on the claim to 'Truth.' The underlying assumption of LEAF's factum in *Butler* is that women constitute a subordinate social group and that it is only from this perspective that the impact of pornography and obscenity law can truly be seen. LEAF's approach to constitutional equality, as a whole, has proceeded from the premise that women's experience of subordination provides an interpretive lens through which constitutional claims must be assessed. Women's standpoint of marginality, in other words, is embraced as a privileged foundation for interpreting Charter equality. Much like feminist-standpoint epistemology, women's experience here acquires the status of an Archimedian point capable of accurately revealing the nature of social relations. Because women lack power, LEAF's approach implies, the standpoint of women offers a clear and undistorted insight into the operations of power. In *Butler* and in each of its cases, LEAF has thus urged the judiciary to view Charter contests from the perspective of women's disadvantage and to assess how laws and practices may reinforce that disadvantage.[19] This standpoint is asserted as a site of epistemic privilege. The irony of such an epistemic strategy is that while admitting to being so situated, it cannot admit to the partiality of its own vision. In this process, what is a clearly locatable position – that of women's subordination – becomes transformed into infinite, perspectiveless vision (Brown 1991, 73; Gotell 1995, 106). From the subordinate vantage point of women, this approach proclaims, we can know the reality of women's oppression and this, in turn, leads to correct and unified feminist and jurisprudential positions. This approach and its related claim to 'Truth' informs LEAF's factum in the *Butler* case.

The thrust of LEAF's position in this case, like that of the government actors and GAP, was to emphasize the pressing and substantial objectives underlying s.163 and, in this manner, to defend obscenity legislation against constitutional challenge. Unlike the other defenders of obscenity legislation, however, LEAF's factum does not represent an explicit embrace of the status quo; in particular, the moral-conservative foundations of Canadian obscenity law are emphatically rejected by this litigant. Drawing significantly on the work of American anti-pornography feminist Catherine MacKinnon (who by her own admission helped to write this factum), LEAF argues that '[h]istorically obscenity law was justified on the basis of morality, a rationale which has been the subject of much criticism and obscures pornography's discriminating effects on women' (LEAF 1991a, 2; MacKinnon and Dworkin 1994, 2; MacKinnon 1987). According to this position, obscenity law as it has traditionally been understood emphasizes decency and indecency and excludes an understanding of the impact of obscenity from 'women's point of view.' As explained by MacKinnon, who is in turn cited in this section of the factum, 'Obscenity law is concerned with morality, specifically morals from a male point of view. The feminist critique of porn is a politics, specifically politics from women's point of view, meaning the standpoint of the subordination of women to men. Morality here means good and evil; politics means power and powerlessness' (MacKinnon 1987, 147). Through its attack on the moralistic basis of obscenity legislation, LEAF, like MacKinnon, is trying to draw a distinction between the feminist objection to pornography and the conservative objection that all sex outside marriage is 'dirty.' A 'women's point of view' is presented as the appropriate point of entry into an analysis of the impact of pornography. According to this factum, the judicial interpretation of s.163 through the 'community-standards test' has been preoccupied with explicitness. This preoccupation underlay the vagueness and subjectivity of obscenity law; but, more critically, this moralistic approach obscured, in LEAF's words, the 'actual harms pornography does to women' (LEAF 1991a, 3). The law ignored, as LEAF argued, the 'exploitation of women' and thereby 'functioned as an instrument to legitimize and enforce women's disadvantaged status' (ibid., 4). The community-standards test was, therefore, 'not properly anchored in a harms based principle that found harms to women to be determinative' (ibid., 4–5).

It is useful to distinguish between LEAF's critique of conservative moralism and obscenity law and the critique that was advanced in the factums of the BCCLA and the CCLA/MARL. For the BCCLA and the CCLA/MARL, moral conservatism must be challenged because it constrains sexual expression and represses sexual diversity. For LEAF, by contrast, moral-conservative approaches to obscenity regulation are 'wrong' because they prevent us from seeing, and in turn from regulating, the 'actual harms' that pornography causes for women. While the BCCLA/CCLA/MARL critique supports deregulation, LEAF's argument seeks to justify a different and intensified form of regulation, one that is attentive to the 'actual' or 'True' impacts of pornography.

The unequivocal assertion that 'harm' is the essence of pornography is the fundamental and central claim that underlies LEAF's factum, grounding its constitutional arguments on obscenity law. In this factum, LEAF constructs pornography as if its only 'Truth' is harm, and in this way it cements an entirely negative view of sexual expression. It is significant that in its more recent explanation and defence of its *Butler* intervention, LEAF attempts to qualify this position and to reframe and restate what it argued in the Supreme Court. According to LEAF's post-hoc statement, the effects of sexual representation are not entirely 'negative.' In this statement, it is conceded that part of the feminist project must involve 'exploring women's sexualities' and that some forms of pornography may play a role in this endeavour (Busby 1994, 182). LEAF's statement further stresses its commitment to 'affirming the social and sexual identities of lesbians through the law' and suggests that it is 'heterosexual pornography' that has been most responsible for harms towards women (ibid., 182, 172). These kinds of qualifications are, nevertheless, simply not present in the text of the *Butler* factum. In the factum, LEAF advances an absolute and definitive conception of pornography as the very embodiment of gendered harm.

This is first apparent in the manner in which this factum defines pornography – that is, as a 'practice of sex discrimination against individual women and women as a group' and as a 'systematic practice of exploitation and subordination based on sex that differentially harms women'

(LEAF 1991a, 2, 7; Busby 1994, 171). Implicit in this definition is that pornography is something that is 'done' to women by men. This is made explicit at other points when LEAF states that '[p]ornography is made to produce male sexual excitement, erection and masturbation' (LEAF 1991a, 16). So the factum defines pornography as a practice of gender-based exploitation. Nowhere does it attempt to make a distinction between forms of pornography that may harm women and those that may not. Nowhere does the factum acknowledge that some women make pornography that is explicitly for women (Williams 1993a; Loach 1993; Rodgerson 1993). All pornography is simply brushed away with the same broad stroke – that is through its complete equation with 'harm.' Nor does the factum set pornography as 'harm' apart from other categories of sexual representation. For example, it does not claim (following from the work of some feminist critics of pornography) that pornography is different from erotica, which is something 'not harmful,' defined by 'consensual and egalitarian' depictions of sex (see Rubin 1993a, 28, for a discussion). While, as Rubin highlights, this distinction is highly subjective and therefore difficult to draw and sustain, at least by invoking it LEAF would have indicated that not all sexual representations are uniformly oppressive. By omitting any references to positive forms of sexual expression from the factum, pornography is constructed as a practice innately harmful to women. In fact, the factum even goes so far as to argue that an 'Appellant [be required to] demonstrate that the subject matters do not limit women's rights before the protection of [freedom of expression] can be claimed' (LEAF 1991a, 8). What is clearly implied here is that all representations of sex are by definition 'exploitative' unless proven otherwise. As Rubin has commented in a critique of this form of definition, 'This is argument by tautology. If pornography is defined as that which is inherently degrading to women then by definition it cannot be reformed ... This tactic completely finesses the necessity of providing some demonstration that what is generally thought of as pornography is actually denoted by this definition' (Rubin 1993b, 27).

LEAF, however, does not shy away from the task of elaborating, in great detail, the harms that it alleges flow from pornography. As it states, 'The harms of pornography to women documented in [the] literature include dehumanization, humiliation, sexual exploitation, forced sex, forced prostitution, physical injury, child sexual abuse and sexual harassment. Pornography also diminishes the reputation of women as a group, deprives women of their credibility and social and self worth, and undermines women's equal access to protected rights' (LEAF 1991a,

7). To establish these connections between pornography and harm LEAF relies, first, on the same body of social-scientific evidence deployed by the other litigants in this case. By now it should be apparent that this research is highly indeterminate; it can and has been used to vastly different ends in the legal debates about pornography and censorship (Rubin 1993b, 30; King 1993). For the CCLA/MARL and the BCCLA, the inconclusiveness of this research was stressed in order to bolster arguments for striking down criminal obscenity legislation. For the government actors and GAP, by contrast, this research became 'evidence' and was used to support the claims that pornography both harms women and undermines the family.

Despite its obvious malleability, however, LEAF treats this literature as if it were conclusive. Furthermore, it reports the findings of this work in a highly selective manner. It ignores findings that have been used to promote moral-conservative agendas – for example, that pornography produces less belief in marriage, greater dissatisfaction with one's own sex life, and greater tolerance for homosexuality and sexual variety.[20] In turn, LEAF places its own particular interpretations upon this body of research, stressing support for the claim that pornography causes gendered harm. LEAF argues, first, that 'direct physical violence ... is inflicted to make some pornography'[21] (LEAF 1991a, 9–10); and it treats this category of pornography as if it were widespread, contrary to the claims of many sex-trade workers themselves (Rubin 1993b, 33). Second, LEAF contends that materials which combine sex and violence cause an increased risk of violence against women. This finding is phrased in particularly unequivocal language. As LEAF states, 'it is uncontroversial that exposure to such materials increases aggression towards women' (LEAF 1991a, 11). At the same time, however, the leading researcher in this field (who is extensively cited in the LEAF factum) has cautioned against overinterpretation of his findings (see Rubin 1993a, 30; Lacombe 1994, 37). Third, LEAF argues that materials which combine sex with aggression produce attitudinal changes including desensitization to sexual violence (LEAF 1991a, 14). Finally, non-violent materials that 'degrade and dehumanize women' are associated with a whole range of extremely negative effects, including 'lower inhibitions on aggression by men against women, increase[d] acceptance of women's sexual servitude, increase[d] sexual callousness toward women, decrease[d] ... desire by both sexes to have female children ... and increase[d] belief in male dominance in intimate relationships' (ibid.).

LEAF's attempt to demonstrate the incontrovertible relation between pornography and women's subordination does not end with its description of social-science research. In order to draw the reader even further into the narrative that pornography harms women, the LEAF factum employs a rhetorical and epistemic strategy drawn from its approach to Charter equality. According to this approach, as we have seen, women's experience in asserted as a privileged site of knowledge. In the *Butler* factum, this form of experiential 'Truth' is called upon to bolster LEAF's conclusions regarding the entirely negative effects of pornography. As the factum states, 'these laboratory studies merely document *what women know from their lives*. Many women report that men abuse them through pornography' (my emphasis) (LEAF 1991a, 14–15). What is implied in this quote is that women's claims about their own experience must be valued, because women are powerless and therefore women's words constitute the hidden 'Truth' of women's existence (and of pornography).

This is a rhetorical strategy that seeks to legitimize its 'Truth' through connection to worldly powerlessness. It assumes, as Brown writes, that 'Truth is always on the side of the damned or the excluded, hence truth is always clean of power, always reproaches power' (Brown 1991, 76). This form of argument, therefore, carries with it enormous weight. As Smart argues, for example, experiential claims and the use of personal testimony as a form of intervention 'can have an authority denied the theorist or statistician' (Smart 1993, 188). Through its use of experiential claims, LEAF is essentially saying that pornography is harm because its 'victims' know that it is harmful. This argumentative strategy is one that renders the harms of pornography obvious. Furthermore, it is a rhetorical tactic that serves to insulate LEAF's arguments from critique and contestation. To challenge the relation between pornography and harm is not simply to challenge the voices of those relatively privileged lawyers making this argument in the court; it is also to question those 'victims' who have given testimony of abuse (ibid., 190). By challenging LEAF's conclusions, one appears to be denying the realities of these less privileged women for whom LEAF claims to speak.

In sum, LEAF constructs an extremely powerful and unequivocal narrative on pornography, one that is highly consistent with dominant cultural constructions of sexuality and also with the claims advanced by the defenders of the status quo. Despite its assertions post-*Butler*, LEAF's factum develops a conception of sexuality as an unambiguous and uncontainable danger zone for women. To the extent that women's sexuality is discussed in the factum, it is located within sexual violence.

Women are presented as abused and diminished and entirely dominated through an innate male aggression. In turn, the potential of
women's sexual pleasure and agency is erased and eclipsed within this
narrative. While LEAF does not directly say that pornography is a fundamental cause of women's oppression, this assertion can nevertheless
be inferred from this factum.[22] For if pornography is responsible for the
broad-ranging impacts attributed to it here, one can only conclude that
this practice must play a significant role in subordinating women.

The LEAF factum presents women as powerless victims of male sexual violence. In this manner, it reflects a traditional conception of women
as sexually passive and helpless and in need of (male) protection. Just as
the defenders of the status quo deploy a strikingly similar construct in
order to justify the imperatives of criminalization, so too does LEAF's
narrative work to render the value of regulation self-evident. As Vance
has written of anti-pornography feminist rhetoric, 'the dominant cultural ideology elaborate[s] the threat of sexual danger, so the anti-
pornography movement responds by pushing for sexual safety via the
control of public expression of male sexuality' (Vance 1984, 6). LEAF's
equation of pornography and harm and its assertion of sexuality as danger underpin its constitutional arguments for the maintenance of criminal obscenity regulation. If pornography is harm, as LEAF tells us, then
'prohibiting pornography promotes equality' (LEAF 1991a, 17).

The first thread of LEAF's constitutional argument is to claim that
some pornography is a violent form of expression and therefore not protected under the expression guarantee of the Charter (LEAF 1991a, 9–
11). This is an argument that LEAF had developed over several years in
interventions on hate literature – interventions that were clearly laying
the groundwork for a constitutional position on obscenity and pornography (MacKinnon and Dworkin 1994, 2; LEAF 1991b, 1, 10). Second,
LEAF argues that other forms of pornography must also be excluded
from constitutional protection because of pornography's role in promoting women's disadvantage (LEAF 1991a, 12–17). In making this argument, LEAF asserts that section 28, the sexual-equality clause of the
Charter, is a pre-eminent guarantee, which has the effect of trumping all
other constitutional rights claims (ibid., 12). Thus, according to this factum, a balancing of rights must occur within the analysis of freedom of
expression, and in this contest women's equality claims must take prece-
dence over those invoking the protections of section 2(b).

In constructing the argument that pornography is not a form of
expression protected under freedom of expression, LEAF echoes the

defenders of the status quo. LEAF states very clearly that sexual expression is a lesser form of expression that is far away from the intent of s.2(b). As the factum argues (in very similar language to that used in the factums of the A.G. of Canada, the A.G. of Manitoba, and GAP), 'It is not made to further any search for truth. It is not a critique of the status quo or a dissenting but repressed voice ... [I]t is not a form of political speech as traditionally protected' (LEAF 1991a, 16). Pornography thus has no 'Truth'; its only 'Truth' is harm. Moreover, sexual expression is viewed as if always and entirely empty of and separate from political content. Like the defenders of the status quo, LEAF relegates pornography to the realm of the 'base,' which is, by definition, without any meaningful content. But adding to the arguments advanced by the A.G. of Canada, the A.G. of Manitoba, and GAP, LEAF also contends that pornography is not expression because it tells 'lies about women and their sexuality.' It is not, in other words, 'Truth' from 'women's point of view.' Pornography, according to LEAF, has worked to 'silence' women and to repress their expression (ibid.). Of course, this unequivocal argument ignores that women's voices might sometimes be articulated through sexual expression.

LEAF uses the claim that pornography is not expression in order to justify its assertion that the restriction of pornography does not infringe upon section 2(b). In the alternative, however, LEAF argues that the regulation of pornography can clearly be seen as a pressing and substantial government objective under section 1 of the Charter. In attempting to give constitutional support to the objectives of s.163, however, this litigant does not engage in a defence of conservative moralism or its expression through the 'community standards test.' This approach to obscenity has already been rejected because of its failure to emphasize the gendered harms of pornography. Yet, as LEAF argues, '[w]here a statute can reasonably bear an interpretation that conforms with the Charter it should be interpreted in that manner' (LEAF 1991a, 18). That interpretation, as the factum contends, can be found within what has been referred to as the 'degradation' test and its focus on social harms (ibid., 5–9). In effect, LEAF argued that the legal definition of obscenity must be recast to encompass the perspectives of women 'victimized' through pornography. It thus encouraged the court to abandon the conservative moral discourse that has long framed the definition of obscenity, in favour of an approach based on the harms pornography causes for women. Under this test, obscenity would be defined as material that is 'dehumanizing' and 'degrading' for women (ibid., 19).

Once again, the similarity between LEAF's arguments and the arguments of defenders of the status quo becomes apparent. While government actors and GAP affirmed their support for the continued application of the community-standards test, they also lauded the 'degradation' test as a legal standard capable of demarcating the boundaries of the criminally obscene. And underlying all of these factums is the assumption that the category of obscenity is amenable to clear legal definition. Like the defenders of the status quo, LEAF thus embraces the view that pornography/obscenity is open to literal interpretation. This view assumes that pornography can be understood universally and decontextually and it neglects how the context within which images are produced may influence their interpretation (Vance 1993b, 40–1; Smart 1993, 188). Similarly, this view ignores the very ambiguity of sexual texts, the role of subjectivity in shaping how sexual images are understood, and the fact that the same image is capable of producing conflictual responses, sometimes within the same reader/viewer. Indeed, as Vance has commented, 'Anti-pornography feminists have always favoured a single and universal reading of sexual imagery. They have elaborated a mechanistic theory about the myriad of ways in which sexual imagery causes harm ... Just like moral-conservatives, they reject interpretative schemes that admit the complexity and ambiguity of images, as well as the diverse responses of viewers' (Vance 1993b, 36).

But the embrace of a literalist interpretive scheme is only the first element of slippage between obscenity law's status-quo defenders and LEAF's arguments regarding the clarity of the degradation test. If LEAF assumes that pornography possesses a singular and apparent meaning, so too does it assume with confidence that the judiciary is capable of discerning that meaning. The task of defining what is 'degrading and dehumanizing' is seen to be open to objective legal determination. And in this manner, legal objectivity is reified.[23] LEAF's claims, like those of the government actors and moral-conservative intervenors, rest upon an appeal to law's power. While LEAF acknowledges that legal interpretations have been biased in the past, excluding an understanding of pornography from 'women's point of view,' it nevertheless presupposes that legal standards can be reframed from this standpoint.[24] Underlying this pro-censorship position is the belief that should the Supreme Court endorse a definition of pornography as 'harm against women,' then this would become the universal legal standard for the interpretation of obscenity. In other words, guiding this intervention is not only an appeal to legal objectivity, but also a conception of law as a unified instrument. In its struggle to transform obscenity law from 'women's point of view,' LEAF simply assumed that feminists can insert their concerns into law and law itself would be recast in this process.

Both the notion of degradation as a universal legal standard and the idea of law as a unified instrument, however, rest upon shaky analytic ground. First, as I have illustrated, the concept degradation has no inherent meaning. In the legal arguments of this case, the Supreme Court has already been presented with three distinct definitions of what is degrading. Degradation has been encoded in moral-conservative discourse, such that it denotes that which 'most people would consider humiliating' (the A.G. of Manitoba's definition). It has been encoded within a gender neutral framework, such that it denotes that which is an affront to the 'dignity of individuals' (the A.G. of Canada's definition). And here LEAF encodes this term within a gender-specific paradigm, such that it means that which is 'harmful to women.' In short, degradation is a highly subjective concept; its meaning depends upon the content that is poured into it. And as we will observe in chapter 3, multiple meanings have indeed been poured into this concept, both in the *Butler* decision and the legal decisions on obscenity that have followed.

Second, the notion that law possesses a unity must be interrogated in light of the obvious disunity of the criminal-justice system. Obscenity law has always been applied and elaborated upon by a disparate collection of state actors, including the courts, customs officials, provincial attorneys general, and police. This disunified regulatory environment has, of course, persisted in the post-*Butler* period. In this context, the difficulties of constructing and maintaining universal legal standards are numerous. As Snider has astutely observed, when feminists are organized and vocal, law can be forced to respond, and tightening up social control is consistent with both its interests and history. Nevertheless, '[f]eminists do not determine the mobilization or enforcement of the law. Once external pressure stops and attention shifts to other issues, normal patterns within the criminal justice system will reassert themselves. And these patterns will reflect the need of the criminal justice system to maintain itself, to process cases efficiently, to focus on real crimes and to act in ways which are congruent with dominant structural forces in society' (Snider 1990, 161–2). The criminal-justice system is, in other words, always a highly unreliable ally of feminists. In light of this, LEAF's assumption that a new and 'feminist'-inspired legal revolution could follow from its *Butler* intervention has been criticized as optimistic, simplistic, and naive (McCormack 1993b, 33). And LEAF has, in turn, responded by acknowledging that '[r]eliance on state power is always an incomplete, imperfect strategy and its use in relation to pornography is no exception' (Busby et al. 1994, 175). It remains true, however, that no such subtleties are apparent in LEAF's *Butler* factum, or in the strategy that framed this intervention. This intervention quite clearly relied on the view that law can be an instrument of feminist struggle.

In sum, LEAF's intervention in *Butler* is heavily reliant on foundational claims, and in this manner it represents a clear articulation of the 'new feminist politics of anti-pornography.' LEAF appeals to scientific 'evidence,' to legal objectivity, and finally to experiential 'Truth' (the privileged vantage point offered by women's point of view) in order to support its claim that the universal essence of pornography is 'harm.' Furthermore, LEAF's arguments are presented in categorical terms, as if it were revealing a singular feminist position to the judiciary – 'prohibiting pornography promotes equality' (LEAF 1991a, 17). The *Butler* factum embodies the characteristic narrative style of legal argument. It is closed and unequivocal; it refuses complexity and contingency. It is marked by what Yeatman refers to as generic closure. As she explains, generic closure is the assertion of an 'impersonal voice of authority, where propositions appear as features of fact, formal principles of order are fundamental to shaping the text and there are no indications of process, uncertainty or contest' (Yeatman 1990, 167).

The absence of contestation is, in fact, central to LEAF's rhetorical strategy in *Butler*. When LEAF invokes the 'victims' of pornography, it is simultaneously constructing a moral claim. According to this moral narrative, women are victimized through pornography and, therefore, pornography from women's standpoint, from a feminist point of view, is incontestably harm. While LEAF rejects conservative moral discourse, the form of its argument speaks directly to a traditional, unreconstructed moral paradigm (Smart 1993, 197). It claims to speak for and from the vantage point of those diminished through pornography, and the position that emerges is, in this way, constructed as both good and true. LEAF claims the moral high ground in feminist debates about pornography and it assumes that those feminists who challenge its anti-pornography and pro-censorhip position are either misguided or else not really feminist at all.

This can quite clearly be seen in the aftermath of *Butler*. In the heightened pornography conflicts that have followed the Supreme Court's decision, some of which are analysed in chapters 4 and 5 of this book, LEAF's 'pornography as harm' position has since been consistently

challenged by a diverse group of feminists who have resisted the construct 'women as victims' and all that it entails.[25] These women, among
them artists, writers, lesbians, bookstore workers, media workers, and
sex-trade workers, have reacted with outrage to LEAF's wholehearted
endorsement of state censorship. They contend that far from constituting a feminist legal victory, *Butler* merely provides a new feminist language to legitimize and modernize what is really an old conservative,
moral agenda. Anti-censorship feminists assert that this decision, and
LEAF's participation in it, have contributed to a climate of repression
marked by the restriction of gay/lesbian materials by judges employing
the notion of porn as 'harm'; the increased targeting of lesbian/gay
materials by Canada Customs; the harassment of sex-trade workers; and
the increased self-censorship of cultural workers dealing with sexual
representations. While diverse, what unites these voices is the assumption that sexuality is a terrain of struggle in which feminists must
engage. From this perspective, state censorship thwarts feminist
attempts to re-map the terrain of sexuality, operating to silence those
voices who challenge dominant sexual norms.

This construction of women – as 'agents' with 'voice' – contrasts
sharply with the 'passive, silent victim' that grounds LEAF's anti-
pornography stance. Ironically, it is this 'victim' who has been called
upon to insulate LEAF's position from the criticisms of anti-censorship
feminists. At a meeting with the recently formed Ad Hoc Coalition of
Anticensorship Women, LEAF attempted to respond to charges that its
unequivocally pro-censorship position was not 'representative,' through
invoking the vantage point of 'victimization.' As one member of the
National Litigation Committee responded, in *Butler* LEAF had attempted
to 'represent' the needs of 'victims' of male violence, of 'battered' women,
of those women 'most marginalized' and not present to defend themselves (Ad Hoc Coalition of Anticensorship Women, Notes of meeting, 17
June 1993). It was on the basis of this vantage point that LEAF defended
its position; from the perspective of 'victims,' as LEAF representatives
claimed, pornography is 'harm' and the Supreme Court's decision in *Butler* a 'feminist' victory. In this way, the *Butler* factum became unassailable,
placed above the push and pull of feminist contestation.

LEAF has consistently declined to reconsider the position that it
advanced in *Butler*. It has explained and qualified its intervention,
although, as I have argued, there is a clear gap between what LEAF
claims to have said and the text of its factum. Moreover, in attempting to
grapple with the legal aftermath of the Supreme Court decision, LEAF

has not retreated from the assertion that *Butler* can be viewed as a clear feminist victory. Instead, legal decisions that target gay and lesbian sexual expression and homophobic customs seizures have been explained away as a 'failure to properly apply the law' (MacKinnon and Dworkin 1994; Busby 1994, 184–7). What is ignored in this explanation, however, is the manner in which LEAF's position reflected, reinforced, and appealed to what I have termed the new politics of anti-pornography. LEAF's responsibility for legally articulating this 'new politics,' alongside and together with government actors and moral-conservatives, has not been properly acknowledged.

Conclusion

In effect, LEAF's intervention in *Butler* and its aftermath starkly calls out the tensions between what Brown calls 'deriving norms epistemologically' and 'deciding them politically,' and illustrates LEAF's preference for the safety that resides in the former (Brown 1991, 77). I have argued in this chapter that anti-pornography feminist discourse, the moral-conservative discourse of the New Right, and the increased political support for anti-pornography regulation all share the same tendency towards reactionary foundationalism. Reactionary foundationalism is at heart a form of discursive strategy in which 'Truth' trumps politics and one with a broad appeal in these times of postmodern anxiety. The legal arguments framed in the *Butler* case must be placed within the broader context of these times and seen in relation to discourses of sexual panic and danger that currently circulate through dominant cultural meaning systems. These discourses, in turn, are called upon and affirmed by those supporting the criminal regulation of obscenity. As I have stressed, the distinctions between the positions of government actors, GAP, and LEAF are much narrower than they first appear; and it is perhaps the case that their resounding similarity, rather than LEAF's uniqueness, is what influenced the Supreme Court's decision in *Butler*.

The assertion that *Butler* constitutes a feminist success story in law is, therefore, an interpretation that can and must be challenged. As Brenda Cossman demonstrates in the following chapter, if feminist anti-pornography discourse appears to shape the Supreme Court's reasoning, so too does the decision rest upon a conservative, moral sexual subtext. *Butler* may indeed enunciate the alleged links between pornography and gender-based harm, and in this sense LEAF may claim the decision as a victory. But it is also true that *Butler* supports the legal regulation of sexual morality and can equally be seized as a victory by government actors, and by conservative anti-pornography activists such as GAP. In any case, as we insist here, legal conflicts and decisions are inseparable from their wider social context. Thus, the *Butler* decision can only at a most superficial level be understood as a simple reflection of legal arguments. The decision must be situated within and viewed as an integral part of the construction of a 'recessionary erotic economy,' and its connections to extralegal anti-pornography politics and discourse must be thoroughly mapped.

If there is a lesson to be learned from LEAF's intervention in *Butler*, it is not about how feminist legal actors can effect changes in the law; it is rather a lesson about the legitimacy of feminist legal actors as 'spokespeople.' LEAF's intervention in *Butler* was premised upon a claim to speak the 'Truth' of pornography from the position of all women. In articulating this monolithic and universal truth-claim, LEAF was not only able to construct an argument that was consistent with law's preference for foundational and authoritative discourse, it also escaped the messy business of negotiating its position on pornography politically with extralegal feminist actors. In this process, LEAF effectively silenced all feminists who might disagree with its unequivocally anti-pornography stance, casting any critical voice as naive, or even anti-feminist. As we emphasize in this book, however, to silence legitimate normative debate among feminists about our collective conditions and strategies is antithetical to democratic feminist practice. What is urgently needed is an opening up of political spaces for arguing about feminist norms and not their restriction through the new politics of anti-pornography. As Brown forcefully argues, politicization of feminism requires that we make room for conflicts among feminists that cannot simply be set aside or settled by invoking some universal 'Truth' (Brown 1991, 77). We need to reinvent within feminism an appreciation of debate, of wars of position, of respectful conversation and heated argument. Sexuality is a critical field of feminist struggle, and pornography, as one way in which sexuality gets represented, will continue to occupy a central if always contradictory space in our efforts to reconfigure sexual norms. To restrict this field of struggle, to participate in a political agenda that has as its objective the creation of all women as silent victims, to speak as if the only 'Truth' of pornography is 'degradation,' is, I would argue, both wrong-headed and dangerous. This position underlies our critical analysis of the post-*Butler* context and our attempts to elaborate upon a feminist politics of subversion in these admittedly repressive times.

NOTES

1   Karen Busby together with Shiela McIntyre, Andree Cote, Helena Orton, et
    al. 'LEAF and Pornography: Litigating on Equality and Sexual Representa-
    tions,' June 1994, 7. In this paper, the feminist litigation organization the
    Women's Legal Education and Action Fund seeks to explain and defend its
    controversial pro-censorship intervention in *Butler*. This paper appears
    within a list of official LEAF documents. A version of it had been published
    as a journal article; see Karen Busby, 'Litigating on Equality and Sexual
    Representations,' *Canadian Journal of Law and Society* 9, no. 1 (Spring 1994):
    165–92.
2   The Group Against Pornography is a Manitoba-based anti-pornography
    coalition. This coalition embraces a conservative critique of pornography
    and, although not exclusively religious, organizes extensively through
    churches. It holds a yearly 'White Ribbon Against Pornography' campaign.
    It intervened in the *Butler* Supreme Court appeal to advance a distinctly
    conservative moral defence of obscenity regulation.
3   What is foundationalism? Foundationalism, as a concept, is used in this
    chapter to denote discourses that, in keeping with Brown's definition, dis-
    play a preference for 'truth (... uncontestable) over politics (flux, contest,
    instability); for certainty and security (safety, immutability ...) over freedom
    (vulnerability ...); for discoveries (science) over decisions (judgments);
    for separable subjects armed with established rights and identities over
    unwieldy pluralities adjudicating for themselves and their futures on the
    basis of nothing more than ... persuasion' (Brown 1991, 69). As Butler
    argues, foundational discourses are those that rely on primary premises that
    in turn function as authorizing grounds. Foundations (while variously
    defined – reason, experience, God) constitute the unquestioned and unques-
    tionable – a set of norms that are constructed as beyond power, above con-
    testation, and capable of distinguishing between true/false, right/wrong
    (Butler 1992, 6–7). Admittedly, the category foundationalism is broad,
    encompassing all modernist discourses. Many versions of feminism are
    clearly foundationalist, relying on women's 'experience' as an authorizing
    ground, a vantage point for revealing social relations and emancipatory
    strategies. Postmodern feminism, by contrast, challenges feminist founda-
    tionalism, emphasizing the constructed character of experience, the instabil-
    ity of the feminist subject, the contingency of all knowledge claims, and the
    irreducible complexity of the social world. As Butler argues, postmodern
    feminism takes as one of its central tasks the interrogation of foundations,

that is, what precisely the theoretical move that establishes foundations excludes or forecloses (ibid., 7).

4   Foucault used the term 'truth' to refer to the 'ensemble of rules according to which true and false are separated and specific effects of power are attached to the true' (Smart 1995, 73). In this chapter and throughout the book, big T 'Truth' is used to denote discourses that present themselves as impersonal voices of authority, as capable of determining the 'true' character of social life. In many ways, as Smart argues, law like science exemplifies such a foundational form of discourse. Through the correct and neutral application of legal method, law claims to produce always correct depictions of social reality (ibid., 73–4).

5   For a critical discussion of assumptions underlying feminist foundationalism see Brown 1991, 69.

6   As Lacombe documents, anti-pornography feminist organizations entered into formal alliances with Right organizations during the 1980s, working closely with churches and other groups in the anti-pornography campaign. In 1984, for example, a Symposium on Media Violence, held in Toronto, brought together several feminist and conservative organizations. See Lacombe 1994, 47, 52–3.

7   Lacombe's book (1994) provides the most comprehensive overview of the development of pornography conflicts in Canada. For another discussion of the emergence of diverse pressures for Canadian obscenity-law reform, including those from civil-libertarian, conservative, and anti-pornography feminist sources, see Campbell and Pal 1989, 119–21.

8   The Fraser Commission on Pornography and Prostitution, commissioned by the Liberals, reported in 1985, soon after the Conservative's remarkable electoral victory. The Fraser Commission served to legitimize the identification of pornography as a policy priority; but its report reflected an orientation that would differ quite markedly from Tory anti-pornography discourse. On the whole, the Fraser Commission appeared to capture the mood of pornography policy during the previous Liberal regime. While the Commission had heard witnesses representing diverse perspectives, anti-pornography discourse, and in particular anti-pornography feminist discourse, clearly informed the Commission's report (Lacombe 1994, 97). The *Fraser Commission Report* proposed a new pornography law founded upon a harms-based rationale; it located the problem of pornography within a discourse of equality and human rights; and it recommended tougher penalties on child pornography, on 'degrading' and violent pornography, while endorsing the decriminalization of non-violent and 'soft-core' pornography (Canada, Spe-

cial Committee on Pornography and Prostitution, 1985). In effect, the Commission supported a criminal-law framework for addressing the 'problem' of pornography, but sought to construct a new balance between freedom and equality within this framework.

9 For a discussion and analysis of Bills C-114 and C-54, see Campbell and Pal 1989, 135–50; and Lacombe 1994, 99–136.

10 This approach is based on the notion that pornography has a clear and unambiguous meaning that depends on neither context nor the perspective of the consumer. For a discussion and critique of this approach, see Vance 1993a and Arcand 1991, 24–5.

11 See, for example, the recommendations of the Canadian Panel on Violence Against Women (1993), which proposes the amendment of obscenity provisions to 'reflect prohibitions of sexually violent and degrading material' and the creation of civil remedies for women 'abused in the consumption of pornography' (Canadian Panel on Violence Against Women 1993, 56).

12 I do not mean to suggest that the state behaves in an instrumentalist, conspiratorial manner. Nevertheless, I want to stress how state discourses emphasizing a sexual danger zone have become increasingly significant; these discourses, in turn, do have the effect of reinforcing the association of sexuality with danger, as well as the construction of women as passive victims. This discursive construction serves a purpose for neoconservative state actors, creating popular support for and consent to the institutionalization of the law-and-order state.

13 The BCCLA's argument is normative in its assertion of sexual plurality and freedom of sexual expression as pre-eminent and fundamental political values. Similarly, the interventions of GAP and of government actors are normative in their assertion of the fundamental importance of maintaining a common and uniform sexual morality.

14 It is significant that in making these claims, both the A.G. of Manitoba and GAP rely heavily on the report of the U.S. Attorney General's Commission on Pornography (Meese Commission). The Meese Commission's conclusions on the links between pornography and harm are presented as unequivocal. Nevertheless, it is widely acknowledged that the proceedings and report of the commission were extremely biased. The commission was established with the express objective of finding 'more effective ways in which the spread of pornography could be constrained.' Before being appointed to the commission, seven of its eleven commissioners had taken public stands against pornography. Its list of witnesses was tightly controlled, and by far the majority of those appearing before the commission supported tougher regulations on pornography. The commission made lib-

eral use of the existing social-science research on pornography. Immediately afterwards, its interpretation of this literature was denounced by some of the leading researchers in the field. As some analysts of the Meese Commission have suggested '[t]he Commission's goal was to implement a traditional conservative agenda on sexually explicit images and texts.' See Vance 1993b and Berger, Searles, and Cottle 1991, 25–8.

15 In most mainstream political-science analyses of the Charter, the complex topic of 'feminism and the Charter' becomes reduced to a discussion of LEAF. In fact, the dominant argument in mainstream texts is that Canadian feminists (i.e., LEAF) have been the most successful Charter actors – an argument that would be seen as exceedingly naive by most feminist analysts. See, for example, Knopff and Morton 1992, 79, 123; and Cairns 1991, 77.

16 See LEAF 1993 and LEAF 1990, 14.

17 At a meeting between LEAF representatives and the Ad Hoc Coalition of Anticensorship Activists, Sheila McIntyre, a member of LEAF 's National Legal Committee, indicated that national consultations had not taken place on *Butler* because LEAF was responding to a three-week time-line. Notes of Meeting, 21 June 1993.

18 As I have argued elsewhere, LEAF's relation to extra-legal feminist actors has been guided by a division-of-labour approach. In this view, boundaries are drawn between law, politics, and feminist service provision, and feminist actors are seen as having a defined expertise and authority within each sphere. Because LEAF claimed legal expertise, law became its domain of authority (Gotell 1993, 410).

19 For a detailed discussion and critique of this approach, see Gotell 1995. Smart makes a similar point in her analysis of standpoint feminism and pornography. As she notes, standpoint feminism claims there is a 'women's position on porn which has been arrived at through the feminist process of consciousness raising' (Smart 1993, 198).

20 LEAF cites the work of Zillman and Bryant, which emphasizes these conclusions (LEAF 1991, 14; *Butler v. R.*, [1992] S.C.R. 452). In addition, it relies extensively on the report of the Meese Commission (see note 9).

21 It relies on the Meese Commission to support this claim (see note 9).

22 Since *Butler* LEAF has taken great pains to distance itself from this argument. As it has stated, 'Contrary to what some have said, LEAF does not assert that pornography is the alpha and omega of women's subordination by men' (Busby 1994, 171). LEAF restates its position on pornography and women's oppression through the statement that '[i]t plays an important part in the social construction of sexual inequality' (ibid., 171–2).

23 See Carol Smart for a critique of the feminist jurisprudence movement. As
    she argues, through the appeal to the power of law feminists reinforce an
    image of law as a purveyor of objective 'truth,' detaching it from the social
    order and treating it as a free-floating embodiment of justice (Smart 1989,
    81).

24 This position, that feminists can effect a jurisprudential revolution within
    law, is most strongly associated with the work of Catherine MacKinnon.
    MacKinnon contends that women's experience of subordination constitutes
    a site of 'Truth' free from the obfuscations of patriarchal power. This 'Truth'
    in turn is capable of challenging the patriarchal standpoint of law. The
    thrust of MacKinnon's work is that women's experience can be used as a
    lever against the law – as a basis for a new legal paradigm that would reflect
    the lives and experiences of women. See MacKinnon 1989, esp. chap. 13.

25 According to artist Elaine Carol, anti-censorship feminist activists in groups
    such as Ontario Coalition Against Film and Video Censorship (OCAFVC)
    and Censorstop reacted with shock to the *Butler* decision and to the position
    that LEAF had taken in it. These women formed a task force charged with
    contacting LEAF to voice criticism. Ultimately these anti-censorship femi-
    nists formed an Ad Hoc Coalition of Anticensorship Women, which drew
    together representatives from OCFVAC, Maggies (a group of sex-trade
    workers), the Lesbian and Gay Film Festival, *Fireweed* (feminist periodical),
    Toronto Women's Bookstore, Playwrights Union of Canada, York University
    Centre for Feminist Research, Glad Day Bookshop, and lawyers and aca-
    demics. Interview, Elaine Carol, 6 June 1993. Minutes of meeting, Ad Hoc
    Coalition of Anticensorship Women, 17 June 1993.

3

Feminist Fashion or Morality in Drag? The Sexual Subtext of the *Butler* Decision

BRENDA COSSMAN

In *R. v. Butler* (1992), the Supreme Court of Canada upheld the constitutionality of the criminal prohibition of obscenity under section 163 of the Criminal Code of Canada (R.S.C., 1985, c. c-46). The Court held that although this provision violated free speech as guaranteed by section 2 of the Canadian Charter of Rights and Freedoms, it was a reasonable limit under section 1. In so doing, the Supreme Court tries to tell us that the obscenity laws are no longer concerned with corrupting morals, or with courts as the guardians of public morality. Rather, in the court's view, the obscenity law is justifiable in its objective of preventing harm, particularly harm towards women, and in promoting the equality and dignity of women.

This has become the official story of *Butler* – it is the story that the Court tries to tell within the text of the decision, and it is the story that feminists who support the obscenity provisions have told before, during, and after the decision (McAllister 1992–3; Busby 1994; Landsberg 1992). But there is another story to be told about the *Butler* decision. *Butler* is also a decision about sex: it is a decision about the role and status of sex, sexuality, and the representation of sexual practices in our society. When we scratch beneath the surface, we find a conservative sexual morality that sees sex as bad, physical, shameful, dangerous, base, guilty until proved innocent, and redeemable only if it transcends its base nature. It is a sexual subtext informed by the basic assumptions that have traditionally informed the dominant ideological discourses of sexuality in Western society: sexual negativity <sex is bad>, sexual essentialism <sex is biological>, sexual monism <there is one way to have sex>, and sexual hierarchy <some sex is better than others>.

In this chapter, I will deconstruct the *Butler* decision in an effort to reveal this sexual subtext. A textual analysis of the decision will reveal the extent to which the discourse of the decision is informed by the same conservative sexual morality that has traditionally framed obscenity law in Canada, with its problematic assumptions about the nature of sex and sexuality. The chapter will argue that, contrary to the claims of anti-pornography feminists, the most significant change in the law represented by the *Butler* decision is one of language alone. Now the law is dressed up in feminist discourse, that of preventing harm towards women, of equality and dignity. The test for obscenity as reviewed and synthesized by the Supreme Court of Canada in *Butler* simply provides a new discourse for what is in fact a very old objective – the legal regulation of sexual morality, and the legal repression of sexual representation. The *Butler* decision and its discourse of harm against women is really just sexual morality in drag.

Further, I will argue that this sexual subtext is essential in understanding how *Butler* has set the discursive stage for the subsequent judicial applications of the *Butler* test, in which gay and lesbian sexual representations have been held to be obscene. The first two obscenity cases to have reached the courts since *Butler* were both against Glad Day Bookshop – a gay and lesbian bookstore in Toronto. While prosecutions have since been brought against heterosexual pornography as well, the particular way in which this law has been used against gay and lesbian sexual representations should alert us to this discursive drag. Yet, feminists who support the *Butler* decision continue to argue that this targeting of gay and lesbian sexual representations constitutes a misapplication of the *Butler* test (Busby 1994, 185). Contrary to these arguments, I will argue that the underlying conservative sexual morality of *Butler* has set the discursive framework for this targeting. The sexual subtext and its good sex / bad sex distinction is particularly dangerous in the context of gay and lesbian sexual representations. The heterosexist assumptions informing this sexual morality operate to locate these representations on the bad side of the dichotomy, and thus pave the road for a particular judicial determination of obscenity.

The *Butler* Decision: Sex and the Supreme Court

The majority decision of the Supreme Court of Canada in the *Butler* case was written by Mr Justice Sopinka.[1] The decision is divided into two parts. In the first part, the court reviews and clarifies the law of obscenity. In the second part, the court then examines whether this law of obscenity is constitutional, that is, whether it violates the right to freedom of expression guarantees of the Charter, and if so, whether it is a reasonable limit on that right. In reviewing the text of both parts of the decision, this section will challenge the dominant representation of the *Butler* decision, by illustrating the sexual subtext of the decision – a sexual subtext informed by the same assumptions of sexual morality that prevailed before the *Butler* decision.

The Law of Obscenity

In the first part of the decision, the Court reviews and clarifies the law of obscenity as set out in s.163 of the Criminal Code. Obscenity is defined in subsection 163(8) as 'any publication a dominant characteristic of which is the undue exploitation of sex, or of sex and any one or more of the following subjects, namely, crime, horror, cruelty and violence.' The question of what constitutes the 'undue exploitation of sex' has been the subject of considerable judicial analysis. Sopinka J. thus begins by reviewing the various tests that have emerged to determine when the exploitation of sex is undue.

Community Standards

The first and most important test developed by the courts to determine when the exploitation of sex is undue is the community standards of tolerance. The Court begins by quoting a passage from *R. v. Close* (1948), which was first adopted by the Supreme Court in *R. v. Brodie* (1962) and has been cited by the Supreme Court of Canada in its obscenity case law ever since: 'There does exist in any community at all times – however the standard may vary from time to time – a general instinctive sense of what is decent and what is indecent, of what is clean and what is dirty' (as cited in *Butler* 1992, 464). Within this passage, which has set the discursive framework within which the Supreme Court of Canada has repeatedly interpreted the undue exploitation of sex, obscenity is cast in the language of indecency and dirt. Not all sexual representations are obscene; only indecent or dirty sexual representations are obscene.[2] Within this framework, there is a distinction made between good and bad sex – a binary opposition between clean and dirty, decent and indecent. Bad sex is dirty sex. There is no positive theory of sexual expression that tells us what makes sex good. The best the courts have been able to do is establish a test of some generality to defer to community standards – that is, to allow 'the community' to draw the lines between clean and dirty sex.

Sopinka J. further observed that this community standard has been found to be a national standard; that expert evidence is not required to establish the community standard, and that the community standard may change over time (*Butler* 1992, 465). Finally, the community-standards test is not based on taste, but tolerance, and the measure of tolerance is not what Canadians would themselves tolerate, but 'what they would tolerate other Canadians being exposed to' (ibid., 465–6). It attempts to escape the subjective nature of individual taste by directing attention away from 'what Canadians think is right for themselves' to the ostensibly broader standard of 'what Canadians would not abide other Canadians seeing because it would be beyond the contemporary Canadian standard of tolerance to allow them to see it'[3] (*Towne Cinema* 1985, as cited in *Butler* 1992, 465–6).

According to this test, individual Canadians may have different tastes, but we all subscribe to the same standard of tolerance. Although this standard of tolerance may change over time, at any one moment it is monolithic. In other words, at any moment in time, there is in the eyes of all Canadians a clear and singular distinction between what we will tolerate others seeing and what we will not – between what is clean (good sex) and what is dirty (bad sex) – even though this may not correspond to each of our own personal tastes of good sex and bad sex. And the obviousness of this distinction is underscored by the fact that no expert evidence is required to establish it. The line between good sex and bad sex is an 'instinctive' matter – a matter of common sense for a judge who will, presumably, simply recognize it when he sees it.

Degradation and Dehumanization

The Court examines a second and more recent test for determining whether the exploitation of sex is undue. This test emerged in the 1980s, as anti-pornography feminism began to shape the discourse within which pornography was debated, and was first endorsed by the Supreme Court of Canada in *R. v. Towne Cinema* (*Towne Cinema* 1985, 202–3). According to this test, materials that 'may be said to exploit sex in a degrading or dehumanizing manner will ... fail the community standards test' (*Butler* 1992, 466). In elaborating on the meaning of this test, the Court tells us that it means materials that harm women: 'Among other things, degrading or dehumanizing materials place women (and sometimes men) in positions of subordination, servile submission or humiliation. They run against the principles of equality and dignity' (ibid., 466). According to this approach, material that is degrading and dehumanizing fails the community-standards test, 'not because it offends morals, but because these materials are 'perceived by public opinion to be harmful to society, particularly to women' (ibid., 467). The Court notes that although 'this perception is not susceptible to exact proof,' there is nevertheless a body of literature that supports the view that these materials are harmful to women.[4]

In this passage, the Court has begun its attempt to shift the objective of obscenity law from the legal regulation of morality to the legal regulation of material that is harmful to women. It emphasizes that material is obscene not because it offends morals, but because it is harmful to women. The shift in the discourse used to articulate and justify the obscenity provisions obscures the extent to which, as Lise Gotell has argued in chapter 2, the feminist discourse of harm does represent a moral claim. Moreover, this effort to shift the discourse from morality to harm has not displaced the underlying conservative sexual morality that has informed the law before *Butler*. Rather, this sexual morality – its opposition between good and bad sex and its strictly negative theory of sexual expression – continues to inform the court's approach. According to this degrading and dehumanizing test, any sexual representation involving aspects of dominance is bad sex. But this test does not tell us what is good about sex, or what good sex is. By implication, good sex must be the opposite of bad sex. If bad sex is sex that places any of its subjects 'in positions of subordination, servile submission or humiliation,' then good sex must be sex that does not place its subjects in such positions. Good sex must be what bad sex is not.

In this good sex/bad sex distinction, the Court tells us that consent is not necessarily determinative. 'Consent cannot save materials that otherwise contain degrading or dehumanizing scenes. Sometimes the very appearance of consent makes the depicted acts even more degrading or dehumanizing' (*Butler* 1992, 466–7). Again, the Court does not tell us what good sex is, but, simply, what it is not. Good sex is not necessarily sex with consent. Sex with consent can be really bad sex; in fact, it can make bad sex even worse. There is no positive theory of what makes sex good; only the further articulation of sex that might be bad. The good sex/bad sex distinction continues to appear in even more troubling forms. It is seen in the passage cited from Madame Justice Wilson, in *Towne Cinema*: 'the public has concluded that exposure to material which degrades the human dimensions of life to a subhuman or merely physi-

cal dimension and thereby contributes to a process of moral desensitization must be harmful in some way' (*Towne Cinema* 1985, 217–18, as
quoted in *Butler* 1992, 468). We see in this passage from Wilson J., as
affirmed by Sopinka J., a particular vision of sex and sexual representation. The merely physical dimension of sex is subhuman. The opposition
of good and bad sex reappears in a somewhat different guise. Bad sex is
subhuman sex. Bad sex is sex that emphasizes the merely physical
dimension of sex.

We begin to see here the underlying binary opposition. It is the distinction between mind and body, between the intellectual and physical,
between the emotional and sensual, that has long informed Western
thought.[5] In this opposition, the body, the physical, the sensual, are seen
as base, as bad, in need of control and, ultimately, transcendence. Sex is
physical, it is about the body and the sensual pleasures of the body.
Being of the body, it is natural, essential, and unchanging[6] (Rubin 1989,
275). And, being of the body, it is, by reference to the mind/body opposition, bad. This conflation of sex with the physical operates to sustain
what Gayle Rubin describes as sex negativity, that is, the idea deeply
rooted in Western culture that sex is 'a dangerous, destructive, negative
force' (ibid., 278; Weeks 1986). But sex is saved from complete damna-
tion by another opposition – good sex/bad sex – which builds on the
mind/body opposition. Good sex, then, is sex that is not only physical;
it is not only sensual. Good sex must transcend the very nature of sex as
physical pleasure. Good sex, then, must be sex with more, it must
appeal to the other side of the opposition, and thus be part of the mind,
the intellect, the soul.

The interaction between these two oppositions, while saving sex from
itself, operates to destabilize the underlying assumptions about sex, and
to constitute sex and sexuality as a highly contradictory category. The
good sex/bad sex opposition, for example, brings into question the
assumption of sex negativity <that sex is always bad>, as well as that of
sexual essentialism <that sex is physical, natural, and unchanging >. If
sex is, by definition, bad, how can it be made good? If sex is of the body,
how can it be made not of the body? And if sex is unchanging, how can
it change? The good sex/bad sex opposition introduces all of these possibilities – possibilities that sit awkwardly with the underlying assumptions about the nature of sex. Yet, these assumptions are never
completely undermined. Sex continues to be presumed to be bad, unless
it can be made good.[7] Sex continues to be of the body, unless it can be
made to be of the mind. And sex continues to be natural and unchanging, unless it is changed <that is, made good and of the mind>. Accord-

ing to the good sex/bad sex distinction, sex can now become that which, by definition, it is not. Sex can now become more than sex.

Internal Necessities/Artistic Defence

The theme of 'sex with more' is continued in the third and final test reviewed by the Court. Sopinka J. begins by quoting the internal-necessities test as set out in *Brodie*: 'What I think is aimed at is excessive emphasis on the theme for a base purpose. But I do not think that there is undue exploitation if there is no more emphasis on the theme than is required in the serious treatment of the theme of a novel with honesty and uprightness' (*Brodie* 1962, 181, as quoted in *Butler* 1992, 468). The Court in *Brodie*, in evaluating the work in question – D.H. Lawrence's *Lady Chatterley's Lover* – held: 'It has none of the characteristics that are often described in judgments dealing with obscenity – dirt for dirt's sake, the leer of the sensualist, depravity of the mind of an author with an obsession for dirt, pornography, an appeal to a prurient interest etc. The section recognizes that the serious-minded author must have freedom in the protection of work of genuine artistic and literary merit and the quality of the work must have real relevance in determining not only a dominant characteristic but also whether there is undue exploitation' (*Brodie* 1962, 181 quoted in *Butler* 1992, 468). According to the Court, this artistic defence has been considered to be the last step in determining whether the exploitation of sex is undue. If sexual material is 'required for the serious treatment of a theme,' then it will not be held to be 'undue.' '[T]he internal necessities test ... has been interpreted to assess whether the exploitation of sex has a justifiable role in advancing the plot or the theme, and in considering the work as a whole, does not merely represent 'dirt for dirt's sake' but has a legitimate role when measured by the internal necessities of the work itself' (*Butler* 1992, 469). According to this test, the representation of sex in and of itself constitutes 'dirt for dirt's sake.'[8] We again see the view that sex is dirt – it is dirty, it is bad. Within this vision, art cannot be sex for sex's sake. By definition, sex is not art. Sex is not a legitimate focus for art. It can at most be part of the larger artistic purpose, but sexuality in and of itself is not art. Within the courts' view, this is one area of human activity (or subhuman activity) that is inappropriate for artistic portrayal.

Art, like good sex, is defined in relation to the mind/body opposition. Art is that which appeals to more than our physical nature. It is, by definition, that which appeals to our higher dimensions – to our intellectual, emotional or spiritual aspirations (Nead 1993a, 145; 1993b, 281–2).

Accordingly, only sex with more, sex that appeals to the other side of the mind/body distinction – that is, sex that transcends its physical nature by appealing to the intellect, the emotions, the soul – can become good sex and, thus, be the subject of art. In other words, only sex that is not sex can be a legitimate focus for art.[9]

Relationship between the Tests

Sopinka J. then attempts to clarify the relationship between these tests, which he acknowledges has been unclear in the case law. He begins by dividing pornography into three categories: '(1) explicit sex with violence (2) explicit sex without violence but which subjects people to treatment that is degrading or dehumanizing and (3) explicit sex without violence that is neither degrading nor dehumanizing' (*Butler* 1992, 470). The Court notes that there is some disagreement in society as to which materials would constitute the undue exploitation of sex. Some would argue that all three categories should be prohibited; others would argue that none of the categories should be prohibited. Sopinka J. further observes that this is not an issue 'that is susceptible to proof in the traditional way' (ibid.). In order to avoid these determinations being made according to the subjective opinions of individual judges, there must be a 'norm that will serve as an arbiter in determining what amounts to an undue exploitation of sex. That arbiter is the community as a whole' (ibid.). According to the community-standards test, the courts must decide what 'the community would tolerate others being exposed to on the basis of the degree of harm that may flow from such exposure' (ibid.). 'Harm in this context means that it predisposes persons to act in an antisocial manner as, for example, the physical or mental mistreatment of women by men, or what is perhaps debatable, the reverse. Antisocial conduct for this purpose is conduct which society formally recognizes as incompatible with its proper functioning' (ibid., 470–1). The community-standards test continues to play a central role in the *Butler* test for obscenity, although it is now more carefully articulated in the discourse of harm, avoiding any obvious references to morality. Under the revised test, the guideline of community standards is intended to allow courts to categorize pornography into one of the three discrete categories, according to an objective legal norm. This categorization approach is based on the assumption that the meaning of pornography can be objectively established. We can begin to see in this test the Court's literalist approach to representation. Like the approach of anti-pornography feminism discussed in the previous chapter, in the Court's view, the meaning of sexual images can be determined in isolation from the context of these images; meaning is thus separated from context.

The Court then returns to the three categories of pornography. In Sopinka J.'s view, the first category <sex with violence> is explicitly mentioned within s.163(8) and will almost always constitute the undue exploitation of sex. The second category <sex without violence, but that is degrading or dehumanizing> may be undue exploitation of sex if the risk of harm is substantial. The third category <sex without violence, and that is not degrading or dehumanizing> is generally tolerated, and will not, with the exception of the involvement of children, constitute undue exploitation of sex. The Court then turns to the question of the internal-necessities test, and how it fits into this new scheme. Sopinka J. states that the artistic defence – that is, whether the undue exploitation of sex is the main object of the work, or whether the portrayal of sex is essential to a wider artistic, literary, or other similar purpose – remains the last step in determining if the material is obscene. 'The portrayal of sex must then be viewed in context to determine whether that is the dominant theme of the work as a whole. Put another way, is undue exploitation of sex the main object of the work or is this portrayal of sex essential to a wider artistic, literary, or other similar purpose' (*Butler* 1992, 471). The court must determine whether the community would tolerate the sexually explicit materials when seen within the broader context of the work as a whole.

According to this test, not only can pornography be objectively and unequivocally classified into one of three discrete categories, but this categorization becomes determinative as to whether the material will be considered to be obscene. This categorization further underscores the absence of a positive theory of sex and sexual expression in *Butler*. The very definition of good sex – the third category – is framed in purely negative terms. Good sex does *not* involve violence, it does *not* involve children, it is *not* degrading or dehumanizing, and it does *not* create a risk of harm. The Court does not tell us what makes sex good; it only tells us what makes sex bad. Good sex, then, is defined only in opposition to what it is not: bad sex. Within this categorization of pornography, the major contested site of sexual representation is degrading and dehumanizing sex.[10] The courts must determine whether particular sexual representations are degrading and dehumanizing, and if so, whether these degrading and dehumanizing representations are likely to cause harm. This is the dividing line between good and bad sex. Drawing the line between good and bad sex continues to be the job of the community-standards test. Notwithstanding the repeated claims to the contrary, this determination can only be made by reference to an underlying sexual morality. The very exercise of drawing a line between good sex and bad sex presumes an underlying conservative sexual morality in which sex is divided between good and bad, and in which there is a hierarchy of sexual practices.

The use of a community standard in this exercise further presumes an underlying sexual morality in which sex and sexual practices are, or should be, essential and monolithic. It continues to assume that there is a national standard that can judge which sexual practices are acceptable and which are not; a national standard that presumes that there is, or should be, a monolithic view of good and bad sex. Not only is sex simply of the body, but this biological imperative is such that sex always and only ever takes one form. As Gayle Rubin has argued, 'sexuality is supposed to conform to a single standard. One of the most tenacious ideas about sex is that there is one best way to do it, and that everyone should do it that way' (Rubin 1989, 283). These assumptions of sexual essentialism and sexual monism – of a single and essential nature of sex, any deviation from which is condemned as 'unnatural,' and thus bad – continue to operate, barely beneath the surface of the *Butler* test.

Finally, by simply incorporating the artistic defence as the last step in determining whether material is obscene, the Supreme Court has reinscribed the underlying oppositions of sex and art, of good and bad sex, of mind and body, that have long informed the internal-necessities test. Indeed, in articulating the new relationship between these various tests, the Supreme Court can be seen to have rearticulated the sexual subtext, and its underlying oppositions, that has long informed each of these tests. Sex remains a highly contradictory category. Sex is of the body, it is physical, not mental, it is sensual not intellectual, it is pleasure, not pursuit. Sex, being of the body, is bad unless it can be made good, by transcending the body and its physical pleasures. Sex can only be made good by transcending its very nature. Good sex is discursively constituted as a contradictory category – it is sex (which is of the body) that has been made of the mind: it is sex that is not sex. According to the test set out in *Butler*, drawing the line between good sex and bad sex continues to be a determination made by reference to this underlying sexual morality.

The Constitutionality of Obscenity

In the second part of the decision, the Court examines whether s.163 violates the right to freedom of expression guaranteed by the Charter. The Court's discussion of the constitutionality of obscenity is divided into two parts, which will be examined in turn: (1) whether the law violates the right to freedom of expression as guaranteed by s.2(b) of the Charter, and (2) if so, whether the violation is a reasonable limit on the right, as contemplated by section 1 of the Charter. In upholding the law from the constitutional challenge, the Court tells us, over and over again, that the objective of the obscenity law is preventing harm, particularly harm towards women. At the same time, in taking a deeper look at why the criminalization of sexual expression is justifiable, the Court continues to expose its views on the value of sex, sexuality, and sexual expression. As I will attempt to illustrate, beneath the official story of preventing harm and promoting equality is the same sexual subtext as found in the first part of the decision, and the same sexual morality that informed the law of obscenity before *Butler*.

Sexual Representation as Expression

The Court first considers whether s.163 violates freedom of expression as guaranteed by section 2(b) of the Charter. Sopinka J. rejected the argument made by the government that physical activity, such as sexual activity, could not be considered expression. In the Court's view, the fact that the subject matter of the materials was 'clearly physical' did not mean that the materials did not 'convey or attempt to convey meaning' (*Butler* 1992, 472). In previous decisions, the Supreme Court of Canada has consistently adopted an expansive approach to the protection provided by s.2(b), holding that the content or meaning cannot exclude the activities or statements from the scope of protection accorded by s.2(b), no matter how offensive those activities or statements may be to the Court.[11] 'Meaning sought to be expressed need not be "redeeming" in the eyes of the court to merit the protection of s.2(b) whose purpose is to ensure that thoughts and feelings may be conveyed freely in non-violent ways without fear of censure' (ibid., 473). Sopinka J. held that both the purpose and effect of s.163 was to restrict 'the communication of certain types of materials based on their content' (ibid.). As a result, the law prohibited expressive activity, and violated s.2(b) of the Charter.

While the Court rejected the view that 'purely physical activity does not convey meaning,' implicit in the Court's language is the view that sex constitutes purely physical activity.[12] It is of, and only of, the body. At the same time, however, the Court recognizes that the portrayal of this physical activity 'conveys ideas, opinions, or feelings' (*Butler* 1992,

472). For example, the Court notes that the portrayal of this physical activity involves the production of meaning by film-makers: 'in creating a film, regardless of its content, the maker of the film is consciously choosing the particular images which together constitute the film. In choosing his or her images, the creator of the film is attempting to convey some meaning' (ibid., 474). In the Court's view, although sex is purely physical, sexual representations are not. Rather, the process of representation necessarily involves the other side of the mind/body distinction, and thus constitutes expression, regardless of the content of that expression.

Obscenity as a Reasonable Limit

The Court then considered whether this violation of s.2(b) by s.163 of the Criminal Code is a reasonable limit within the meaning of section 1 of the Charter. The discussion proceeds along the lines of the well-established *Oakes* test, which requires that there be an objective that is sufficiently pressing and substantial to justify the violation of the Charter right, and that the violation of the right be proportional to this objective.[13] In addressing the question of objective, Sopinka J. observed that, historically, the objective of obscenity legislation was the prohibition of 'immoral influences' and the imposition of a 'standard of public and sexual morality' (*Butler* 1992, 476). In the Court's view, this objective is no longer sustainable. 'The prevention of "dirt for dirt's sake" is not a legitimate objective which would justify the violation of one of the most fundamental freedoms enshrined in the *Charter*' (ibid.). The Court does not say that Parliament cannot legislate on the basis of morality. However, it does say that the objective of s.163 'is not moral disapprobation but the avoidance of harm to society' (ibid., 477). The Court cited with approval the description of the harm of pornography in the Report of the Standing Committee on Justice and Legal Affairs (1978, 18:4). 'The clear and unquestionable danger of this type of material is that it reinforces some unhealthy tendencies in Canadian society. The effect of this type of material is to reinforce male-female stereotypes to the detriment of both sexes. It attempts to make degradation, humiliation, victimization and violence in human relationships appear normal and acceptable. A society which holds that egalitarian, non-violence, consensualism and mutuality are basic to any human interaction, whether sexual or other, is clearly justified in controlling and prohibiting any medium of depiction, description or advocacy which violates these principles' (*Butler* 1991, 477). The objective of s.163 is thus not the imposition of a sexual morality but, rather, the prevention of the harm that pornography causes to women.

Much has been made of these statements of the objective of s.163, particularly by feminists, who support the *Butler* decision. LEAF, for example, has argued that this represents a fundamental shift in obscenity law, away from the regulation of sexual morality and towards a feminist reformulation of the harm of pornography (Busby 1994, 176). However, the Court's effort to reconceptualize the objective must be read within the framework of the decision as a whole. It must be considered alongside the actual test for obscenity set out by the Court in the first part of the decision, as well as considered in light of the rest of the section 1 analysis. When evaluated within the discursive framework of the decision as a whole, and its sexual subtext, the assertion that the statement of objective signifies a radical transformation in the law of obscenity is, at the very least, contestable.

Indeed, even the discussion of the objective of the law itself is contradictory, in so far as the Court is not able to sustain the distinction it is attempting to make between morality <the old law> and harm <the new law>. The sexual morality of the old law is apparent even in the language of the decision. Although the Court specifically states that regulating a standard of public and sexual morality would be inappropriate – that is, it is not an acceptable objective to prohibit 'dirt for dirt's sake' – the Court continues to use the term 'dirt for dirt's sake' as a synonym for pornography in several places in the decision. Again we see the extent to which, in the eyes of the Court, sexually explicit materials constitute dirt. Of course, according to the official story, the point is that the court has to find another reason to regulate and prohibit this 'dirt.'

In attempting to locate the harm as something other than moral disapprobation, the distinction between morality and harm is further disrupted. In previous decisions, the Supreme Court has held that the purpose of a law cannot be seen to change or shift over time.[14] The purpose of a law is, in effect, written in stone at the time that the legislation was drafted and enacted. As a result, the Court in *Butler* was confronted with a problem: did this effort to recast the objective of the law as preventing harm, particularly harm against women, violate this shifting-purpose doctrine – that is, did it constitute an effort to change the purpose of the law from the regulation of morality to the prevention of harm? The Supreme Court of Canada said no. Yet, in so doing, the Court is forced to retreat from its earlier position that morality and harm were distinct. '[T]he notions of moral corruption and harm to society are not distinct ... but are inextricably linked. It is a moral corruption of a certain kind which leads to the detrimental effect on society' (*Butler* 1992, 477). Since the objective of the law cannot change, Sopinka J. holds that the prevention of harm is intricately related to morality. Now, morality and harm are not different. According to Sopinka J., the only thing that has changed is our understanding of the harm caused by pornography. 'The prohibition of such materials was based on the belief that they had a detrimental impact on individuals exposed to them and consequently on society as a whole. Our understanding of the harms caused by these materials has developed considerably since that time; however, this does not detract from the fact that the purpose of this legislation remains, as it was in 1959, the protection of society from harms caused by the exposure to obscene materials' (ibid., 478). The Court spins around a tautological circle: the harms that are intended to be addressed by obscenity legislation are the harms that are caused by obscenity. If this circular reasoning is valid, we now have a generic objective so broad that it can be applied to virtually any piece of legislation. Just fill in the blank: the objective of the <pornography, traffic congestion, security fraud> law is to prevent the harm that <pornography, traffic congestion, security fraud> causes to society. According to this generic, or 'no-name' objective of preventing harm, there will be little difficulty avoiding the net of the shifting-purpose doctrine whenever it is convenient to do so.[15]

Further, in these passages, the Court's views on the relationship between harm and morality is inconsistent. First, Sopinka J. tells us that the law is not about morality, but about harm (morality is bad, and distinct from harm). But, then he tells us that harm is not actually distinct from morality, so there is no shifting purpose (morality is OK, and related to harm). And, finally, he tells us that the harm intended to be addressed is the harm caused by pornography, which used to be immorality but now is harm to women (morality is bad, and distinct from harm). So morality is bad, except when it is related to harm, in which case it is no longer morality. The Court's effort to cast the objective of s.163 as something other than moral approbation is, at best, on rather shaky ground.

The sexual morality underlying the decision is made further manifest in the subsequent analysis of the proportionality requirement.[16] This sexual morality is most clearly revealed in the Court's brief discussion of the nature of the expression at stake in the legal regulation of pornography, which in its view is important in deciding whether the proportionality requirement has been met. Sopinka J. examines whether the nature of the expression at issue in the regulation of pornography is in any way related to the three values that underlie the right to freedom of expression, namely, 'the search for truth, participation in the political process, and individual self-fulfilment' (*Butler* 1992, 481). In evaluating the nature of the expression, the Court reviews the contrasting positions of the Ontario Attorney General and the British Columbia Civil Liberties Association. The former argued that 'only individual self fulfilment and only at its most base aspect, that of physical arousal, is engaged by pornography' (ibid.). The latter argued that 'pornography forces us to question conventional notions of sexuality and thereby launches us into an inherently political discourse' (ibid.). Interestingly, the Court then quotes a passage from Robin West (cited in the BCCLA factum), who argues, 'Good pornography has value because it validates women's will to pleasure. It celebrates female nature. It validates a range of female sexuality that is wider and truer than that legitimated by the non-pornographic culture. Pornography when it is good celebrates both female pleasure and male rationality' (Robin West as quoted in *Butler* 1992, 481). The Court seems to adopt West's view of the positive value of sexual expression, in noting that '[a] proper application of the test should not suppress what West refers to as "good pornography." The objective of the impugned provision is not to inhibit the celebration of human sexuality' (*Butler* 1992, 481).

This is as close as the Court comes to articulating a positive theory of sexual expression. Pornography is divided into good pornography and bad pornography (good sex/bad sex). Good pornography is sexual expression that affirms women's agency (*will* to pleasure, not just pleasure). It is the will, the appeal to agency that comes from the intellect, the mind that transforms sex from bad to good. It is good because it has transcended its purely physical nature. It is also good because it 'celebrates female nature' – a nature that although unarticulated is more than the body; it is of the whole female person – which must include the mind, the spirit. Female pleasure rooted in female nature seems to be posited as something more than physical self-fulfilment. Finally, sexual expression is good when if affirms 'male rationality' – that is, when male sexuality transcends its base and corporeal nature; when it is no longer just of the body, but of the mind. We catch a glimpse of the deeply gendered nature of these oppositions: men are associated with rationality <which is of the mind> and women with pleasure <which is of the body> (Hekman 1990). This articulation of a positive theory of sexual expression is thus firmly rooted in the underlying conservative sexual morality and its good sex / bad sex, mind / body oppositions.

This positive theory of sexual expression is further limited when the Court shifts back, in the next sentence to its focus on the negative value of sexual expression. '[I]t cannot be ignored that the realities of the pornography industry are far from the picture which the B.C. Civil Liberties Association would have us paint' (*Butler* 1992, 481). This assertion of 'the realities of the pornography industry' is supported only by reference to another court decision that describes pornographic materials; it is a reality apparently so obvious that the Court does not even have to take judicial notice, nor refer to expert evidence or secondary literature. These 'realities of the pornography industry' are such that the Court is compelled to adopt the position of the Ontario Attorney General on the nature of the expression, namely, that it appeals only to the most base aspect of individual self-fulfilment (see Gotell, this volume). Sopinka J. concludes: 'the kind of expression which is sought to be advanced does not stand on equal footing with other kinds of expression which directly engage with "core" of the freedom of expression values' (ibid., 482). While the Court had found that sexual expression was expression within the meaning of s.2(b) of the Charter, it subsequently holds that sexual expression is an inferior form of expression, and thus not entitled to the same degree of protection. While, for the purpose of s.2(b), all expression is equal, for the purpose of s.1, the Court appears to be of the view that some expression is more equal than others.[17]

Why is sexual expression a lesser form of expression? All the Court tells us is that it is not related to any of the three core values underlying expression – the pursuit of truth, participation in the political process, or individual self-fulfilment. The Court's answer begs the deeper question – that is, why is sexual expression not related to the pursuit of truth, or to political participation, or to individual self-fulfilment? Sopinka J. only addresses the third value, that of individual self-fulfilment. In his view, 'this kind of expression is far from the core of the guarantee of freedom of expression. It appeals only to the most base aspect of individual fulfillment' (*Butler* 1992, 488). In this passage, Sopinka J. seems to endorse the position advocated by the Ontario Attorney General, which, as noted, described this most base aspect of self-fulfilment as physical arousal. Sexual expression is a lesser form of expression because it appeals only to our most base – that is, our physical – dimension.

A now familiar subtext emerges: sexual arousal, rather than being an important part of our human dimension, is seen as base. And sexual arousal is seen as purely physical arousal – as a purely physiological reaction devoid of any mental elements. Again, sex is only of the body, not of the mind. Since individual self-fulfilment is valued only when it is promoting arousal of something more than the body – arousal of the mind or the spirit – it does not apply to sexual arousal or fulfilment. And again, we see the mind/body opposition, in which sex is located firmly within the body; it is bad unless it can be made good by transcending its corporeal nature. It is, then, this appeal to the body that makes sexual expression a lesser form of expression. As Linda Williams has argued, we can begin to see the extent to which pornography is 'a volatile issue not simply because it represents sexual acts and fantasies, but because in that representation it frankly seeks to arouse viewers. Perhaps more than any other genre its pleasures are aimed at the body' (Williams 1989, 46). It is the very fact that this expression is directed at the pleasures of the body that makes it a lesser form of expression. It is based on an understanding of sex and sexual pleasure as being only of the body. There is no recognition of the role of our minds or our imaginations in sexual arousal and sexual pleasure. Nor is there any recognition of the social construction of sexuality. We again see the assumption of sexual essentialism operating: sex is biological, it is of and only of the body and, as such, unaffected by social relationships or culture.

Ironically, this assumption of sexual essentialism sits in stark contrast to the understanding of sexuality that informs the feminist anti-pornography position. The work of anti-pornography feminists has been based on the idea that sexuality is socially constructed – that sex and sexual desire are a product of the patriarchal society in which we live, and that sexual arousal (particularly, male sexual arousal) is negatively affected by images that represent women as sexual objects. Indeed, the sexual essentialism of the decision sits awkwardly with the Court's own assertion of the relationship between pornography and harm to women. Yet, it is only through this biological essentialism of sex, as of and only of the body, that the Court can sustain the assertion that sex appeals only to the most base aspect of physical fulfilment, and, in turn, the conclusion that sexual expression is a lesser form of expression.

The question of why sexual expression is not related to the other two values of expression – the search for truth and political participation – is not directly addressed by the Court. This silence, however, speaks volumes as to the underlying sexual morality. It is based on an unstated understanding of the truth about pornography – what it is, and what it is not; a 'truth' that upon further deconstruction reveals a multiplicity of assumptions about sex and sexuality. In the Court's view, there is a 'truth' to pornography, which is asserted to dismiss the idea that it could in any way be related to the values underlying freedom of expression. It was the truth about pornography – that it appeals only to the most base dimension of physical fulfilment – that allowed the Court to reject any connection between sexual expression and individual self-fulfilment. It is similarly this truth about pornography that allows the Court to implicitly reject any connection between sexual expression and the pursuit of truth.

For example, the efforts of the BC Civil Liberties Association to frame sexual expression as a challenge to conventional sexuality and, in turn, as a political discourse (see Gotell), were simply rejected on the basis of the 'realities' of the pornography industry. According to the Court, the realities or truth of the pornography industry are that it is characterized by a particular form of sexual representations of women, that is, of women as sexual objects for men. In this view, there is no possibility of a diversity of sexual representations within the pornography industry. Nor is there any room to admit that these sexual representations may be subject to different interpretations (Williams 1989). Again, we see the Court's literalist approach to representation, according to which pornography is seen to have a single and universal meaning, readily available to any viewer. This reality of the pornography industry, along with the monolithic nature of its representations, the meaning of which is uncontestable, precludes the possibility that pornography could be implicated in what we otherwise value – the search for truth. The 'truth' of the pornography industry is in effect asserted to preclude the possibility that pornography could be implicated in the search for truth.

It is similarly the truth about pornography that precludes the possibility that pornography could in any way be involved in promoting the second value of freedom of expression – that is, participation in the political process. Pornography, or more specifically the pornography industry, which by definition undermines women's equality and dignity, becomes the antithesis of participation. The arguments that sexual representation is for some communities part of an inherently political process of forging community identities were not, in the Court's view, even deemed worthy of mention. The question 'participation for whom?' thus remains unaddressed, as does the question of participation in relation to what issues.

This rejection of the potential value of sexual expression in promoting participation in the political process also implies that sex is not worthy of the political process – that sex is not a matter for the political process. Yet the very history of the legal regulation of sex demonstrates how extensive this regulation has been. The failure to consider any possible connection between sexual expression and political participation obscures the extent to which sex has long been a subject of legal regulation and repression. Indeed, the sexualities of the very individuals who are now seeking to forge their identities in and through these sexual representations – lesbians and gay men, sex-trade workers, feminist artists – have long been the subject of legal regulation and repression, without their consent.

Contrary to the historical realities of legal regulation, the sexual subtext of the decision is based on the idea that sex is not a matter for politics, or for political debate. Not only is the subject not worthy of politics, but we see again the underlying assumptions of the monolithic nature of sexuality. The truth about sex is that sex is just sex – basically it's bad, unless it's good, and we all know which one it is when we see it. There is no room for disagreement or dissent, or for the possibility that there may be diverse sexualities. Nor is there any room to acknowledge that the exploration of diverse sexualities may have value in and of itself.

Sex, being of the body, cannot be the subject of debate. As a function of biology, of pure physical arousal, there is nothing to debate. This sexual essentialism is further reinforced by the assumption of sexual monism. Because there is only one way to have sex, or at least, one good way to have sex, there is nothing to be gained from sexual expression. It is not a subject that can contribute to or be advanced by political debate. These various assumptions of sexual morality – sexual essentialism, sexual monism, and sexual negativity – combine and interact to produce a truth about the nature of sexual expression, a truth according to which sexual expression is not in any way related to political participation, or to any of the other core values that underlie freedom of expression.

Again, we can begin to see the tensions in this sexual subtext. The assumption of sexual monism sits awkwardly with the good sex/bad sex distinction and the sexual hierarchy implicit in this distinction. The idea that there is only one way to have sex is at odds with the idea that there is good sex and bad sex. The latter suggests that there is in fact more than one way to have sex, although one way is good and the other bad. Notwithstanding this tension, these two assumptions – of sexual monism and sexual negativity – operate together to the effect that there is only one way that we should have sex.

In the context of sexual expression, this sexual subtext operates to reinforce the idea that nothing is to be gained from such expression, and, in fact, much is to be lost. Since there is only one way to have sex, sexual expression may only lead others astray; it may encourage people to have bad sex (which in the Court's view is what pornography does). This view is reinforced by the truth about the pornography industry – that is, that it only represents bad sex. The very problem with sexual expression, then, is that it will cause people to have sex or sexual desire in ways that they should not. The repression of such expression, by contrast, will ensure that sex will be as it should be, in the natural order of things, which is still bad, unless it can become good, which if left to the natural order of things <marriage, heterosexuality, and reproduction> it can.

In the subsequent discussion of the three dimensions of the proportionality test, the Court continues to articulate its now popular refrain – obscenity laws do not prohibit all sexual materials, only those sexual materials that cause harm, particularly harm towards women. The sexual subtext of this refrain is also articulated again and again. On the question of minimum impairment, for example, the Court finds that s.163(8) does not proscribe all sexually explicit material, but only that which is violent, degrading, and/or dehumanizing. The provision does not prohibit good sex, that is, 'sexually explicit erotica without violence, that is not degrading or dehumanizing' (*Butler* 1992, 485). Nor does the section include sexually explicit materials that have scientific, artistic, or literary merit. The Court here rearticulates the distinction between sex and art, noting that materials that involve 'aesthetic expression, and thus represent the artist's attempt at individual fulfilment' would not be captured by the provision. The same good sex/bad sex, mind/body, art/sex distinctions continue to appear.

Concluding Remarks on the Butler *Decision*

The result of the *Butler* decision was twofold. The Supreme Court reformulated the test for obscenity under s.163 and subsequently found that although s.163 violated the right to freedom of expression, it was a reasonable limit on this right, and thus constitutional. The meaning of the decision remains highly contested. Those who take the position that *Butler* represents a feminist victory have argued that the objectives of s.163 now require that degrading and dehumanizing be read in a new light, and that the meaning of community standards has been so fundamentally transformed as to resemble the previous test in name alone (Busby 1994, 176). I have tried to map out a very different reading of the *Butler* decision, within which the underlying sexual morality, and its assumptions of sexual negativity, sexual essentialism, and sexual monism, can be seen to leave s.163 transformed in language alone. The classification of sexual representations into one of the three categories of pornography according to the community-standards test of harm can only be done by an implicit reliance on an underlying sexual morality. The very concept of sex that is or could be degrading and dehumanizing only makes sense through the underlying discourses on sexuality – of good sex/ bad sex, of mind/body distinctions, and of the assumptions of sexual negativity, essentialism, monism, and hierarchy on which these distinctions are based. Similarly, community standards only make sense in relation to a prevailing, and generally accepted, understanding of sexual morality, in which some sex is good and some sex is not.

In this reading of the *Butler* decision, the sexual subtext can be seen to inform the Court's discussion of the objective of the legislation, and indeed the discussion of the constitutionality of the law as a whole. Notwithstanding the Court's best efforts to cast the objective of the law as the prevention of harm, particularly of harm towards women, the underlying sexual morality continues to infuse and shape the discourse of the decision. We do not have to look very far to find the continued references to morality, to sexual morality, to good sex and bad sex, to sex being of the body and thus bad, unless it can be made something more, and thereby good. Yet, there is no explicit articulation of what makes sex good. Rather, good sex is simply implied as that which bad sex is not: not base, not physical, not violent, not degrading or dehumanizing, not involving children. The sexual subtext of the *Butler* decision is informed by the discourses on sexuality that have dominated Western thought since the nineteenth century: sexual negativity <sex is bad>, sexual essentialism <sex is biological>, sexual monism <sex is singular>, and sexual hierarchy <some sex is better than other>.

These different assumptions informing prevailing understandings of sexuality sit in awkward relationship to one another, and operate to constitute sex as a highly unstable category. For example, the idea that sex is bad sits in awkward juxtaposition to the idea that it can be made good, which in turn does not seem consistent with the idea that sex being of the body can be made good only by becoming that which it is not – of the mind. The very idea of sexual hierarchy – that some sex <marital, heterosexual, reproductive> is better than other <non-marital, non-reproductive, homosexual> sits inconsistently with the idea of sexual monism – that there is only one sexuality. Sexual hierarchy seems to be based on an implicit notion of sexual diversity, and yet operates at the same time to condemn that diversity. The diversity is reduced to a simple binary opposition of good and bad sex. In *Butler*, these assumptions interact in multiple and seemingly contradictory ways to constitute sex as a highly unstable category – yet not so unstable as to be easily displaced. This unstated sexual morality remains powerfully entrenched as the ideologically dominant discourse of sexuality.

Beyond *Butler*: Obscenity and the Representation of Gay and Lesbian Sexuality

Since the *Butler* decision, gay and lesbian sexually explicit materials continue to be targeted by customs officials and police. The continued criminalization of gay and lesbian sexual representations raises some difficult questions around the ostensible rejection of sexual morality in obscenity law. According to *Butler*, the purpose of s.163 is to prevent harm, particularly harm towards women. The understanding of harm is based on the tenuous, but judicially accepted, link between pornography and violence against women. Men watching pictures in which women are objectified as sex objects is seen to cause men to mistreat women. It is an understanding of harm set in a heterosexual framework. The pornography is male heterosexual pornography, and its harm is that heterosexual men are likely to mistreat women. The feminist literature on which this understanding of harm is based has similarly operated within this heterosexual discursive framework. In the work of its leading exponents, (hetero)sexuality is identified as the site of women's oppression. It is in and through (hetero)sexuality that men are constituted as aggressive and dominant, and women are constituted as passive and subordinate (MacKinnon 1987, Dworkin 1981).

This heterosexual framework raises a serious question about applying the *Butler* test, and its conception of harm, to gay and lesbian materials. Many gay men and lesbians have argued that gay or lesbian sexual representations have absolutely nothing to do with the harm towards women associated with heterosexual pornography. Carl Stychin has contended, for example, that the sexually explicit images of gay male pornography do not reinforce patriarchal male sexuality, but, rather, directly challenge dominant constructs of masculinity by displacing the heterosexual norm (Stychin 1992, 857). Lesbian writers, such as Barbara Smith and Lisa Henderson, have similarly resisted the equation of lesbian pornography with heterosexual pornography, insisting instead on the cultural specificity and the cultural transgression of sexually explicit imagery created for, by, and about lesbians (Smith 1988; Henderson 1992). Within this view, since gay and lesbian sexual representations do not operate within a heterosexual framework, these images cannot and should not be measured against a heterosexual norm.

It would therefore not be unreasonable to suggest that the heterosexual framework of the *Butler* test should limit the applicability of this obscenity doctrine to heterosexual pornography. At a minimum, this heterosexual framework would seem to require that courts at least address the question of how the understanding of harm could be applied to gay and lesbian sex. How does men watching pictures of men having sex with men, or women watching pictures of women having sex with women, contribute to the type of harm to women identified in *Butler*? In the case law that followed on the heels of the *Butler* decision, however, the courts have neither limited the *Butler* test to heterosexual materials nor explored how this heterosexually defined concept of harm can be applied to gay and lesbian imagery. The first two obscenity cases after *Butler* involved Glad Day Bookshop (a gay and lesbian bookstore), and the courts used the obscenity test as set out by the Supreme Court of Canada to find sexually explicit gay and lesbian materials to be obscene. Not only was the question of the relationship between gay and lesbian sexual imagery and harm to women not answered in these cases – the question was not even posed.

Indeed, it is in this application of the *Butler* test, and of its model of harm to gay and lesbian sexual representations, that the discursive drag of the *Butler* decision can be most directly challenged. It is within the context of gay and lesbian materials that the distinction between morality and harm is most difficult to sustain, and that we can most clearly see the extent to which obscenity laws are still predicated on the legal regulation of sexual morality. Gay and lesbian sexual representations are not produced within the heterosexual framework of the more mainstream pornography to which the *Butler* decision addressed itself – the images are of gay/lesbian sexuality, produced by gay men/lesbians, to be consumed by gay men/lesbians. Yet, these sexual representations have been charged and found guilty pursuant to the *Butler* test for obscenity. In this section, I will argue that the criminalization of these gay and lesbian sexual materials does, however, make sense within the discursive context of the sexual subtext of the *Butler* decision. I will illustrate the extent to which the sexual morality underlying the *Butler* decision has framed and informed these two obscenity decisions against

Glad Day Bookshop. The sexual subtext, and its good sex/bad sex oppositions is particularly dangerous in the context of gay and lesbian sexual representations. The heterosexist and often homophobic discourses of this conservative sexual morality operate to locate these representations on the bad-sex side of the dichotomy.

Glad Day Bookshop v. Canada

In the case of *Glad Day Bookshop* (1992), the dangerous implications of the *Butler* decision, and of its understanding of sex and sexuality, for gay and lesbian sexual representation has begun to come clear. This case arose in the context of a customs seizure of gay male pornography en route to Glad Day Bookshop. Glad Day appealed from a determination of the deputy minister of National Revenue for Customs and Excise, declaring the materials to be obscene and, thus, prohibited from import into Canada.[18]

After reviewing the case in considerable detail (and dismissing the expert evidence called by the defence) and the law of obscenity as established in *Butler*, Hayes J. turned to the material in question. The Ontario Court (General Division) reviewed each of the seized materials. Hayes J. briefly described each publication, and concluded that each magazine, story, and comic strip was 'degrading and dehumanizing.' Throughout the decision, each publication is dealt with in two or three paragraphs: one paragraph describes the sexual representation; the second paragraph is conclusory in nature – that is, the Court concludes that the material is degrading, that the material does violate community standards. For example, in relation to *Oriental Guys* no. 4 (Spring 1989), which contains explicit representations of gay oral and anal sex with no violence, the Court held: 'The description in the magazine of this sexual activity is degrading, I am of the opinion that this particular material does indicate a strong inference of a risk of harm that might flow from the community being exposed to this material. I am of the opinion that the community would not tolerate others being exposed to this item. The dominant characteristic is an undue exploitation of sex. It is obscene' (*Glad Day Bookshop* 1992, 15). There is almost no analysis as to why particular materials are degrading. Rather, in each case, the Court simply asserts that the material is degrading, that there is a risk of harm, that the community would not tolerate others being exposed to it.

To the extent that the Court gives any reason as to why the material is degrading, the theme that emerges, in single sentences and passages, is the ostensible absence of 'real human relationships.' For example, with regard to *Movie Star Confidential*, a sexually explicit comic strip, the Court writes: 'It does not contain any real human relationship. In its grotesque figures and their sexual activity, it is completely degrading and dehumanizing' (*Glad Day Bookshop* 1992, 16). On *Spartan's Quest*, Hayes J. writes: 'It is a sexual encounter without any real meaningful human relationship' (ibid.). On *Humongous – True Gay Encounters*, a collection of short stories, which includes explicit gay sex with strangers: 'The manner in which they express explicit sexual activity is described is degrading [sic] to human beings. *There is no real human relationship'* (ibid., 17; emphasis added). On *Sex Stop*: 'The introduction to this book ... clearly indicates the base purpose of the material which has no human dimension and is degrading and dehumanizing' (ibid., 18). On *Advocate Men*, a magazine with explicit representations of oral and anal sex: 'The description and activities are degrading and without any human dimension. The dominant characteristic is the undue exploitation of sex' (ibid., 19).

According to Hayes J., any explicit sexual representation without a 'human dimension' or 'human relationship' is degrading and dehumanizing, and constitutes the undue exploitation of sex. The implication throughout the decision is that sex is not human – a sexual relationship is not a human relationship. Our sexual dimension is not part of our human dimension – our sexual dimension makes us base, makes us subhuman. This understanding of sex is informed by and reinforces the binary opposition between good and bad sex, in which sex – which in and of itself is bad – gets to become good if it can transcend its subhuman nature and become human. Sex becomes good if it can transcend the purely physical, purely pleasurable, dimension and become something more. Sex becomes good if it can become that which by definition it is not.

In Hayes J.'s view, sexual representations are bad, unless they can be redeemed by emotional relationships. The *Glad Day Bookshop* decision makes clear that what is needed to make sex (which is inherently bad) good is an intimate, loving, monogamous relationship. However, since even *Advocate Men*, the gay male equivalent to *Playboy*, was found to be obscene, it is difficult to imagine what, if any, representations of gay male sex and sexuality would meet this test. It seems as if it is the representation of gay male sex in and of itself that is without a 'human dimension' and thus degrading and dehumanizing.

According to the *Glad Day Bookshop* decision, sex with strangers, group sex, sex with bondage are all degrading and dehumanizing. Not only are the actual sexual practices considered to be inappropriate, but the mere representation of sexual fantasies are also prohibited (such as comic books, which represent the fantastical, not the real). Even the fantastical 'without a human dimension' is degrading and dehumanizing. There is, in Hayes J.'s sexual morality, no distinction between the real and the fantastical, between reality and fantasy. The *Glad Day Bookshop* decision has been argued by some to be a misapplication of the *Butler* test, and it is currently under appeal. There is no question that the Court failed to engage with the *Butler* test. There was no consideration of why particular materials were degrading and dehumanizing, nor why these materials would cause harm. They were simply deemed to be degrading and dehumanizing and, in turn, deemed to cause harm. However, the failure of the Court to engage with the *Butler* test should not be taken as a vindication of the *Butler* test. First, the *Glad Day Bookshop* decision exemplifies what lower courts can do with an inherently vague test like 'degrading and dehumanizing,' and with a community-standards test that does not require evidence. The vagueness of the test opens the door to, and invites the application of, a subjective determination on the nature of the sexually explicit materials. Second, it is not at all clear that the finding in Hayes is at odds with the sexual subtext of the *Butler* decision. Rather, in its assumptions of sexual negativity and sexual essentialism – sex is of the body and bad, unless it can be made good – the Hayes decision is quite consistent with the sexual morality of *Butler*.

The main point of potential conflict between the *Glad Day Bookshop* decision and the *Butler* decision is in the application of a heterosexist model of harm to gay sexual representations. The Court does not engage with the fundamental question of what the *Butler* model of harm has to do with gay sexual representations. Indeed, the Court makes no reference to harm in terms of harm towards women. The only reference to harm by Hayes J. is in terms of causing 'anti-social conduct.' The ostensibly feminist objective of the law evaporates. Rather, the application of the law is simply the application of a conservative sexual morality. The harm, according to the Court, is the harm of sexually explicit materials. The sexual subtext of the *Butler* decision – the good sex/bad sex distinction – is given a particularly homophobic spin in *Glad Day Bookshop*, whereby the representation of explicit gay sexuality becomes, by definition, bad sex.

R. v. Scythes, Glad Day Bookshop

On 30 April 1992, two months after the *Butler* decision, the Toronto police seized the magazine *Bad Attitude* – a magazine of 'lesbian erotic fiction' – from Toronto's Glad Day Bookshop, and charged the store and the store's owner, John Scythes, with the possession and sale of obscene material, in contravention of s.163 of the Criminal Code. After a five-day trial in December 1992, Justice Paris of the Ontario Court (Provincial Division) delivered a six page judgment in February 1993, in which he found *Bad Attitude* to be obscene, and the accuseds were convicted of violating s.163.

At trial, the Crown focused on a number of parts of the magazine: the fictional articles containing accounts of lesbian sadomasochist sex, and the accompanying photographs of explicit lesbian sex. In the decision, however, the Court focused on one article entitled 'Wunna My Fantasies,' in which writer Trish Thomas tells a story about the sexual practices of two fictional lesbian characters. One lesbian character stalks another in a shower room, and the two women engage in s/m sex.

The brief decision is a journey through heterosexual assumptions and neo-Victorian sexual morality. Interestingly, after briefly reviewing the *Butler* decision, the Court specifically turns to the question of heterosexuality. Paris J. denies that the 'sexual orientation' of the sexual representations have anything to do with his decision.

I have detected during this trial a concern that the Court will find relevant the sexual orientation of Bad Attitude. In recent years, many courts and tribunals have struck down laws and practices held to discriminate against gays. This is an indication that our society has moved beyond tolerance to the actual recognition that homosexuals form an essential part of our community. It follows then that as members of a sexual minority they have the right to communicate publicly on the subject that bind together. That right however will on occasion be curtailed in the public interest. The community tolerance test is blind to sexual orientation or practices. Its only focus is the potential harm to the public. Any consideration given to the sexual orientation of the material would constitute an unwarranted application of the test. (*Scythes* 1993, 4)

In the Court's view, sexual orientation is irrelevant, and the community-standards test must be applied in a formally equal manner. In the name of formal equality – which does not exist for gays and lesbians in Canadian law – the Court has ensured that the particular context of lesbian sexuality and representations will not be considered relevant. The test for community standards is supposed to be formally neutral to sexual orientation. But what this standard of formal neutrality obscures is the extent to which the standard is one deeply informed by heterosexual assumptions. The community standard is a heterosexual standard, and it is this heterosexual standard that becomes the norm by which all representations of sexuality are to be judged.

In the next paragraph, Paris J. finds that the article contains representations of both sex and violence, and thus falls within the definition of s.163(8). He then briefly turns his attention to the question of consent: 'The consent in this case, far from redeeming the material makes it degrading and dehumanizing' (*Scythes* 1993, 4). In a slick discursive move, provided courtesy of the Supreme Court of Canada in *Butler*, the consensual nature of the sexual practices is not simply rendered irrelevant, but, in the Court's view, actually contributes to making the material degrading and dehumanizing. This discursive shift, in which consent becomes degradation, ensures the erasure of the specificity of lesbian sexual practices.

Consent is a cornerstone in lesbian s/m sexual practices, and in lesbian sexual/cultural production. As Lisa Henderson has argued, consent appears as a subtext throughout lesbian s/m sexual/cultural production.[19] As Becki Ross discusses in greater detail in the next chapter, the defence counsel in the case tried to explain this consensual nature of the sex in 'Wunna My Fantasies' to the Court. This attempt to explain the importance of consent within lesbian s/m culture, however, proved futile.[20] Even if established, in the reasoning of the *Butler* decision, consent only makes the sexual representation more degrading. After citing the *Butler* decision's passage on consent, Paris J. writes: 'This material flashes every light and blows every whistle of obscenity. Enjoyable sex after subordination by bondage and physical abuse at the hands of a total stranger' (*Scythes* 1993, 5). In Paris J.'s sexual world, there is no legitimate space for s/m sex, no room for bondage, no room for fantasizing about sex with a stranger. None of these sexual practices and fantasies could or should lead to enjoyable sex. Moreover, Paris J. seems unable to comprehend the extent to which the story represents a sexual fantasy. In the Court's view, the sexual representations combined too many elements of bad sex: sex with strangers, sex with bondage, sex with submission, or even sexual fantasy.

Paris J. then commits the ultimate act of judicial heterosexism: 'If I replaced the aggressor in this article with a man there would be very few people in the community who would not recognize the potential for harm. The fact that the aggressor is a female is irrelevant because the potential for harm remains' (*Scythes* 1993, 5). To determine whether the text in question is obscene, the Court replaces the woman aggressor with a male aggressor. This substitution is allowed by the framework that the Court sets out at the beginning of the decision, which insists that sexual orientation is not relevant in determining community standards. Since sexual orientation is not relevant, then, in the Court's eyes, it does not matter whether the sex is occurring between two women, or between a woman and a man. The court is able to use its understanding of heterosexual sex to evaluate whether the representation of lesbian sex is obscene.[21] Through this judicial technique of heteroswitching, the specificity of lesbian sexuality, and of lesbian s/m cultural practices, are negated. All the arguments of the defence counsel, on the need to consider the specific cultural and ideological context under which lesbian sexual images are produced and given meaning, are, in a single heterosexual sweep, rendered irrelevant. And the heterosexual norm of the ostensibly neutral community standards is thereby reinforced.

In the final paragraph of the decision, the Court rejects the comparison the defence attempted to make between *Bad Attitude* and Madonna's book *Sex*. Defence counsel argued that the sexually explicit representations in *Sex*, which includes both heterosexual and homosexual s/m practices, demonstrated a shift in community standards. The commercial success of *Sex* in the Canadian market was presented as evidence that these kinds of sexually explicit representations do not violate community standards. The Court, however, was unpersuaded. 'Madonna's book called Sex was offered to show the public tolerance to this type of material. One photograph of particular relevance shows a so called playful rape in a school gymnasium. I received very little information on the distribution of this book. I am told however that few were available and were sold immediately. I find the sample too small to be a reliable indication of the public's reaction to its distribution' (*Scythes* 1993, 6). The strongest argument on the nature of community standards, and the challenge to the assumed heterosexism of the standards, was simply rejected on the grounds that there was not enough evidence. The *Butler* test reaffirmed that there is no need to enter evidence of the community standard. Yet, here, the arbitrary and discretionary nature of the community-standards test is used to say that there was not enough evidence to show that the community standard has been changed. In other words, while no evidence is required to prove community standards, evidence is required to prove that these standards have changed.

In *Bad Attitude*, the representation of s/m lesbian sex, which in the Court's view involves explicit sex with violence, is, by the standards laid down by the Supreme Court of Canada, bad sex. There was no need to entertain the question of whether the representation constituted good sex, because the representation 'blows every whistle of obscenity.' Again, we see the Court expound on the negative values of sexual expression, on what is bad about sex. Sex with bondage, with domination, with strangers, is bad sex. And in order to insulate itself from charges that it was reverting back to the regulation of sexual morality, and not the prevention of harm towards women, the Court simply turned lesbian sex into heterosexual sex. It was only by virtue of this heteroswitching that the Court was able to conclude that the sexual representations harmed women, within the heterosexual framework of the *Butler* decision. Indeed, within this framework, no gay or lesbian sexual representations will be safe from review on the ground that there is no harm towards women. Rather, through this new-found judicial technique of heteroswitching, gay sexual representations can always be transformed by replacing a man with a woman; and lesbian sexual representations transformed by replacing one of the women with a man.[22]

R. v. 931536 Ontario

Gay and lesbian sexual representations have not been the only focus of criminal prosecutions. Heterosexual pornography has also been subject to prosecution under s.163 in the aftermath of *Butler*. Interestingly, some of the so-called straight porn that has been prosecuted has included scenes of lesbian or gay sexuality.[23] In *R. v. 931536 Ontario*, this lesbian imagery played a central role in the Court's finding of the material to be degrading and dehumanizing. In this case, eight videos were alleged to be obscene. At trial, the Court held that seven of the videos did exploit sex, and thus had to determine whether this exploitation was 'undue.' According to the Court, six of the remaining videos did not fall within the categories proscribed by *Butler*: they did not involve sex with violence, they were not degrading or dehumanizing, and did not create a substantial risk of harm. But one video, entitled *Cherry Tricks*, was held to be obscene on the basis that 'its dominant theme is the degrading and demeaning treatment of women, combined with unobjectionable heterosexual and lesbian acts of sex.' While this reference to lesbian acts of sex as unobjectionable might suggest that lesbian sexuality was not a relevant factor in the case, a deeper look at the reasoning brings this claim into at least some doubt.

In reviewing the video, the Court tells us that women are degraded throughout the video in their portrayal as 'stupid, with no skills or ability, except sex.' The women are 'required to and are prepared to have sex with men who are either their employers, acting teachers, or men in positions to give them a job.' The Court describes that each sex act begins *after* a scene in which a woman is humiliated. 'The only actual overlapping of sex and humiliation occurs when two women are requested to suck and lick each other so that the men can choose the appropriate person for a job (a pun made in the movie), while the men look on. The women in the scene are shown as consenting and enjoying the sex' (*R. v. 931536*). The Court concludes, on the basis of *Butler*, that the 'film is degrading and dehumanizing because it places the women in positions of subordination or humiliation, and runs against the principles of equality and dignity of all human beings.' The Court repeats that 'the sexual acts, themselves, taken in isolation, are not degrading.'

It is the lesbian sex act that nevertheless stands out. It is in this sequence that the women are humiliated at the same time as they perform an otherwise 'unobjectionable sex act.' In the Court's view, there is a connection between the degrading mental treatment and the sex act. 'There is the false consent, and the sex is always related to the woman's servile and subordinate position in relation to the men. The non-degrading sex taken in isolation is so interwoven with the reasons the women are having sex that it becomes degrading itself (*R. v. 931536*). It is interesting that this ostensibly 'false consent' and the depiction of women in subordinate positions is present in other scenes, which the Court describes but does not focus on in finding the video to be an 'undue' exploitation of sex. Women are shown as only able to advance in their modelling or acting careers by having sex with their male employers or teachers. There is also the depiction of what the Court describes as a 'non-violent sexual assault,' in which a woman consents to sex with a man on the basis of mistaking his identity. Yet, these are not the images that attract the Court's attention – apparently because the humiliation immediately precedes the sex. The Court does not tell us why humiliating women just before sex (and, presumably, into having sex) is any less degrading and dehumanizing to women than if the act of humiliation continues during the sex.

Nor does the Court tell us why this particular sex act is any more humiliating than the others, in which women are compelled to have sex with their male employers or teachers. The Court insists that it is not because the act is a lesbian act. Lesbian sex is, according to the Court, unobjectionable in isolation. This position is consistent with the Court's conclusion on two of the other videos, which also contained scenes of explicit sex between women, but which were not held to be degrading and dehumanizing. While lesbian sex may be unobjectionable, forcing women to have lesbian sex is, apparently, a different story. Indeed, it appears to be a different story than forcing women to have sex with men. The subtext is difficult to escape: what is particular objectionable is coercing women to have lesbian sex.

Lesbian sexuality is not irrelevant. While it may not be sufficient in itself to make sexual representations bad sex (which is certainly a step forward from the *Glad Day Bookshop* decision), it does operate as a factor that pushes sex across the line into bad sex. Compelling women to have sex with male employers to get a job may not exactly be good sex – in the Court's view, it is clearly sexist – but it is not sufficient to push the sex into the bad-sex category. Compelling women to have sex with other women to get a job, however, is bad sex. This is not to suggest that if the Court had focused on the other scenes in *Cherry Tricks*, then the finding that the video was degrading and dehumanizing would have been justified. It is simply an attempt to illustrate the underlying assumptions of sexual morality that continue to operate – assumptions in which sexual orientation is not a neutral factor. Neither the *Butler* test nor the sexual morality within which it is interpreted or applied is neutral on sexual orientation. While the decision in *Cherry Tricks* is evidence that this sexual morality has shifted, in so far as the Court is willing to say that lesbian sexuality is not in and of itself obscene, this is not the end of the story. Underlying the decision is still a sexual morality informed by the assumption of sexual hierarchy, in which some sex is better than others. Lesbian and gay sex may not be bad sex in and of itself, but it is certainly not as good as straight sex.

Good Girls (and Boys) Don't: Gay and Lesbian Sexual Representations as Bad Sex

The question that remains unanswered in these cases is what gay and lesbian sexual representations have to do with harm against women? While in *Cherry Tricks* the sexual representations of women having sex with women were, arguably, not inappropriately interpreted within the heterosexual context of the video, the same does not apply to the first two cases involving specifically gay and lesbian material. In the *Glad Day Bookshop* decision, the Court did not even attempt to answer the question. In *Scythes*, the Court engages with the question, although it hardly provides an acceptable answer. The Court simply falls back on the heterosexual discursive framework of *Butler*, and assumes that the same harms would flow. At this level, it would seem that both of these obscenity charges against Glad Day Bookshop could reasonably be seen as a misapplication of the *Butler* test. And this is the view taken by feminists who support the *Butler* decision: that *Butler* has been misapplied, and that gay and lesbian representations are being unfairly targeted (Busby 1994, 184–7).

At a deeper level, however, it is considerably less clear that these cases can simply be dismissed as a misapplication. The sexual subtexts of the cases is quite consistent with the sexual subtext of the *Butler* decision. Each of these cases is characterized by assumptions of sexual negativity, sexual essentialism, sexual monism, and sexual hierarchy. While these assumptions are troubling enough in a heterosexual context, they are disastrous in a gay or lesbian context. If heterosexual sex is at risk of being bad sex, then gay or lesbian sex is most certain to be bad sex (sexual negativity). If (hetero) sex is a natural force, then gay or lesbian sex is most likely to be unnatural (sexual essentialism). If there is only one way to have (hetero) sex, then it is almost certain that it is not the way of gay or lesbian sex. And in the hierarchy of sexual activity, gay or lesbian sex most certainly ranks well below heterosexual sex.

Gayle Rubin, in her description of the sex hierarchy, observes that some areas of previously contested sex are now 'inching across the line of acceptability': 'Unmarried couples living together, masturbation, and some forms of homosexuality are moving in the direction of respectability. Most homosexuality is still on the bad side of the line. But if it is coupled and monogamous, the society is beginning to recognize that it includes the full range of human interaction' (Rubin 1989, 283). In the context of representations of gay and lesbian sexuality, sexually explicit representations risk pushing this sex back across the line of bad sex. Sexually explicit materials focus attention on sexual interaction, which, in turn, seems to detract from viewing gay and lesbian sexuality within this fuller 'range of human interaction.' Good sex for gay men and lesbians must not only be monogamous and loving – it must also be private and, preferably, in the absence of cameras. The mere representation of gay and lesbian sex risks pushing the new-found acceptability back across the line of bad sex. Gay sexuality can be represented within a higher artistic context – witness films such as *M. Butterfly, The Wedding Banquet, Torch Song Trilogy,* and *Strawberry and Chocolate,* which illustrate the so-called fuller human dimension of gay men's lives, in which sex is only a small part. But, the representation of gay and lesbian sex for the explicit purpose of sexual arousal is in a different category – a category more likely than not to fall on the side of bad sex. Gay and lesbian sexuality may not be degrading and dehumanizing in and of itself – it is just the *representation* of gay and lesbian sexuality that is degrading and dehumanizing. Gay and lesbian sex is not bad sex, but representations of gay and lesbian sex might be. And the more the representation hints at other forms of traditionally 'deviant' sexuality, the more likely it is to be bad sex. Bondage and leather is virtually guaranteed to be bad sex. However, even non-monogamous or non-intimate sex, which abounds in heterosexual pornography, risks becoming bad sex if it is situated in the context of gay and lesbian explicit sexual representations.

As I have tried to argue, the *Butler* decision is not neutral on sexual orientation. The analysis of harm within *Butler* is based on a particular analysis of heterosexual sexuality. Yet, it is being deployed in ways that assume that the analysis of harm can be applied to all sexually explicit representations. And as such, the decisions are beginning to expose this underlying heterosexism of the *Butler* test. In *Glad Day Bookshop*, this heterosexual norm was most notoriously exposed: it was simply the representation of gay sex that made the sex bad. In *Bad Attitude*, the heterosexism was somewhat less visible, but no less significant. Lesbian sex was not in and of itself degrading and dehumanizing. Rather, lesbian sex was turned into heterosexual sex, and then judged by heterosexual norms. Even in *Cherry Tricks*, a 'straight porn' video, the heterosexual norm of the degrading and dehumanizing test was again apparent, in so far as 'otherwise unobjectionable' lesbian sex was judged by harsher standards than heterosexual sex.

Neither the discursive framework of the *Butler* test, nor the dominant sexual morality within which this test is applied, is neutral on the question of sexual orientation. The relevance of sexual orientation within this sexual morality has shifted over time, to the extent that sexual orientation has now become a contested site. It is a sexual morality in which some courts are willing to state that gay and lesbian sexuality is not in and of itself obscene. This is an important change, but it does not signal the end of sexual orientation's relevance. There is still a conservative sexual morality informed by the assumption of sexual hierarchy, in which some sex is better than others. Lesbian and gay sex may not (always) be bad sex in and of itself, but it is certainly not as good as straight sex. Lesbian and gay sex continues to run a much higher risk of being pushed back across the dividing line between good and bad sex, back from its tenuous legitimacy, into its all-too-familiar condemnation as bad sex.

To return to the argument that some feminists have made that the gay and lesbian community is being unfairly targeted and that these decisions by lower courts are a misapplication of the *Butler* decision, I believe that a different reading is possible. While I agree that these are not particularly exceptional examples of judicial decision-making, I disagree that these decisions represent some fundamental deviation from the principles established in *Butler*. The very argument that gay and lesbian sexual representations have been misclassified by the courts – that these representations should not be bad sex – is based on the tacit acceptance of the good sex/bad sex distinction of the *Butler* test, a distinction that only makes sense when put within the framework of the dominant discourses of sexuality. Further, the *Butler* decision still involves an appeal to a community standard – a standard that is national in scope and can be established without evidence. It is a standard that only makes sense in the context of dominant discourses of sexuality that remain informed by a profoundly conservative sexuality morality, in which heterosexuality, and only certain forms of heterosexuality, remain privileged.

While the discourse of *Butler* justifies the law of obscenity in relation to harm towards women, and the promotion of equality and dignity, the sexual subtext of the decision has provided the lower courts with the arsenal they need to repress sexual representation – particularly, sexual representation by sexual minorities. The anti-sex agenda of the *Butler* decision paved the road for the particular judicial approach to gay and lesbian sexual representation.

At the same time, it is important to recognize that the legal regulation of sexual representations in the post-*Butler* era continues to be a site of contest, conflict, and change. Neither the Supreme Court of Canada nor any of the lower courts has yet had their last word in the development and application of obscenity doctrine. In *R. v. Hawkins*, the Ontario Court of Appeal entered the fray and attempted to correct what it considered to be evidentiary problems in the early application of the *Butler* test.[24] The site of contest in *Hawkins* was, again, the second category of the *Butler* typography of pornography – degrading and dehumanizing. The Court of Appeal revisited the specific requirements set out in *Butler* for this category of materials. The Court emphasized that not all sexually explicit materials that are degrading and dehumanizing are obscene, but rather must also, according to the *Butler* test, create a substantial risk of harm to society. And, like any element in a criminal trial, 'such risk must be proved beyond a reasonable doubt and that proof must be found in the evidence adduced at trial.' In considering the facts of each case, and whether sufficient evidence had been adduced at trial to conclude that the materials did create a substantial risk of harm, the Court of Appeal dismissed all but one appeal, in which the Court held that the trial court had incorrectly found the materials to be obscene.[25]

Hawkins is an important development in the post-*Butler* obscenity jurisprudence, particularly in its re-emphasis that the Crown must prove that degrading and dehumanizing materials create a substantial risk of harm. In so doing, it may operate to protect against some of the more flagrant abuses of *Butler*, by ensuring that the Crown meets the regular standard of proof in a criminal case. The ruling casts further doubt on the *Glad Day Bookshop* decision, in which there is a strong argument to be made that the trial judge erred in finding the materials to be obscene, without adequate evidence that the materials caused harm.

However, *Hawkins* does not represent a departure from the *Butler* test, nor from its sexual subtext. It simply re-emphasizes the objective elements of the crime that the Crown must establish. And in so doing, the Court of Appeal can be seen to be reinscribing the good sex/bad sex distinctions that underlie *Butler*. For example, in attempting to clarify the degree of proof that is required to establish the material causes harm, the Court held:

In some cases, as, for example, in films portraying necrophilia, bondage or bestiality, or sex associated with crime, horror, cruelty, coercion or children, it may be concluded from the contents of the films themselves, without expert or other evidence, that they may predispose persons to act in the antisocial manner contemplated by *Butler*. In other cases, as, for example, in films in which the participants appear as fully willing participants occupying substantially equal roles in a setting devoid of violence or the other kinds of conducts just noted, the risk of societal harm may not be evident. Further evidence may be required to prove that exposure to the impugned materials will create a substantial risk of an identifiable harm that may cause persons to act in a manner inimical to the proper functioning of society. (*Hawkins*)

According to the Court of Appeal, some sexual representations are so bad that no further evidence is required to prove that they are bad. Other sexual representations that are not so bad will require further evidence in order to prove that they are bad sex. A new dualism thus arrives on the obscenity scene: bad sex that is really bad, and bad sex that is not really bad. This somewhat recast good sex/bad sex distinction (really bad sex/not really bad sex) is thus deployed to establish the degree of proof required to draw the lines between good and bad sex. In other words, the line between good and bad sex is used to help draw the line between good and bad sex. Ironically, the more the Court attempts to establish objective standards of proof, the more it falls back on its subjective distinctions between good and bad sex.[26]

Hawkins, then, is at best a cause for cautious optimism, in the continuing conflict over the legitimacy of sexual representations. As a legal text, it too is the site of contradictory assumptions about the place and status of sexual representations, assumptions that include instinctive notions about what is good and what is bad. And leave to appeal to the Supreme Court of Canada has been granted in one of the cases included within the *Hawkins* appeal.[27] This appeal means that within the foreseeable future, the Supreme Court of Canada will have another opportunity to address the law of obscenity. And more generally, the appeal is yet another indication that the struggle over the legal representation of sexual representation is far from over. The law of obscenity, along with the place and status of sexual representations in our society, continues to be a site of contest and change.

Conclusion

My efforts in this chapter to reveal and deconstruct the conservative sexual morality of the *Butler* decision should not be seen as a condemnation of any concept of sexual morality. To critique the conservative sexual morality is not necessarily to adopt a position of sexual libertarianism according to which 'anything goes.' My argument is not that we can transcend sexual morality, and that the Supreme Court of Canada has failed in not doing so. Rather, my concern is with the content of that sexual morality. We delude ourselves with the attempt to cast the legal regulation of sex as something other that what it is. We must, as Carol Smart has argued, recognize that feminism has not transcended moral questions, and begin to address feminism's failure to confront moral questions 'sufficiently reflexively' (Smart 1993, 187; see also Gotell in this volume). The legal regulation of sex will necessarily involve a sexual morality – of what is good and what is bad about sex. My point is that the sexual morality of the *Butler* decision is one about which we should be very concerned.

I believe that we need to turn our minds to the question of sexual morality, not away from it. Recognizing and critiquing the deeply problematic nature of the dominant sexual morality that informs the *Butler* decision need not mean that we relinquish the terrain of discursive struggle about sexuality. As feminists and queer theorists have revealed, our sexualities are deeply political. We can and must continue to engage in political argument about the sexual world that we want to inhabit. We need to re-image our sexualities in ways that embrace their deeply political nature and the diversity of human sexual experiences. We need to develop more positive theories of sex and sexual expression; of what makes sex a good and positive dimension to our humanity. We need to move beyond the assumptions of sexual essentialism and sexual monism – to recognize the ways in which our sexualities are products of the communities in which we live, and the ways in which our sexual desires and practices are different. We must transcend the mere denunciation of diversity if we are to construct a sexual morality that is based on respect.

A revisioned sexual morality, based on a radical sexual pluralism, could still allow us to be attentive to the subtle workings of power in sexual discourses. We can still be attentive to the ways in which these subtle workings of power deprive many women from engaging in consensual sex. Yet, we must do so in a way that does not make sweeping generalizations about the way other people engage in consensual sex, including s/m practices of consensual nonconsensuality. Such a sexual morality would further allow us to rethink the legal regulation of sex. Sex laws that seek to impose a conservative sexual morality, in which sex is bad – such as obscenity and the criminalization of prostitution – should be abolished. Sex laws, by contrast that seek to eliminate coercive sex – sexual assault and child sexual abuse – should be retained, and even strengthened. We need not relinquish normative judgment, nor even the drawing of lines between good and bad sex, and, in turn, between good sex laws and bad sex laws. But, we must radically rethink the way in which we do so.

NOTES

1 Lamer C.J.C., LaForest, Cory, McLachlin, Stevenson, and Iacobucci, JJ. concurred with Sopinka J. Gonthier J. wrote a minority decision, in which he agreed in the result of the majority, although he offered different reasons.

L'Heureux Dubé J. concurred in this minority decision. It is the majority decision that is the focus of this discussion.

2 In this respect, the community-standard test did represent a significant
change from the *Hicklin* test. Under *Hicklin*, virtually any sexual representation could be (and was) found to be obscene, since it was sexual images
themselves that were bad. With the community-standards test, it was no
longer necessarily the case that sexual representations were in and of themselves bad, but only those representations that were dirty, indecent, or illicit.
The community-standards test introduced into obscenity law the possibility
of distinguishing between good sex and bad sex. See Kendrick 1987.

3 Another assumption underlying this test seems to be that tolerance is not
only more objective than taste, but that it is also broader. This distinction flies
in the face of the history of the legal regulation of obscenity, where the
explicit justification for prohibiting its distribution was that certain particularly vulnerable groups in society – notably, poor, uneducated men, and all
women, particularly young women – must not be exposed to its influences.
Although pornographic images were acceptable for the educated male elites,
they must not be massly distributed. The history of pornography reveals that
tolerance was in fact considerably more narrow than taste.

4 The Court cites some of the literature that has been seen to establish a connection between pornography and violence against women, including the
U.S. Attorney General's Commission on Pornography (the Meese Commission) of 1986. For a critique of the Meese Commission in particular, see Vance
1993b. For a critique of the literature attempting to find a causal connection
between pornography and violence, see Segal 1993 and Thelma McCormack,
'Making Sense of the Research on Pornography,' in *Women Against Censorship*, ed. V. Burstyn (Vancouver: Douglas and McIntyre 1985).

5 This mind/body opposition, which has formed a cornerstone of Western
thought since Descartes, rests on and reinforces a series of foundational dualisms: rational/irrational, culture/nature, subject/object. As feminist theorists have argued, these oppositions are also deeply gendered. 'In each of the
dualisms on which Enlightenment thought rests, rational/irrational, subject/
object, and culture/nature, the male is associated with the first element, the
female with the second. And in each case, the male element is privileged over
the female' (Hekman 1990, 5). The gendered nature of the mind/body distinction, in which men are associated with the mind, and women with the
body, makes several brief, but significant, appearances in the text of the decision.

6 Gayle Rubin describes this assumption of sexual essentialism as 'the idea
that sex is a natural force that exists prior to social life and shapes institutions

... [it] consider[s] sex to be eternally unchanging, asocial and transhistorical' (Rubin 1989, 275).

7 As Gayle Rubin argues, '[s]ex is presumed guilty until proven innocent. Virtually all erotic behavior is considered bad unless a specific reason to exempt it has been established' (Rubin 1989, 278). And that reason must have something to do with the other side of the mind/body distinction.

8 Some readers might be inclined to dismiss the relevance of this language – since it comes, after all, from an old case, which the Court is only reviewing, not unequivocally adopting. Indeed, some commentators point to the fact that the Court expressly rejects this objective of obscenity law later in the decision. However, I believe that this language is not insignificant. Similar language is deployed throughout the decision. Sopinka J. resorts to the language of sex as dirty, of 'dirt for dirt's sake,' on several occasions in the decision. His use of quotation marks, signalling both the adoption of this language from earlier decisions and, presumably, his distance from this language, is somehow intended to sanitize his deployment of the language. These are not his words, after all. Yet, he chooses to use them – again and again. Even in quotation marks, the effect of the repetition of this phrase is to reinforce the underlying binary opposition between good and bad sex (between dirty and clean sex). This repeated deployment of the discourse of sex as dirty is significant in the production of meaning, and in revealing the sexual subtext of the decision.

9 As Lynda Nead's work has illustrated, pornography and art have been set up as binary oppositions, in which each is defined as that which the other is not. 'If art is a reflection of the highest social values, then pornography is a symptom of a rotten society; if art stands for lasting, universal values, then pornography represents disposability, trash. Art is a sign of cleanliness and licit morality, whereas pornography symbolizes filth and the illicit' (Nead 1993b, 282).

10 This second category is not the only contested site. Rather, the question of what constitutes 'sex with violence' within the first category is also a highly contested site, particularly within the context of s/m sex. S/m-sex advocates argue that s/m sex is not violence, and thus ought not to be classified as 'sex with violence.' Gayle Rubin, for example, writes: 'S/M materials are aimed at an audience that understand a set of conventions for interpreting them. Sadomasochism is not a form of violence, but is rather a type of ritual and contractual sex play whose aficionados go to great lengths in order to do it and to ensure the safety and enjoyment of one another. S/m fantasy does involve images of coercion and sexual activities that may appear violent to outsiders' (Rubin 1993a, 22). Yet the mere appearance of these images is

within the context of the *Butler* test, likely to lead to their classification as 'sex with violence.' As a result, consensual s/m sex, as well as depictions of sex with bondage, is (mis)classified as 'sex with violence.'

11 See *R. v. Keegstra* (1990), 61 C.C.C.(3d) 1; *Reference re:ss.193 and 195.1(1)(c) of the Criminal Code* (1990), 56 C.C.C.(3d) 65.

12 There is some inconsistency in the Court's description of sex as physical activity. At 472, the Court distinguishes between purely physical activity, like parking a car, and physical activity, such as sex. However, at 474, the Court again uses the phrase 'purely physical activity' as synonymous with 'purely sexual activity.' The point seems to be that although sex may not be so purely physical as to be devoid of any expression, it is, nevertheless, still physical. In relation to the mind/body distinction, it remains of the body, which foreshadows the Court's subsequent discussion of the 'nature of expression.'

13 Section 1 of the Charter provides that all rights and freedoms are 'subject only to such reasonable limits, prescribed by law, as can be demonstrably justified in a free and democratic society.' The Supreme Court of Canada has established a test for this section 1 analysis (*R. v. Oakes*). According to this test, the Government must first establish that there is a pressing and substantial objective that justifies overriding the violation of the Charter right. Second, the Government must establish that the violation of the Charter right is proportional with the objective of the legislation.

14 Although the Court tends to use the words 'objective' and 'purpose' interchangeably, the word 'purpose' is often used specifically in relation to the 'shifting purpose doctrine.' Shifting-purpose doctrine refers to the idea that the purpose of a law can change over time. This doctrine was rejected by the Supreme Court in *R. v. Big M Drug Mart Ltd* [1985] 1 S.C.R. 295. Dickson J. (as he then was) held that 'Purpose is a function of the intent of those who drafted and enacted the legislation at the time and not of any shifting variable.' In considering the objective of the legislation, courts are thus not permitted to consider a new purpose, but rather must focus only on the purpose of the drafters of the legislation.

15 It is interesting to note, however, the way in which the shifting-purpose doctrine has been used in other cases by the Supreme Court of Canada. In a subsequent s.2(b) case, *R. v. Zundel* (1992), in which neo-Nazi Ernst Zundel was charged with the crime of spreading false news for his publication of Holocaust denials, the Supreme Court of Canada struck down s.181 of the Criminal Code, on the basis that it violated freedom of expression and was not justifiable under section 1. The shifting-purpose doctrine was an important factor in the decision. The Court rejected the arguments of the Government

that the objective of the legislation could be seen. On the basis of *Butler*, it was open to the Court to cast the objective of the legislation more broadly. Indeed, it is difficult to reconcile the decisions of the Court in *Butler* with its decision in *Zundel* on the shifting-purpose doctrine.

In comparing the use of the shifting-purpose doctrine in these two cases, I do not mean to conflate the regulation of sexual expression with the regulation of hate expression. These two areas, which are often conflated in pro-censorship arguments <pornography is framed as hate speech>, have very different histories, with very distinct legislative objectives. A position for or against the censorship of sexual representations should be seen and evaluated quite separately from a position for or against the censorship of hate speech. Although there may be similar arguments in terms of the relative legitimacy and efficacy of state censorship, the arguments are otherwise quite distinct. As discussed in the introduction, it is not our intention in this book to evaluate the relative merits of the regulation of hate speech.

16 This proportionality requirement involves a three-step test: (1) there must be a rational connection between the legislative provision violating the right and the objective; (2) there must be a minimum impairment of the right; and (3) there must be proper balance between the effect of the legislative provision and the legislative objective.

17 For a further discussion of this marginalization of the s.2(b) guarantees through the section 1 analysis, see Jamie Cameron, 'Abstract Principle v. Contextual Conceptions of Harm: A Comment on R.v. Butler,' (1992) 37 *McGill L.J.* 1135.

18 Tariff Code 9956 prohibits the importation of obscene materials, as defined by s.163 of the Criminal Code into Canada. When materials are seized by Canada Customs, the importer has a right of appeal. The first step involves a request for redetermination, after which ensues an appeal to the deputy minister of National Revenue for Customs and Excise, and, subsequently, to court.

19 Henderson examines the lesbian s/m imagery in *On Our Backs*, a lesbian sex magazine, and Pat Califia's *Macho Sluts*, a collection of short stories about lesbian s/m. She argues that both are filled with references to the consensual nature of the sexual practices of the women. '*Macho Sluts* also addresses a range of readers through its demystifications of s/m practice, particularly around images of consent. Indeed, in her introduction, Califia challenges critics who would argue that amid the sexual coercions of patriarchal society, women cannot truly consent to sadomasochism: "If you don't believe we choose to do s/m, you aren't using the term 'consent' in any meaningful way, but rather, as a synonym for 'mature', 'socially acceptable' and 'politically

correct' ... Virtually all the stories ... make pointed distinctions between sado-masochism and sexual coercion"' (Henderson 1992, 184).

20 This issue of consent in lesbian sexual representations is explored more fully by Becki Ross in chapter 4.

21 We are at least partially indebted to LEAF for this heteroswitching technique. In the *Butler* case, LEAF attempted to support their arguments of the degrading and dehumanizing nature of pornography to women with reference to gay male pornography. Kathleen Mahoney, quoted in *MS. Magazine,* explained: 'We showed them the porn – and among the seized videos were some horrifically violent and degrading gay movies. We made the point that the abused men in these films were being treated like women – and the judges got it. Otherwise, men can't put themselves in our shoes. Porn makes women's subordination look sexy and appealing; it doesn't threaten men's jobs, safety, rights, or credibility' (Landsberg 1992, 14).

Karen Busby, however, denies that LEAF played into homophobic discourses in its arguments, and she specifically takes issue with the allegations that LEAF showed videos of gay sex to the Court, which she insists is categorically untrue, and simply the product of media misrepresentation. It is difficult to know what to make of Mahoney's quote in the Landsberg article, since neither Mahoney, Landsberg, or *MS Magazine* appear to have retracted the comments. While LEAF did not in fact show videos in Court, Mahoney's words suggest that LEAF may have simply tried to make this connection in oral argument. Busby admits that LEAF did refer to gay male pornography, but that the arguments in no way collapsed these materials with the harms-based analysis of heterosexual pornography (Busby 1994, 179–80). It is difficult, however, to reconcile Busby's argument with the submission in LEAF's factum, which Busby herself cites – that is, that 'LEAF submits that some of the subject of pornography of men for men, in addition to abusing some men in ways that it is more common to abuse women through sex, arguably contributes to abuse and homophobia as it normalizes sexual aggression generally.' The submission seems more in line with Mahoney's quote than with Busby's explanation.

22 The technique of heteroswitching can be related to what Eve Sedgwick has described as the trope of 'gender inversion,' according to which lesbians have long been constructed as virile and masculine (and conversely, gay men as effeminate) in order to maintain 'the essential heterosexuality within desire itself' (*Epistemology of the Closet* [Berkeley: University of California Press, 1990] at 87). The construction of sexuality as heterosexuality is thereby not threatened or displaced by the recognition of same-sex sexuality. The heteroswitching is perhaps a particular manifestation of this gender inver-

sion, which within the context of obscenity leaves the heterosexual norm of both sexuality and its model of harm unchallenged.

23 This is hardly a surprising factor, in so far as much straight pornography includes depictions of women having sex with women. The discursive distinction between these sexual representations and the representations of specifically lesbian sexuality is discussed in greater length by Becki Ross in chapter 4.

24 *R. v. Hawkins* involved appeals from five separate criminal charges, in relation to four different accused persons: Hawkins, Ronish, Smeek, and Jorgensen: Jorgenson had two different charges against him – one against his adult video store in Hamilton, and one against his store in Scarborough. The Crown appealed the acquittals of Hawkins and Ronish at trial. The defendants Jorgensen and Smeek appealed their convictions.

25 In *Hawkins*, the Crown had adduced no evidence to establish harmful effects, and the material had been approved by the Ontario Film Review Board for 'restricted audiences,' which absent any evidence rebutting this finding could be taken as a significant indication of the community standard of tolerance. The Crown's appeal of the acquittal was dismissed.

In *Ronish*, the evidence adduced by the Crown did not prove to the satisfaction of the judge that social harm would result from exposure to the films. The Crown's appeal of the acquittal was dismissed.

In *Jorgensen* (Scarborough), the trial judge correctly concluded that the content of the three videos included the depiction of sex coupled with violence and coercion and created the requisite risk of harm. The approval of the materials by the OFRB was found not to be determinative. Rather, the trial judge had properly treated this evidence as indicative of community standards of tolerance, but concluded that it did not outweight the evidence before her that the material coupled sex with violence and created a substantial risk of harm. The defendant's appeal was dismissed. In *Jorgensen* (Hamilton), the record in the case did not contain evidence to support the conclusion that community standards require that 'sexual activity take place within the context of love, affection, commitment, or emotional involvement.' The evidence, including the testimony of the Chair of the OFRB, indicated the opposite – that is, that 'explicit depiction of human sexuality in a context devoid of any meaningful relationship does not exceed contemporary national community standards of tolerance.' The defendant's appeal was allowed.

In *Smeenk*, the violence, vampirism, and necrophilia depicted in the films was, according to the Court of Appeal, 'patently such as to bring the films within the second of the *Butler* categories.' The depictions were degrading and dehumanizing, and created a risk of harm. The defendant's appeal was dismissed.

26 Further, in this passage, the Court articulates its own view of which particular sexual practices constitute really bad sex. These bad representations include those specifically mentioned in s.163 – sex with 'crime, horror, cruelty,' as well as those specifically mentioned in *Butler* – sex with children. But, these representations also include sexual practices that are not explicitly mentioned in s.163, or by the Supreme Court of Canada in the *Butler* test – necrophilia, bondage, bestiality, coercion. There may in fact be a strong argument to be made on the face of the *Butler* reasoning, and its underlying sexual morality, that these practices are within these categories of bad sex. But, these practices were not specifically so designated within the *Butler* decision. Nor does the Court of Appeal articulate its reasoning for including these practices within these proscribed categories. Rather, it simply asserts these practices as obvious examples of really bad sex – so obvious, that no reasoning is required to bring them within the *Butler* categories.

27 The Crown's application for leave to appeal in the acquittals of *Hawkins* and *Ronish* was dismissed, but the defendant's applications for leave to appeal their convictions in *Jorgenson* was allowed.

4

'It's Merely Designed for Sexual Arousal':* Interrogating the Indefensibility of Lesbian Smut

BECKI L. ROSS

Good women ... possess no language and no terminology, either for their feelings or their anatomy.

Dr Howard Kelly, 1913

Our pictures felt like proof that our reality could be altered, that the world we lived in and were part of was not the only world, and that within our imaginations dwelt another reality that was mysterious and potent. For me this reality included the possibility of women together, and signified that beneath the outer trappings of our everyday masks and costumes there existed a body that hungered and thirsted for freedom. That beneath the artifice there existed another 'self,' another, more authentic body – in my case, a lesbian body that was struggling to name itself by imagining and then imaging its own unspeakable yearnings.

Susan Stewart, 1994

On 2 April 1992, Constable Patricia McVicar, a female member of Project P, the joint OPP/Metro Toronto Police anti-pornography squad, seized *Bad Attitude* (1991) – a 'lesbian erotic fiction' magazine (published bimonthly in Cambridge, Massachusetts) from Toronto's Glad Day Bookshop. Outfitted in plain clothes, undercover officer McVicar targeted *Bad Attitude* because 'the magazine contained sexually explicit materials with bondage and violence ... that were degrading and obscene and not what Canadians would abide other Canadians seeing.'[1] Almost a month later, on 30 April 1992, McVicar charged John Scythes, owner of Glad Day Bookshop – the city's lesbian and gay bookstore – and manager Tom Ivison with possession and distribution of obscene material. Seven months later, in December 1992, the case was heard in the Ontario Court (Provincial Division). It marked the second 'lesbian pornography' trial in Canadian history – the first, involving the lesbian pulp novel *Women's Barracks*, was held in Ottawa in 1952 (Adams 1993, 21).

On 16 February 1993, Judge Claude Paris found the accused, Scythes and Ivison, guilty of the possession and sale of *Bad Attitude* (specifically, the story 'Wunna My Fantasies') because of its combination of sex and violence. Referencing the Supreme Court's decision on *R. v. Butler* (1992) Paris J. ruled in favour of 'protecting' the general public from lesbian material that would 'predispose individuals to anti-social behaviour' (*R. v. Scythes* 1993, 3). He convicted Scythes and Ivison of violating section 163(8) of the Canadian Criminal Code, and fined the store two hundred dollars. In moral tones suggestive of nineteenth-century social-purity reform, Paris advised the criminals to refrain from selling the magazine in the future.

In this chapter, I explore the vulnerability of lesbian-made images, in particular s/m images, to legal judgments governed by the Canadian Supreme Court's *Butler* decision. Having been called upon as an expert witness to testify in the *R. v. Scythes* case, I draw from the Ontario Provincial court transcripts and the judge's ruling. Specifically, I examine the legal privileging of a school of social-science research that delivered certainty in the stunning absence of empirical evidence. And I counterpose this privileging to my (futile and failed) efforts as an expert witness to explicate and contextualize the specificities, nuances, and complexities of lesbian s/m fantasy, alongside the sociopolitical meanings it engenders within lesbian s/m subcultures. Rather than attribute my experience of futility and failure to 'poor performance,' I argue that my refusal to interpret lesbian s/m as 'harmful to women' was simply unintelligible to gatekeepers of obscenity law in Canada. It seems clear to me in retrospect that the battle to defend *Bad Attitude* was lost before it began.

I maintain that the obscenity charge and eventual conviction against Glad Day Bookshop in 1993 are indicative of the makings of a moral panic reminiscent of anti-VD campaigns, postwar purges of homosexuals from the Canadian civil service, and the citizens' lobby to ban romance literature and crime comics in the 1940s and 1950s.[2] Paradoxically, the current moral panic has been met by independent producers of lesbian/queer pornography in Canada whose counter-hegemonic volleys I survey at the end of this chapter. In all, the case of *R. v. Scythes* invites me to examine how competing knowledge claims about sexuality, morality, and the zone of fantasy are bound up in operations of power. Empirically knowable, these operations of power do not function in the mode of repression and negation: they mark, in Michel Foucault's terms, an incitement to speak about and administer sex (Foucault 1980, 11, 24). Indeed, *R. v. Scythes* reveals mechanisms by which so-called 'crimes against nature' continue to be speechified and regulated in the late twentieth century (ibid., 32).

Social-Scientific 'Truths' about Lesbian Pornography

To lead off discussion of the magazine *Bad Attitude* in *R. v. Scythes*, American psychologist Neil Malamuth was called as an expert witness by the prosecution to outline the media effects of pornography on human attitudes and behaviour. A professor of communication and psychology at the University of Michigan, Malamuth has built his reputation as one of a handful of social-science experts proclaiming and defending a causal link between (heterosexual) pornography and violence against women. He was invited by the prosecution *because* his clinical research indicates this link, despite the acknowledged inconclusivity of 'effects studies' as a whole. In fact, Malamuth's work in large part supplied the 'scientific' foundation for the *Butler* decision, and it appears as the 'Truth' about pornography in the factums submitted by the Attorney General of Manitoba, Attorney General of Canada, and the Group Against Pornography (see Gotell, this volume). And his previous engagement as a consultant for the prosecution in two Canada Customs cases involving lesbian and gay materials only served to enhance his expert status.

During the Crown's process of establishing Malamuth's credentials before Judge Paris, defence counsel Clare Barclay intervened to argue that Malamuth had never made the effects of lesbian/gay images a focus of his research, therefore he should be disqualified as an expert on lesbian pornography. Barclay was overruled by Judge Paris, who agreed to accept Malamuth as an expert on communications, psychology, and laboratory-based analyses of (heterosexual) pornography. Explaining his rationale for accepting Malamuth (in ways that foreshadow his final decision), Judge Paris added that he did not feel that 'there was a need to make a distinction between [representations of] heterosexual sex and homosexual sex.' Much later, I ruefully noted that Malamuth's obvious lack of expertise in no way undermined or delegitimized his efforts to render an objective, positivist interpretation of the 'offending' lesbian material. In fact, because Judge Paris accepted Malamuth's contentions before he had even spoken in the trial, I'm left to wonder why it was necessary for him to testify at all.

Over the course of his testimony, Malamuth flatly repeated that he had never studied lesbian and gay erotic material made specifically for members of the lesbian, gay, and bisexual community (Malamuth 1992, 17). Yet to reassure the Crown and the judge of his social-scientific expertise, he pointed to *Bad Attitude* and argued: 'It's very difficult to tell the difference between these [lesbian] materials and heterosexual materials ... One could go through the [lesbian] stories and change three or four words saying it's a woman and a man ... chang[ing] 'she' into 'he' and there would be no difference ... From the perspective of the effects on the public, I think that basic mechanisms and processes are likely to be very similar' (ibid., 18).

Malamuth was asked by the Crown to speculate on the negative effects of lesbian s/m fantasy on readers of *Bad Attitude*. (Here we can see the Crown's unchallenged assumptions at work: a. there *are* effects, and b. they are, matter-of-factly, negative and harmful.) In his content analysis Malamuth stated that the magazine contained 'acts that appear to be designed to humiliate,' images of 'subservience of one person to another,' 'elements of pain and suffering,' 'the depiction of humiliation and demeaning terms,' the 'lowering of rank,' and 'references to participants as animals' (Malamuth 1992, 32, 35–6). According to his 'expert' opinion, *Bad Attitude* 'portrays unequal power relations as being sexy, as being arousing' (ibid., 44). Malamuth repeated several times that lesbian imagery like *Bad Attitude* relied on themes that were derivative of heterosexual materials: he said that if images like those in *Bad Attitude* appeared in a heterosexual magazine they 'would draw tremendous fire from the feminist community' (ibid., 49). Using the rhetorical technique of analogy, Malamuth argued that 'there was an amazing similarity [between the seized copy of *Bad Attitude*] and sadomasochistic materials in the heterosexual community' (ibid., 36). He added that upon considering sadomasochistic portrayals, the consent that may appear in the depictions is 'really not a particularly relevant issue' (ibid., 41). To conclude, Malamuth predicted the harmful effects of *Bad Attitude* on the attitudes and behaviours of some lesbians and gays as well as some heterosexual readers (ibid., 46–9). When I analyse his testimony, I find that Malamuth did not define the terms humiliation and subservience; he did not produce empirical evidence of heterosexual s/m to verify his analogy (which I argue is unverifiable); he had no evidence of actual harm that flowed from exposure to *Bad Attitude*; and he roundly dismissed the crucial lever of consent in a self-consciously Butlerian flourish.

University of Toronto psychologist Jonathon Freedman, in later testifying for the defence, disputed Malamuth's claims on methodological grounds. He warned against simplistic extrapolation from studies of heterosexual, non-consensual pornography on film/TV to homosexual print material such as *Bad Attitude*. As Freedman explained, 'Malamuth took research done on the attitudes of straight men to what he called violent, degrading pornography, and he generalized the results to images of consensual sex between women ... But [in *Bad Attitude*], the whole meaning, context and significance of the images has changed' (Freedman 1992, 39–44). Freedman added that because there are no scientific definitions of 'degradation' and 'humiliation,' Malamuth's application of these terms to *Bad Attitude* reveals his subjective, non-scientific interpretation (ibid., 36).

Delivering Counter-Truths

On 15 December 1992, in a third-floor, church-like room at Old City Hall, now the Ontario Court (Provincial Division), I took the stand to defend *Bad Attitude*. Briefed only two days before I appeared on the stand, I became part of the 'Defence Team' headed up by counsel Clare Barclay. I suspect that I was enlisted by Barclay and Glad Day Bookshop because I am a long-time anti-censorship activist – a former member of the Canadian Committee Against Customs Censorship, a former editor of *Rites*, a gay/lesbian liberation magazine, and a member of Censorstop, a Toronto-based anti-censorship organization. I hold a PhD in sociology with a specialization in feminist theory and lesbian/gay studies. Unlike Malamuth, at the time of the trial I did not hold a full-time university post: I was under-employed at the University of Toronto teaching one course a term. On the stand, I was immediately subjected to a two-hour attack by the Crown, who strove to discredit my scholarly qualifications and drastically narrow the purview of my testimony. Finally, I was sworn in as an expert witness on lesbian sexuality, culture, and community. Except for brief appearances by law student Suzanne Jarvie and lesbian photographer Jennifer Gillmor, I was the only other woman to testify.

Dire financial constraints meant that John Scythes, owner of Glad Day Bookshop, was unable to call additional witnesses such as Carole Vance,

Pat Califia, Dorothy Allison, and Gayle Rubin – well-known American writers and academics who have argued vehemently against state censorship of feminist and lesbian/gay materials for twenty years, in some cases as lesbian s/m participants themselves. It is likely that most of these women would have agreed to testify had there been money, but it is not clear what impact they might have had. It is significant that in the 1994 challenge by Little Sister's bookstore to seizures of lesbian and gay materials by Canada Customs, the Crown decided to forgo cross-examination of almost all the writers and artists in what appeared to be a move to convey their perceived irrelevance (Fuller and Blackley 1995, 60).

I felt intense pressure *to perform* feminist pro-pornography analysis in ways that did its pioneering proponents justice, and in ways that convinced Judge Paris that the Supreme Court justices in *R. v. Butler* were wrong. And as the *Bad Attitude* trial progressed, I felt acutely uneasy about my role as a speaker *for* members of lesbian s/m communities. I am connected to these communities, but I am not an active member of them. Indeed, I remain steadfastly critical of the fact that no lesbian s/m aficionados were called forth in *R. v. Scythes* to instruct the judge on the subtleties of s/m fantasy from their own standpoints.

Before my testimony, during the process of 'qualification,' Crown Attorney Charles Granek repeatedly tried to discredit me as a defender of child pornography and intergenerational sex. He insinuated that I was someone with an appetite for 'kiddie porn' by pointing to my support for *The Body Politic* newspaper's right to publish the controversial 'Men Loving Boys Loving Men' feature in 1977 (the paper was charged with obscenity and eventually acquitted in 1983). 'Youth pornography' has become a favourite target of police and politicians of all ideological stripes and one that was recently and hastily codified in the punishing youth pornography law, Bill C-128 (see Bell, this volume). This is not to say that issues of incest and the abuse of power by adults over children/ youth are unimportant. Rather, it is my view that the stubborn and never-substantiated equation of gays and lesbians with child molestation motivated the Crown's line of questioning, and was deployed to intimidate me. It is noteworthy that there is absolutely no mention of cross-generational sex in the seized copy of *Bad Attitude*. So, though Granek seemed off topic, I later realized that he highlighted my research/writing on obscenity law to establish for the judge my 'biased,' subjective, and value-laden, anti-censorship stance. Importantly, neither Crown nor defence pigeonholed psychologist Neil Malamuth's bias as pro-censorship. In fact, the opposite occurred: his stance as an 'objective' and 'value free' scientist was incontrovertible. As the trial unfolded, it became crystal clear to me: I was partisan, Malamuth was neutral; Malamuth was the expert, I was the exhibit[3] (see Valverde 1996, 213).

On the stand, almost sixty-five years after Radclyffe Hall's classic lesbian romance *The Well of Loneliness* was banned and burned in England and named 'a moral pestilence' and a 'vile poison,' I argued passionately for the historical and contemporary significance of lesbian-specific images (sexual and non-sexual) in a culture that institutionalizes, privileges, and mandates compulsory and compulsive heterosexuality. I battled to situate the seized issue of *Bad Attitude* on a spectrum of lesbian-produced images alongside the *Dyke Sex Calender* (1990), the San Francisco lesbian porn magazine *On Our Backs*, the British *Quim*, *Getting Wet: Tales of Lesbian Seduction* by the Women's Press (1993), and the writings of Susie Sexpert (Susie Bright 1990, 1992), Joan Nestle (1987), Jewelle Gomez (1987), and Carolyn Gammon (1992). While naming these works in court, I remember the rueful feeling that each of these works was at risk of falling under the censuring gaze of the OPP/ Metro Toronto anti-pornography squad. I then sensed that none of them was safe if they could be named and fingered by law enforcers.

Inside Lesbian Imagery

Consistent with anti-porn feminists who have historically identified s/m as the 'epicentre of harm,' during the *Bad Attitude* trial the Crown (and the judge) relentlessly centred and recentred sadomasochism as evil incarnate.[4] On the stand, I maintained that lesbian-made sexual imagery, including s/m imagery, articulates particular social meanings and is received by intended lesbian audiences and performers in very specific ways. For example, in issues of *Bad Attitude* and *On Our Backs*, in Pat Califia's *Macho Sluts* (1988), Carol Allen and Rosamund Elwin's *Getting Wet* (1993), Karen Barber's *Bushfire* (1991), and Lady Winston's collection, *The Leading Edge* (1987), the stories involve openly lesbian characters in varied settings. Barber situates her sexual and romantic encounters at an art gallery, at a downtown delicatessen, and in the construction trade. *The Leading Edge* delivers a wealth of polymorphously perverse lesbian sexcapades designed to entertain, to educate, and to honour the pussy. In her contribution, Jewelle Gomez skilfully depicts lusty sex between two women: one African American and one white (Gomez 1987, 161–71).

Photographs in lesbian-published magazines depict sex between women who are focused on, and engaged in, sex with each other; their mutual pleasure is of paramount concern. The photographic camera angles, lighting, cropping, positioning, and framing, combined with the lesbian-directed narratives, are all constructed to enhance a lesbian reader/viewer's enjoyment of, and vicarious participation in, the fantasy scenes. The narratives and pictures are made sense of by skilled members of lesbian leather and s/m subcultures who are intimately familiar with the expressed codes, techniques, etiquette, cues, argot, and rule-governed practices. Hence, as I described in detail to the court, the material context in which the images are produced and consumed is of utmost significance. Lesbian-made s/m images inscribe codes specific to lesbian s/m practice: role-playing and the exchange of power, confession, attention to rules and restrictions, staged sexual scenes, costume, drama, and ritual. To me, the contemporary images seem to draw inspiration from nineteenth-century French, German, and British s/m photographs (captured lovingly in the coffee-table collection *Jeux de dames cruelles, 1850–1960*) that feature women dressed as maids, school marms, nurses, school girls, or harlots spanking, gagging, biting, paddling, and whipping each other with gusto (Nazarieff 1988).

Queer theorist Judith Butler argues that 'Femininity is not the product of a choice, but the forcible citation of a norm, one whose complex historicity is indissociable from relations of discipline, regulation, punishment' (Butler 1993, 23). Lesbian s/m fantasy, which is often inflected with butch/femme signs, exposes the naturalized status of femininity (and masculinity) in ways that disrupt the power of heterosexualizing law. Indeed, I argue that portrayals of s/m in *Bad Attitude* enact the theatrical agency of queer performativity, the campy dramatization of leathered queerness that opens up spaces between the norms that regulate gender and sexuality.[5] In effect, we might say that elements of lesbian s/m send up or satirize conventional sexual and gender stereotypes and at the same time borrow from historical traditions of gay camp (Bergman 1993, Newton 1993). The s/m models perform, as do camp artists, for an audience – in this case, readers.[6] When I analyse lesbian s/m porn, I note the use of artifice, role-playing, masquerade, flamboyance, and exhibitionist abandon. In part, the camp of lesbian s/m emerges out of the incongruity between conventional images of suitable, rewarded femininity and distinctly anti-feminine images of bad girls decked out in combinations of leather corsets, dog collars, harnesses and silicon dildos, wrist bands, motorcycle boots, nipple rings, tit clamps, and chains. It seems to me that, contrary to Malamuth's claims, lesbian s/m self-consciously trades in (and re-makes) conventions of gay male s/m much more than it mimics conventions of heterosexual s/m images.[7] Whether dominant or submissive or both, lesbian s/m players subvert the purportedly *natural* sexual submissiveness of women towards men. As such, lesbian s/m offers an intriguing exploration of the very signs of 'male' and 'female' (Creet 1991b, 33).

As part of my testimony I explained how in lesbian s/m fantasy, the 'bottom' actually 'runs the fuck' – a fact that throws into chaos the legally codified (yet highly subjective) notions of 'harm' and 'degradation' enacted via (male) dominance and (female) submission. By orchestrating the sexual encounter, the bottom disrupts popular conceptions that she is passive, subjugated, and exploited.[8] The objective of the top is to provide her bottom with sexual pleasure. As such, the top's own sexual needs/desires are dependent on the pleasure experienced by the bottom, and may even be sacrificed in the process of pleasure-giving.[9]

In sharp opposition to Neil Malamuth's equation of s/m with degradation and humiliation, American lesbian feminist writer Pat Califia explains that '[s/m] participants are enhancing their sexual pleasure, not damaging or imprisoning one another' (Califia 1981, 31). And she adds that even if scenes are acted out, there is no necessary correlation between the roles women assume in s/m sex and how women behave in their ordinary, everyday worlds. During the trial, I recall thinking that my Califia-informed explanations would only confirm my 'prurient interest' in lesbian s/m porn to Crown and judge, and unveil yet another dimension of my 'subjective,' hence problematic, approach. Moreover, I remember wanting to add how lesbians and gay men of colour have intitiated challenges to the racism and anti-Semitism inscribed in some s/m imagery (see below). But for me delivering testimony in courtroom 3-A, there seemed to be absolutely no opportunity to discuss or engage such an important issue.

Reading Trish Thomas

During my testimony, I was asked to give a detailed reading of 'Wunna My Fantasies,' written by California-based lesbian writer Trish Thomas and published in *Bad Attitude* (Thomas 1991, 25–9). It features fully consensual sex-play between two fictional lesbian characters. The narrator imagines herself in s/m gear (leather, nose-ring, chains, etc.) inside a locker room; she approaches the other woman from behind, blindfolds, handcuffs, and then has sex with her. The author Trish Thomas, as I've since discovered through interviewing her for *X-tra!* magazine in 1993, is a 37-year-old grandmother, a shy butch who lives in San Francisco, has s/m sex with women she's in love with, and is not an active member of the public s/m community (Ross 1993, 27). Thomas contextualized 'Wunna My Fantasies,' a story she wrote in 1986: 'It's about a girl I had a class with at San Francisco State and she would pick me up every Wednesday night and take me to class – "Incarcerated Women" taught by Angela Davis. I had a major crush on this girl, and it was a masturbation fantasy for me for months, and finally I decided to write it down.' Thomas continues, 'I would have loved to tell the Judge that the woman who inspired the story read it, was flattered and wanted a copy to act out the scene with her dominatrix girlfriend. But I think he would have regarded me as a monster pervert.' On the witness stand, I interpreted Thomas's story 'Wunna My Fantasies' as one of sexual play and role reversal where the aggressor is left unattended in the end while her prey engineers her own orgasm, watching herself come in the mirror. The fantasy story, printed in *Bad Attitude* in italics to designate its dream-like character, ends like this:

She crawls all the way out of the shower stall and across the wet tile floor, with my hand still in her pussy up to my forearm, until we're over in front of the mirror. I wipe the steam off the glass with the sleeve of my jacket so we can see ourselves. She watches my arm pump into her pussy. And I watch her. And she's checking me out, watching her. Then she grins this wicked grin and pulls herself up off her elbows until she's kneeling straight up with her arms over her head. She pushes her body flat out against the mirror. Still pushing her cunt down onto my fist, she watches her nipples graze the nipples of the woman in the mirror who is herself. Oh man, she's fucking herself. The fucking bitch is fucking herself! (Thomas 1991, 29).

Indeed, the bottom – the woman who is pursued in the shower stall – is wearing a nipple ring, which signifies her membership in the s/m sub-culture. In this fantasy sequence, she is hardly, as the Crown insisted, an innocent, unsuspecting victim. If Thomas's intent was to portray (and legitimize) a rape, she would not have included numerous references to improving the comfort level of the woman pursued, nor details of how 'the pursuee' happily participates in the exchange by 'spreading her legs wide,' 'letting out moans,' and 'wrapping her legs' around her captor (ibid., 25–7). Nor would she be troubled to observe safer-sex practices that accompany the fisting – an act both players plainly enjoy. The top in

'Wunna My Fantasies' is vested with eroticized mastery and yet her open respect for guidance from her 'prey' dispels the enactment of traditional patriarchal authority. Like a dog with a bone, the Crown repeatedly cited decontextualized snippets of description in order to demonstrate what he argued was the narrative's essentially coercive, brutal, and non-consensual thrust.

By contrast, I argued that the consent established between the two female characters in 'Wunna My Fantasies' (and in lesbian s/m literature in general) is the motor that drives the story. Here, consent is the fundamental principle upon which the entire encounter is premised (though why questions of consent *in fiction* are so legally problematic warrants further attention). Rather than making the sexual materials 'more obscene' or 'more violent,' as the *Butler* decision confirms (and as Judge Paris upheld in his verdict in *R. v. Scythes*), the practice of consent guarantees mutuality, communication, and collaboration. Lesbian s/m sex involves a negotiation process between sexual partners whereby certain words are agreed upon and then used to set limits. Jasmine Sterling, publisher of *Bad Attitude* magazine, asserts: 'I write about how you use "safe words," which are mutually agreed-upon words that mean to slow down or stop a scene. I feel I'm empowering women, not promoting violence against them' (Toobin 1994, 74). Indeed, without consent the interaction cannot proceed (or it does and becomes something else, like rape, which is an indictable offence). Moreover, given feminists' longstanding concern for the methods used to produce commercial pornography, it is significant that the photographed models in 'Wunna My Fantasies' were not coerced to participate in the staged scenario – one is the author, Thomas herself and, her partner, Trashina, volunteered.

In court defending her photographs published in *Bad Attitude*, Toronto artist Jennifer Gillmor testified that her model, 'who has an exhibitionist nature,' came up with the ideas for the images herself and, in advance of publication, signed model release forms to formalize her consent and to ensure that she was over eighteen years of age (Gillmor 1992, 16). One of Gillmor's three photos in the seized copy of *Bad Attitude* features her model – a young, white woman in a merry widow and garter belt, lashed with heavy ropes to a cross and tombstone, Christlike, in a graveyard (facing). This is the image that Neil Malamuth described as simliar to sexually violent heterosexual pornography (Malamuth 1992, 34). In another photo the same model appears decked out in full top regalia (p. 165). Gillmor explained: 'She likes to switch roles. On the cross she's submissive. Here, she's wearing a black leather

motorcyle cap and black leather motorcycle chaps, a belt buckle that she designed from a piece of the motorcycle's gas tank, some hockey equipment, armour really, painted black. She has studded leather cuffs that go from her wrist to her elbow. She's wearing black leather boots, a G-string, and she's carrying a whip that she made entirely for show purposes – it's made out of bathtub chain' (Gillmor 1992, 17–18).

During cross-examination, the Crown pounced on Gillmor's defensive allusion to the whip as a fake, a prop (Granek 1992a, 22). He questioned why she felt the need to emphasize that the whip was not functional, not a real whip. When Gillmor responded that 'the idea is not to hurt people,' the Crown pushed her to admit her discomfort with whipping, a tactic that succeeded in bolstering his anti-s/m agenda and in deflecting attention away from the more germane issues of fantasy, representation, and consent.

To date there have been no empirical studies proving the causal link between lesbian (or gay male) s/m images and violence against women (Though, importantly, the *Butler* decision states that actual proof of harm is unnecessary.) In factums submitted to Supreme Court judges in *R. v. Butler*, the Attorney General of Manitoba, the Attorney General of Canada, and the feminist Group Against Pornography (GAP) conclude that, even without evidence, it is reasonable to conclude that significant harms flow from obscene materials (see Gotell, this volume). Not one lesbian, to my knowledge, has ever proclaimed in a court of law that lesbian s/m erotica is degrading, humiliating, and dehumanizing or that it is responsible for her experience of abuse. Furthermore, there is no conclusive evidence, following from the *Butler* decision, that 'harm would flow from exposure' to lesbian s/m materials. Nor is there social-scientific research to determine what 'the community would tolerate others being exposed to' vis-à-vis lesbian sexual depictions. Interestingly, when I raised issues of the inconclusive research during my testimony, Crown Attorney Charles Granek retorted: 'There's no proven causal linkage between smoking and cancer, but they're correlated' (Ross 1992, 63). In retrospect, I might have rebuffed Granek by using the correlation 'Silence = Death' devised by AIDS activists to capsulize my analysis of the effects of state sexual censorship.

Testifying in the case of *Little Sister's Book and Art Emporium v. B.C. Minister of Justice* in late 1994, pscyhologist and well-known 'media effects expert' William Marshall acknowledged that exposure to violent (heterosexual) pornography is not a correlate of sexual aggression against women in natural settings (rather than laboratory experiments)

(cited in Fuller and Blackley 1995, 115). He also testified that exposure to pornography did not result in demonstrable negative changes in the emotions, attitudes, and behaviours of Canada Customs officials. Americans Marcia Pally and Nadine Strossen have independently concluded, upon assessing the literature, that there is no credible evidence corroborating a causal link between exposure to sexually explicit material and violent behaviour (Pally 1994, Strossen 1995). Strossen cites studies that show the *inverse*: a rise in the availability of sexual material correlates to advances in the availability of education on gender equality and sex-positive curricula in schools, along with the unacceptability of sex-related violence (Strossen 1995). Upon reviewing the psychological literature on pornography and harm, British researcher Lynne Segal urges feminists and supporters to abandon the search for some spurious link between men's violence against women and pornography, however defined (Segal 1993, 5–21). Those who trumpet a definitive causal relationship are too (desperately) invested in their own moral agenda to ever probe why they cleave like barnacles to such an untenable 'fact' in the first place. Now when I read the *Butler* decision, I see that the glide from indeterminate empirical evidence to 'reasoned apprehension of harm' amounts to little more than an elaborate, sorcerous hoax.

Lezzie Spreads in Mainstream Porn

Like Jennifer Gillmor, in my testimony I strove to stress the particularities of lesbian-produced sexual texts in part through illustrating what they are not. I presented Judge Paris with the photo series 'Stream of Cuntiousness' in *Hustler* magazine (*Hustler* 1990, 36–41). Though this 'lesbian spread' features two women, it illustrates the photographic, compositional, and ideological conventions intrinsic to heterosexual pornography: masculinist fetishization of hyper-caricatured femininity – large, pouty lips, large breasts, lots of facial make-up, most often white-skinned but sun-bronzed and oiled bodies, long fingernails and nail polish, big, lacquered hair, stiletto heels, colour-enhanced pussys, and so on. In these photographs (which signify a random but highly representative sampling) two white faux-dykes are splayed out across rocks in the middle of a swift-running stream. In the 'Nicki and Bronson: Aquavelvet' spread in *Hustler*'s September 1993 issue, two white 'lesbians,' one blonde, one brunette, cavort on the deck of a sun-drenched power boat (*Hustler* 1993, 96–104). Each photo (which likely cost more to produce than an entire year of *Bad Attitude*) is painstakingly constructed to embrace the male reader – in other words, 'Lesbianism as (heterosexual) Foreplay 101' or girl + girl = straight male titillation.[10] The processes of construction reveal how pornography as vehicle of fantasy is not reality. Through lighting, shading, framing, cropping, texturing, colouring, and so on, the intended male reader is invited to enter and master the scene – that is, to dominate the two women, thereby 'doubling his pleasure.' The women are typically painted as primed for heterosexual intercourse initiated and controlled by men; they appear as overburdened signs of male lust, male sexual appetites and obsessions, not as sexually self-defining subjects.

In contrast to lesbian-produced imagery, the women pictured in 'lesbian spreads' do not attend to each other: they stare out coyly at a male voyeur and their bodies are positioned to maximize both his arousal and their own submission to his needs. They exist on the page to service men. The women tend to be almost identical in shape, size, age, and colour (no butch/femme codes here), and I have yet to see any evidence of safe-sex practice – a regular component of lesbian sexual imagery. (Indeed, the absence of latex suggests the absence of sex altogether.) Lesbianism itself, and more specifically (hot) lesbian sex, is of no or little interest to *Hustler* publisher Larry Flynt. Indeed, in numerous spots throughout *Hustler*, *Forum*, and *Penthouse*, lesbianism is lampooned and trivialized, rendered toxic and dangerous, in keeping with the magazines' deeply heterosexist and homophobic thrust. 'Real' lesbians routinely appear in cartoons as overweight, bra-less, badly dressed, and villainous sex freaks with bad haircuts lecherously seeking to poke cute, unsuspecting blondes in the ass with their deluxe dildos. This is not to say that lesbians (and non-lesbian women) never find straight lezzie spreads arousing or educational. Clearly some do, though lack of alternatives, especially in smaller communities, often determines their choices.

I contend that if the erotic/educational needs of lesbian readers were met by the 'lesbian spreads' in *Penthouse*, *Forum*, and *Hustler*, there would be no desire for, hence no consumers of, lesbian-produced images. If the two were ostensibly interchangeable, why not opt for the vastly easier to find super-slick hetero-spreads? As I observed in court, in terms of the relations of production, lesbian stories/images in *Bad Attitude*, *Girlfriends*, *Lezzie Smut*, *Lickerish*, and *Quim* are nested in a publishing environment whereby lesbian and feminist issues are addressed, be it safe-sex and HIV/AIDS prevention, the threat of gay bashing, the need for pay equity, the power of anti-racist praxis, spousal benefits, access to effective and non-stigmatized artificial insemination, and affordable child care. The seized issue of *Bad Attitude* sports an editorial statement about the rise in street violence directed at lesbians and provides a series of phone lines for women in the Boston, Massachusetts, area (*Bad Attitude* 1991b, 2). Furthermore, without making a claim for the ultimate 'truth' or 'authentic' power of lesbian-made pornography to reveal the essence of lesbian sex, the stories and pictures unambiguously intend a lesbian and bisexual audience through the foregrounding of women's sexual desires and tastes. This context differs dramatically from the sexist, heterosexist, and often racist environment that frames 'lesbian spreads' in *Hustler*, *Forum*, and *Penthouse*. In these magazines, the figuring of 'lesbians' to attract and accommodate the male gaze confirms age-old myths of the gargantuan, ever-ready sapphic appetite best satisfied by a horny, straight he-man.

It is important to recognize that in lesbian-made erotica, including s/m imagery, the protagonists are women, hence the gender-based inequities that pervade commercial pornography (and society in general) are neither represented nor reinforced. Indeed, 'she' is not a 'he.' The economic, physical, and cultural power of men over women that is objectified and sexualized in much (though not all) heterosexual pornography, is not and cannot be accomplished in lesbian sexual imagery because straight men are either absent from, or insignificant to, the scene. Men, almost always gay men, might appear, as they do in Pat Califia's story, 'The Surprise Party,' but their pleasure is secondary to the pleasure sought and found by the female characters (Califia 1988, 211–42).

To me, it is the unique sexual dynamic between two women captured in lesbian porn that constitutes the turn-on. In my opinion, and in my experience, the most arousing images involve the eroticization of sexual tension or difference (butch/femme, top/bottom), which may be positively complicated by age, race, and/or class difference, *in the context of gender sameness*. (There were a number of surreal moments during my testimony in *R. v. Scythes*: one involved my need to clarify for Crown and judge that a photograph of a butch/femme couple was of two women, not a man and a woman.) Pat Califia's short story 'Jessie,' first published in 1981, remains for me one of the hottest pieces of lesbian porn ever written. It was a 'breakthrough' for her, and is reprinted in the state-confiscated *Macho Sluts* (Califia 1988, 28–62).[11] The narrative has violent, rough elements; Califia plays with power, objectification, humiliation, and sexual want. 'Jessie' is not about wholesome, respectable love-making, and this both unnerves me and quickens my lust.

Madonna's *Sex*: Putting Queer Sex Out There?

In today's postmodern, mishmashed world of cross-referenced and borrowed image-making, gay and lesbian images are customarily appropriated, commodified, and sold back to us by astute entrepreneurs. It is worth noting that these images (some of which are silly, ironic spoofs) never seem to incite the wrath of police, crown attorneys, and judges. American First Lady Hilary Clinton appeared as a leather s/m dominatrix, crop in hand, smiling on the cover of *Spy* magazine in February 1993. In an image that oozed butch/femme and s/m overtones, scantily clad Cindy Crawford was pictured shaving a mannish and blissed-out k.d. lang in *Vanity Fair*, August 1993. During the *R. v. Scythes* trial, law student Suzanne Jarvie introduced Helmut Newton's photo spread in *Vogue* magazine (September 1992) entitled 'Chain Reactions' (incidentally, the name of a lesbian s/m sex club in London, England). Jarvie drew attention to sexual poses of the female models and the lesbian s/m codes incorporated into the spread – leather, chains, whips, harnesses, and dog collars. Though Judge Paris refused to acknowledge the context in which *Bad Attitude* and other lesbian-made porn is produced and received, he intervened to assert that *Vogue* was a *fashion magazine*, one his daughters read at home (Jarvie 1992, 25). In spite of evidence that both magazines deploy the signs of s/m fantasy, the judge elected to ignore the blurring of fictional genres. In my opinion, his intimation that *Vogue* was nothing like the nasty lesbian smut on trial reveals his desire to confirm fashion discourse as purely pornography-free, and pornographic discourse, that is *Bad Attitude*, as both unfashionable and unfit for home browsing.

A provocative example of trafficking in lesbian images from a non-lesbian standpoint is Madonna's controversial book, *Sex* (1992).[12] In *R. v. Scythes*, defence counsel Clare Barclay introduced *Sex* as a principal exhibit. Examined on the witness stand by Barclay about the form and content of *Sex*, I pointed out that, ironically, *Sex* contains more graphic and controversial images and references to whipping, bondage, water sports, hot-wax dripping, slapping, paddling, bestiality, intergenerational sex, tattooing, humiliation, group sex, and so on, than does *Bad Attitude*. The first ten pages of the over-sized collection are devoted to images of Madonna being sexually serviced by two New York lesbian s/m specialists, both bald and pierced, one with a Star of David tattooed on her back. Dita, Madonna's 'nom de tart,' is depicted bound to a chair and gagged. One s/m dyke stretches Dita's hands high in the air above

her head, while the other lays a switchblade against her barely con-
cealed crotch. Other scenes place Dita in the role of leather dominatrix
expertly snapping a cat-'o-nine-tails on the shiny, black vinyl butt of her
kneeling female captive; in another, she's adorned in ripped school-girl
garb in the company of two men who appear about to rape her on the
gymnasium floor. Most of *Sex*'s images match descriptions of obscenity
detailed in Memorandum D9 1–1, the obscenity guidelines that govern
the importation of materials at the Canada / United States border.[13]

Chock-full of pirated queer content, *Sex* resided atop the *New York
Times* best-seller list for over four months. Yet it has not escaped queer
tongue-lashing. Photographer Susan Stewart of 'Kiss & Tell' delivers a
stinging critique: 'In *Sex*, Madonna's "blonde ambition" drapes itself
over the dangerous transgressive sexuality of two radical leather dykes,
titillating straight sensibilities with an indrawn breath, a momentary
suspension of safety and its attendant adrenalin-rush value, at the same
time underscoring the certainty that this experience is a mere throw-
away exchange.' In the cheeky reader *Madonnarama* (1993), Pat Califia
complains about 'somebody who has not paid her dues using my community as a series of bizarre backdrops for a photo shoot' (Califia 1993,
177). And gay critics Douglas Crimp and Michael Warner add that
'everything about *Sex* is made possible by Madonna's celebrity, and her
celebrity is constructed, in however complex a way, as *heterosexual*. She
can be as queer as she wants to, but only because we know she's not'
(their emphasis) (Crimp and Warner 1993, 93).

Notwithstanding queer annoyance, *Sex* has sold thousands and thousands of copies internationally. In Canada and Quebec it sells for $60.00
a pop (+ GST and PST), and many public libraries stock it. In late 1995,
three years after the court case, gay journalist Bill Richardson wrote that
the four copies of *Sex* in Vancouver's public library system collectively
bear the weight of 1020 outstanding reserves (Richardson 1995, 17). *Sex*
has not, to my knowledge, been subject to obscenity charges of any
kind. *Sex*'s metal covers serve as a bullet-proof, anti-cop shield held up
smugly by the multinational dynasty Time-Warner and its stable of
crackerjack entertainment lawyers. As is common practice among
media magnates, Time-Warner sought and obtained pre-clearance for
Sex from Canada Customs. Lawyer Brian Blugerman of the prestigious
Canadian firm Osler, Hoskin & Harcourt was hired to instruct customs
officials on how to interpret *Sex*: 'Since there was no penetration we
could say it was just violence, no sex. Violence alone is OK under Butler' (cited in Toobin 1994, 76). Blugerman notes that in order to pre-

empt a censorious strike at the border they could have used the 'internal necessities test' or 'artistic defence,' but they didn't need to. Two years later, at the trial of *Little Sister's Book and Art Emporium v. B.C. Minister of Justice* (1994), the bookstore's lawyer, Joseph Arvay, cross-examined Linda Murphy about her professional evaluation of Madonna's *Sex*. Murphy, the director of the Prohibited Importations Directorate in Ottawa, confessed that there was no written version of her own unit's decision to permit the sale of *Sex* in Canada. Journalists Fuller and Blackley report: 'Murphy was unable to provide either a credible or consistent accounting for *Sex*'s innocence. Murphy agreed that many of the images seemed to involve the "undue exploitation of sex," yet she was frequently evasive' (Fuller and Blackley 1995, 125). Evidently, the safe passage of *Sex* across the U.S./Canada border was eased by the twin lubricants of money and power; the publishers of *Bad Attitude* had no such 'luck.'

Certainly, the dazzling production values of *Sex* and its embeddedness in the legitimizing discourses of high art and fashion photography aid in securing its virtual inviolability. And *Sex* is protected by and marketed through Madonna's status as international pop icon. (As a femme, I find that neither the shots of Madonna-the-heterosex-kitten nor of Madonna-the-object-of-leather-dyke-attention pass my wet test. But there is one very hot image of Madonna from behind affecting a Jimmy Dean–like pose, standing in a door frame, cockily and sweetly butch, that I quite like.)

During the *Bad Attitude* hearing, Crown Attorney Charles Granek dismissed *Sex* as Madonna's 'cynical marketing ploy,' a shrewd manoeuvre to increase sales of her album, 'Erotica' (Granek 1992b, 67). In ways exemplary of the adversarial nature of criminal trial proceedings, he then attempted to pressure me into agreeing that the elimination of certain 'shocking and graphic' images in *Sex* would not compromise the book's integrity. Granek pressed me to assume the role of censor, slicing up and chopping out those images in *Sex* that he had already decided were obscene and harmful. Granek also, ineffectually, attempted to elicit my agreement with his assertion that people only rushed out to purchase *Sex* because they were (mindlessly) curious about Madonna and her celebrity status (which, extending Granek's logic, cancelled out any prurient or 'dirty' rationale for buying the book) (ibid., 68, 71–4). In other words, Granek sought to undermine our analysis of *Sex* by insinuating that people were bamboozled by their own foolishness and by excessive media hype; they were duped into lining Madonna's pockets either because they were stupid or they wanted to buy art, *not because they wanted to get off.*

Annoyed by the Crown's incessant efforts to manipulate and trap me, Clare Barclay and I argued that the commercial success of Madonna's *Sex* signified a decisive shift in community standards. (Because I was disallowed as an expert on community standards, this argument carried little weight.) Most notably, the book has never been proved responsible for inciting 'harm to women' or 'anti-social behaviour,' nor has it been prevented from travelling freely across the Canada/U.S. border. In the end, Judge Paris dismissed our exhibit, *Sex*, and all of our attendant arguments regarding changes in community standards evidenced by the book's mass dissemination and popular appeal, as unpersuasive. Here he was aided by the Crown Attorney, Granek, who stressed in his summation that because *Sex* is sold in a sealed package, the community cannot look at or read it before they buy it; therefore, it is an unreliable indicator of liberalizing community standards (Granek 1992c, 48). Moreover, Granek added that Madonna's book *Sex* 'can be distinguished on the very ground of an artistic defense' while *Bad Attitude* was 'merely a document designed for sexual arousal,' hence any comparison or analogy drawn between the two was necessarily specious (ibid., 50). In so doing, he activated a fundamental premise undergirding the *Butler* decision as identified by legal theorist Brenda Cossman: 'Art cannot be sex for sex's sake. By definition, sex is not art' (see Cossman, this volume).

Lesbian pornography produced by and for lesbians has little commercial currency or public profile: in North America there are fewer than eight lesbian magazines that contain explicit sex, and there are approximately forty sexually explicit lesbian-produced videos that are poorly distributed in Canada and the United States. *Bad Attitude* is a low-budget, bimonthly magazine that sells less than two hundred copies an issue across Canada at self-identified lesbian and gay bookstores. The owner and editor of the magazine, Jasmine Sterling, explains: 'We call it *Bad Attitude* because society says that a woman who takes charge of her own sexuality has a bad attitude, and that's what the magazine is about – women taking charge' (cited in Toobin 1994, 74). At $8.95, *Bad Attitude* is not glossy, the reproduction of images is poor, and the text is littered with typos and grammatical errors. In spite of these shortcomings, I explained to Judge Paris during the *R. v. Scythes* trial that seekers of lesbian-made pornography had a very difficult time finding *Bad Attitude*, and that Glad Day Bookshop rarely received or sold more than twenty copies per issue. (Interviewed after the *R. v. Scythes* case, publisher Jasmine Sterling reported that she used to send fifty copies to bookstores in Canada, but that she had stopped doing it because it wasn't worth the hassle; cited in Toobin 1994, 74). This situation is in contrast to the millions of male consumers who first encounter and form impressions of 'lesbians' in heterosexual porn. I argued that stories/images in *Bad Attitude* (as well as in *On Our Backs, Quim,* and *Deneuve*) typically incorporate safe-sex practice, including latex gloves, condoms on penises, dildoes, and vibrators, and safe-sex information. The more I struggled to establish the cultural and political import of lesbian texts that intend lesbian arousal, the more the judge seemed impatient, bored, and exasperated.

Disciplined and Punished

Because I attempted to contextualize *Bad Attitude*, because I refused to provide the court with the 'exact size of the lesbian s/m sub-community' in Toronto, and because I (on occasion) hesitated to give yes and no answers, I was scolded by judge and Crown for being uncooperative and given to 'hearsay' (Ross 1992, 18). Because I was unable to 'count' s/m lesbians or to admit to their 'fringe status,' my knowledge was not interpreted by the Crown (and judge) as objective social science – my analysis ran counter to the structuring of obscenity law. Though trained as a social scientist, I had no genuinely positivist claims of my own to announce. Unlike Malamuth, I had not conducted experimental research in laboratories, hence I could not generalize from 'hard data' and statistically significant findings. The Crown and judge wanted me to solidify the lesbian s/m subculture as a constitutive group that was mathematically measurable. They sought numbers and certainty and 'solid facts.' As legal scholar Carol Smart argues, 'legal arguments ... that present simple, certain and authoritative pictures of social reality are likely to be privileged within legal discourse' (Smart 1989, 71). Ironically, Malamuth himself had no 'facts' to disclose; however, his authority had been pre-established and needed no further justification.

The Crown urged me to pin down the particulars of lesbian s/m identity; I endeavoured to elucidate the unsolicited layers of s/m discourse. I argued that s/m cannot be easily and neatly packaged: there is tremendous variability of s/m fantasy and action. Elements of s/m enter the lives and imaginations of many women (lesbian and non-lesbian), which makes the quantification of a 'lesbian s/m subculture' impossible.

In all, my postmodern insistence that pornography has many meanings, that sexual expression (including s/m) can promote self-fulfilment and alternative sexualities, and that feminists are deeply divided on issues of representation damaged my worthiness and credibility in court. Try as I could, I was unable to argue for the *specificity* of lesbian s/m fantasy, and at the same time underscore the *fluidity* of sexual desire, and be understood. In other words, I was committed to defending *Bad Attitude* as one product of lesbian sexual dissent, *and* I remember wanting to normalize a blurring of s/m-non-s/m boundaries as a way of flipping the hegemonic caricature of s/m on its head. Like American feminist historian Alice Kessler-Harris in her testimony against the gendered discriminatory practices of Sears in the mid-1980s, I learned that developing subtle distinctions and negotiating fine points of interpretation are skills that must be abandoned in the courtroom (Kessler-Harris 1987, 61). And like Kessler-Harris, when I responded to the Crown's questions by underlining the import of nuance and diversity, my answers were often demeaned (ibid., 61–2). Judge Paris warned me that my attitude was corroding my credibility and the helpfulness of my testimony (Ross 1992, 70). He disciplined me several times over the course of my testimony much as a dominatrix would punish her 'prey.' When I string these occasions of punishment and humiliation together, I find ineluctable, ironic confirmation of the trial itself as ritualized s/m theatre.

Lesbian Invisibility in Court and out

Outside of my testimony, over the course of almost thirty hours of examination and cross-examination, the word 'lesbian' was only mentioned sporadically. Almost two full days were spent debating the responses of white, American, college-educated males to non-consensual images of rape and coercion. The freedom, privilege, and power to make sense of, to comment on, and to judge lesbian s/m fantasy were rolled around like marbles in the hands of white, heterosexual male experts – judge, Crown and witnesses. Even psychologist Jonathon Freedman, in an otherwise superb denunciation of Neil Malamuth and the entire 'porn causes violence' school of media analysis, referred to the image of lesbian fisting in *Bad Attitude* as 'disgusting' (Freedman 1992, 40). Artist Ellen Flanders attended the trial: 'They had these men discussing in a very clinical way what was going on in [the *Bad Attitude*] images, and that was the only time they discussed anything about lesbianism. And they didn't know what they were talking about [laughing]. And I found that incredible: here they were, the supposed experts, the judge and the Crown, discussing fisting and they had no idea what they were talking about' (Flanders 1993, 9). Revealing his profound knowledge of, and sensitivity to lesbians, the Crown Attorney, Charles Granek, used his summation to pontificate: '[We know] that the sado-masochistic group is only one fraction of the lesbian community itself. To suggest, therefore, that lesbians on the whole are discriminated against if we are to ban material like *Bad Attitude* is insulting to that very community' (Granek 1992c, 32). He continued by insisting that the trial was not about lesbians; it was about 'the sadomasochistic community of either sex and of any sexual orientation,' a community 'whose rights are, thankfully, not protected by the Canadian Charter of Rights and Freedoms' (ibid., 32–3). When I read the court transcript now, I am sickened by what I interpret to be the Crown's smug separation of good lesbians/ bad lesbians and his declaration of the subhuman status of s/m prac-titioners. I bristle at Granek's highfalutin inference that he knows what is best for 'the lesbian community.' Indeed, it was the startling invisibility of LESBIAN at a lesbian porn trial that I and others expe-rienced bodily and intellectually as most incredible, angering, and insanity-making.

In his summation, Granek also stated baldly that because *Bad Attitude* was indisputably 'dirt for dirt's sake,' my extralegal interpretation of the lesbian text '[flew] in the face of common sense and ought to be disre-garded' (Granek 1992c, 44). In other words, my knowledge of lesbian sexuality and culture was nothing but anecdotal, confessional, and impressionistic non-sense; it was, in short, dispensable. I now see that it was the law, specifically *Butler*, that had discursive monopoly over 'common sense.' My active, sociological disloyalty to *Butler's* sover-eignty placed me in a position of major strategic disadvantage on the terrain of law. By contrast, Malamuth's testimony – a clever incantation of *Butler's* internal logic and coherence – functioned as a polished mirror for the law's narcissistic contemplation of itself (Valverde 1996, 202). I suspect that from the standpoint of the prosecutorial team, my challenge marked a churlish affront to hegemonic conceptions of s/m porn as *the* trope of brutality, depravity, cruelty, and the exploitation of women. In *Butler*, s/m porn lurks between the lines as the unspoken, consummate apex of 'degradation' and 'dehumanization.' To date across Canada and the United States, the only s/m depictions successfully defended in legal arenas – Robert Mapplethorpe's photographic retrospective 'The Perfect

Moment' – have been defended as art based on 'expert' ideas of art (see Lang 1995).[14] In a Toronto court in December 1992, the Crown Attorney, Charles Granek, argued that *Bad Attitude* could not be exculpated on grounds of artistic merit or intent (Granek 1992c, 56–7).

In the end, Judge Paris, the 'trier of fact,' made a ruling on one issue of the 'lesbian erotic fiction' magazine *Bad Attitude* based primarily on Malamuth's use of extrapolation in the place of scientific evidence. He did not reference the discourses of religion, psychiatry, or biology – discourses that have historically been integral to the pathologization of homosexuality.[15] He did not need to. In his official ruling Judge Paris maintained that by substituting a man for the 'sexually aggressive' woman in the story 'Wunna My Fantasies,' the criminally violent character of the scene is fully revealed (*Scythes* 1993, 5). By crafty sleight of hand, Paris-the-magician transformed one (paper) expression of consensual female homoerotic desire into a (live) non-consensual heterosexual 'rape,' and in so doing obliterated the radical specificity of the lesbian imagery/text. Here, the inadmissability of lesbians and lesbian sexual images was legally secured. At the same time, Judge Paris disallowed the reality that in commercial heterosexual s/m, the men are most often submissive, not the women.[16]

Unable or unwilling to interpret lesbian s/m imagery from inside the interpretive frame that I and others built over the course of the trial, Judge Paris drained the lesbian-specific images of content and context. In superimposing a heterosexual template, he was aided by expert witness Neil Malamuth's 'scientific' postulation that it was possible to generalize and universalize from research findings based on exclusively heterosexual male samples.[17] Indeed, Malamuth's inference provides graphic substantiation of Stanley Fish's perception that 'the law wants social science to tell it that a new problem or social experience can be properly and fairly managed by being construed as analogous to something else' (Fish 1989, chap. 17). To Judge Paris, once the original lesbian image was remade into a heterosexual exchange between a man and a woman, it became instantly intelligible. (Ironically, in their factum to the Supreme Court on *Butler*, LEAF's lawyers recommended the substitution of an 'abused' woman-as-bottom for an 'abused' gay man-as-bottom in gay male porn in order to 'teach' judges about the coercion and violence inscribed in heterosexual pornography.) The gender of the female actors/models in lesbian-made sexual imagery is fundamentally relevant and defies the mental practice of substitution or translation. A reading that denies gender relevancy irreparably ruptures the integrity and intention of lesbian texts made explicitly for lesbian viewers/readers, and the particular context/s in which the work is received. In so doing, it discounts the radical specificity of a lesbian sub-genre that exists outside of, heterosexual male imaging of lesbian sex.

To me, there is no question that Judge Paris's decision is shot through with heterosexist and homophobic assumptions and double standards. Never has it been more clear to me that the relevances of anti-violence and anti-porn discourse are contingent on the sexist and heterocentric suspension, if not the disavowal, of women's self-defined pleasure. In the face of massive resources marshalled to extinguish the 'lesbian threat' – the legal profession, the judiciary, and the police – I am certain that I could find no better evidence of the *instability* of normative heterosexuality. Indeed, the legal judgment rendering *Bad Attitude* 'obscene' seems to substantiate Diana Fuss's eloquent argument that 'heterosexuality secures its ontological boundaries by protecting itself from what it sees as the continual predatory instrusion of its diseased other, homosexuality' (Fuss 1989, 2).

Re-Invoking Social-Purity Discourse in the Late Twentieth Century

The categories of degradation, dehumanization, and harm used repeatedly by the Crown during the *Bad Attitude* case (and enshrined in *Butler*) bespeak a persisting concentration on female victimization that centres women's sexual danger, guilt, shame, and fear. (For much of the *Bad Attitude* trial, the Crown clutched the feminist anthology *Against Sadomasochism* [Linden et al. 1982] to his chest.) Importantly, the construct of female sexual degradation was pivotal to the rhetoric of English Canadian moral reformers in the early 1900s: the National Council of Women (NCW), the Women's Christian Temperance Union's Department of Purity in Literature, Art and Fashion, and the Methodist Department of Temperance and Moral Reform – all of whom lobbied for obscenity legislation and greater legal/sexual/moral protection for women and children. And as historian Mary Louise Adams has discovered, in the early 1950s women took the leadership role in urging state censorship of crime comics and pulp fiction that they believed were destined to corrupt morally impressionable young people (Adams 1994). As the Congress of Canadian Women put it in 1952, 'The mass production and distribution of sensational novels depicting lewd, repulsive and perverted behaviour of the characters as a normal way of life has superceded all other worthwhile publications offered for sale in Canadian stores. Men and women are portrayed as monsters of perversion and the women pictured as Lesbians and modern Messalinas. Added to this is the continuous suggestion that crime and perversion is normal' (Congress of Canadian Women 1952, 149). The continuity between the early and late twentieth centuries seems to be the maternal, and later cultural feminist, fixing of certain norms of femininity and masculinity as natural, unchanging, and essentially rooted in binary opposites: the female is morally superior and in need of rescue from the oversexed, uncontrollably lustful and inherently violent male. Today, given the structuring of woman-as-object-to-be-violated-by-man in pro-censorship feminist, conservative, and legal discourse, woman as sexual subject becomes an oxymoron. Once the paradox becomes inscribed in a law that animates police and court action, how then is it possible to tell different stories?

In his final decision, Judge Paris concluded that 'Wunna My Fantasies' 'blew all the whistles and rang all the bells' (*Scythes* 1993, 4). Clearly, he did not read Trish Thomas's story 'Wunna My Fantasies' as fantasy – a work of the imagination, a symbolic representation. He read it literally as real, actual abuse meted out by an attacker on her victim. Accepting *Butler*'s premise that porn is believed by the Canadian public to cause harm, and that consent 'cannot save materials' deemed to be degrading to women, the judge ruled that it is now a felony to fantasize participating in a lesbian s/m sexual act.

I communicated to Judge Paris that lesbian s/m imagery plays a crucial role in the formation of lesbian s/m identities, networks, and subcultures. I argued that isolating s/m (and anal penetration in gay porn) as punishable depictions strips them from the larger political context of resistance and self-definition by marginalized communities. My elaboration of these themes in court was, in the end, entirely disregarded by Judge Paris. In his final judgment he explained that 'The community tolerance test is blind to sexual orientation. Its only focus is the potential harm to the public' (*Scythes* 1993, 4). Defence counsel Clare Barclay had anticipated this tack, and used her summation to caution that 'The community standards test should not be whether a heterosexual majority is willing to tolerate others being exposed to lesbian or gay sexually explicit imagery, for it is the community as a whole which must be the arbiter' (Barclay 1992, 12). Barclay bravely argued that the exclusion of lesbian and gay Canadians from determinations of community standards would mean discrimination on the basis of sexual orientation. She added that such exclusion would violate section 15 of the Canadian

Charter of Rights and Freedoms, and would be unconstitutional. Barclay then reviewed case law on sexual orientation as evidence that 'community understanding and tolerance of lesbian and gay sexuality has increased immensely' (ibid., 17). Finally, she reintroduced Madonna's *Sex* as evidence of what communities do tolerate in the 1990s, and she reiterated the necessity of evaluating lesbian images in the contexts within which they are produced and disseminated.

In his six-page ruling, Judge Paris conceded a point to Barclay in his willingness to recognize 'the rights of sexual minorities to communicate publicly on the subject that binds them together' (*Scythes* 1993, 4). And then he delivered his view that, in this case, curtailing these rights was justifed 'in the public interest' (ibid.). To me, his decision suggests that lesbian producers and consumers of *Bad Attitude* (and queers in general) are not members of the 'public,' hence their (subhuman) views on community standards do not count, need never matter, and are not officially registrable.[18] Indeed, it seems a short slide from the erasure of lesbian pornographic images to Eve Sedgwick's sobering apprehension of 'an overarching, hygienic Western fantasy of a world without any more homosexuals in it' (Sedgwick 1990, 42).

The moral standpoint that governed both the police raid on Glad Day Bookshop and the judge's conviction of obscenity is legally codified in the *Butler* decision. By deploying *Butler*, Judge Paris consigned lesbian-made images to the private sphere, hidden from view, in Linda Williams's terms, 'off the scene of representation' (Williams 1990, 2). Thus, lesbian-made depictions remain dirty and forbidden while straight male publishers circulate often sexist and racist images that are one-dimensional distortions worked up from inside male fantasy, or sanitized, sugared versions sold via fashion, art, and entertainment magazines. In other words, *R. v. Scythes* shows that a double standard falsely separates respectable from ignominious lesbian images, and heterosexualized from lesbianized female bodies.

Rather than promote (or legislate) women's equality, I argue that the decision made by Judge Paris re-encodes late-nineteenth-century social-purity definitions of women as sexually passive objects in need of manly protection (see Backhouse 1991, Mitchinson 1991, Valverde 1991). As such, this ruling is not simply or merely about lesbians or, more pointedly, 'nasty s/m perverts.' It is about patriarchal preoccupation with re-making good/bad, moral/immoral, madonna/whore, and male/female in ways that re-demarcate boundaries of hegemonic heterosexual norms and reassign what is 'properly' public and private. Arguably, the overt challenge made by lesbian s/m porn to common-sense roles of male dominance and female submission unnerved the Crown and judge. In my opinion, it is possible that the images in *Bad Attitude* (particularly those of fisting) threatened their sense of masculine prowess in part through obstructing their ability to enter and control the pornographic scene. Indeed, portrayals of sexually self-sufficient lesbians may shake heterosexual men's sense of entitlement to power over women in general – not only sexually, but economically, politically, and culturally.

The decision made in *R. v. Scythes* is not without serious implications. We know that the censorship of *Bad Attitude* and the ongoing Canada Customs seizure of lesbian and gay images denies access to valuable information and it relegates much-needed knowledge to a largely unavailable, unreliable underground (Jones 1993, Fuller and Blackley 1995). Removing lesbian sexual depictions, s/m and non-s/m, from circulation creates an open wound that harms the much broader ecosystem of lesbian/gay cultural production and consumption. Among queers, especially those fearful of exposure, printed materials are highly prized and defended because the practice of reading is safer than going to an outwardly visible gay/lesbian bar, a theatre, or Pride Day. Materials about sex and sexual fantasy are especially significant for lesbians and gays who live in small towns and remote areas far from large urban centres. Without access to meaningful images, sexual and non-sexual, lesbians and gay men are consigned to speechlessness, invisibility, and internalized homophobia. We are told that lust is something to be ashamed of, to apologize for, and we are punished for stepping out of line. We are denied knowledge of the breadth and diversity of queerness manifested in different body shapes, cultures, races, ethnicities, ages, abilities, and sexual tastes. This does not mean that we are left with nothing; some queer cultural workers interpret censorship law as an invitation to get busy (see below). However, in the case of *R. v. Scythes*, the single-minded containment of lesbian sexual discourse suggests that queer-made images and the queer bodies they document are terrifying, dangerous, and polluted.

Ambivalences

Over the course of the *Bad Attitude* trial, the number of lesbian, feminist, and pro-feminist supporters in the courtroom averaged ten a day.[19] Gay men routinely outnumbered lesbians. Only a handful of anti-censorship advocates were present on the final day as Charles Granek and Clare

Barclay offered their final submissions. I suspect that the low attendance at the trial reflected a series of factors: (a) the low profile of the case in the local, national, and even alternative press, (b) the limited resources that Glad Day Bookshop had to finance the defence, and (c) the persisting ambivalence vis-à-vis pornography (defined here as sexually explicit materials) expressed by many lesbians and feminists, compounded by age-old skirmishes between feminists, lesbians, and gay men over sexual politics (see Ross, 1993). Indeed, after more than fifteen years of intermittent eruptions and periods of slow boil, the sex debates in Western feminism, and in Canadian feminism specifically, have yielded no consensus.[20] In some cases, it feels to me that the 'pro legal reform/anti-porn' and the 'anti-censorship/pro-porn' tendencies have hardened into cemented polarities. Clearly, on issues of power, morality, pleasure, danger, and the law, there is little agreement.

Deep splits endure among feminists about what pornography is, what it represents, and how to deal with it; the *Bad Attitude* case did not succeed in galvanizing the factions. In Canada, diverse constituencies of feminists including the Women's Legal Education and Action Fund (LEAF) identify pornography as a key site of women's subordination (see Gotell, this volume). In their *Butler* factum prepared for the Supreme Court of Canada in 1992, LEAF submits that 'pornography is a form of hate propaganda against women,' and as such it 'undermines the equality of women' (LEAF 1991a, 16, 19). LEAF lawyers Kathleen Mahoney and Linda Taylor conclude that 'The pervasive presence of pornography thus deters women's equal access to participation in community life' (ibid., 19).

Queer theorist Julia Creet astutely observes: 'A [feminist] movement built on the repudiation of sexual objectification has had a very difficult time embracing sex and its inherent complexity without questioning the tenets of the movement itself' (Creet 1991a, 139). Feminists politicized through anti-violence and anti-rape activism, and through their own and others' personal experiences of sexual danger (for instance, incest, rape, harassment), regularly point to commercial heterosexual pornography as a cause of women's suffering. Because pornography is viewed by many as a graphic embodiment of women's inequality, it has long been the focus of women's anger and outrage. Catharine MacKinnon writes that showing porn to men is 'like saying "kill" to a trained guard dog' (MacKinnon 1993, 12). However, long-time gay activist Chris Bearchell warns: 'Porn is an easy target – it's visible, officially disapproved of and relatively controllable. The abusive situations faced by many women and young people, on the other hand, have tended to be invisible, condoned and very difficult to change' (Bearchell 1993, 40). In others words, erasing porn will not eradicate gendered (as well as racialized and classed) power relations.

There is a long history of feminist criticism of pornography, and a small but significant body of literature that isolates sadomasochism as especially anti-woman hate literature. The feminist anthology *Against Sadomasochism* (1982) contains contributions from Judith Butler and the late Audre Lorde. And there has been a recent revival of feminist commentary on the evils of lesbian s/m in the work of Didi Herman (1994), Janice Raymond (1992), Reina Lewis and Karen Adler (1994), Ann Scales (1994), Sheila Jeffreys (1994), and Karen Busby (1994), among others. Unfortunately, the pinpointing of lesbian s/m fantasy plays directly into the hands of Christian coalitions, right-wing politicians, and other moral conservatives who view pornography, s/m porn especially, as a foul assault on (white, middle-class) family values. Unable to stamp out actual, practised lesbian s/m, critics must content themselves with controlling a proxy: the images of sexual behaviour (see Vance 1989, 43).

Lesbian feminist legal theorist and activist Didi Herman, in an attempt to theorize the *Butler* decision in relation to s/m porn and practice, makes a surprisingly conservative, sex-negative assertion that 'the law has an *inevitable and legitimate role* to play in regulating desire' (her emphasis) (Herman 1994, 6).[21] In a paper delivered to the Canadian Sociology and Anthropology Association in 1994, Herman maintains that s/m porn and practice (both gay and straight) 'violate the core values that anchor our condemnation of genocide and other similar practices – core values such as respect, empathy and substantive equality' (ibid., 12). She concludes that '[s/m porn and practice] are morally reprehensible' (ibid., 13). Given my concerns in this chapter, Herman's invalidation of lesbian s/m imagery on moralistic rather than empirical grounds affirms Judge Paris's ruling in *R. v. Scythes* that such imagery imperils women's equality. Her notion of 'core' values smacks of universalism and has its roots in an ahistorical notion of culture as unchanging and uncontested. She implies that makers, users, and supporters of lesbian s/m imagery are not only disrespectful; they are unconcerned about actual lived violence and despair in women's lives. Moreover, Herman seems to suggest that the eradication of s/m imagery will hasten women's actual, lived equality. In opposition, feminist sociologist Thelma McCormack asserts that censorship of so-called harmful porn overprotects women, infantilizes women, and contributes to the dependency of women; it does not help in achieving women's equality (McCormack 1993b, 30). Herman supports state censorship of what she views as condemnable s/m porn. By contrast, McCormack warns that 'Censorship is the fastest and cheapest way of seeming to deal with the psychological uncertainty we feel about our social lives, our pervasive sense of being manipulated' (ibid., 33).

Herman's emotional equation of s/m porn and practice with genocide and moral corruption neither elucidates the porn's allegedly objectionable properties nor makes room for candid discussion of why s/m imagery pushes her buttons one way, and pushes mine (and others') another, and what, if anything, is to be done about it. In addition, her conflation of s/m porn and genocide trivializes actual instances of genocide and enables, if not fuels, anti-queer backlash. It enjoins right-wing moralizing discourse that calls for policing sexualities rather than encourage democratic discussion of alternative sexualities and pleasures.[22] Herman's endorsement of obscenity law postpones engagement with issues of power that have vexed feminists for over a century and invites further state suppression of lesbian sexual texts that may possess no other raison d'être than readership arousal: dirt for dirt's sake. In effect, arguments such as Herman's, much like obscenity law, act to circumscribe the imaginability of homosexuality itself.

By avoiding analysis of the structure of pornographic fantasy and its place within the field of social power, Herman forecloses talk of contradictions and complexities lived by women (and men) of all sexual persuasions in favour of renewing binaries of us/them, good homo/bad homo, and madonna/whore. Perhaps most significantly, Herman's conception of representation as *debasing and discriminatory action* situates fantasy as the causal link, as if, Judith Butler argues, 'fantasy could suddenly transmute into action' (Butler 1990, 113–14). It is this very 'truth' that is enshrined in the Supreme Court's *Butler* decision, and it is this 'truth' that Judge Paris deployed in his ruling against the lesbian sex magazine *Bad Attitude*. Rather, no pornographic text (s/m or other) operates as a site of singular, univocal meaning: textualized fantasy does not supply a single point of identification for viewers (ibid.). As such, women (lesbian and non-lesbian) are and can be agents of pornographic fantasy. Whoever she is, the woman pictured in erotic texts is not *fixed in meaning* as an injured, assaulted object; her subject position as unilaterally oppressed victim is not stable. Once we accept this, we then recognize that there can be no definitive acts of harm that flow from exposure to sexual images, s/m or not.

Other feminists have been equally adamant in their critique of lesbian s/m porn and practice. In *Women's Studies International Forum*, British writers Reina Lewis and Karen Adler argue that 'Sm's presentation of itself as a hip new lifestyle inhabited by tops and bottoms rather than sadists and masochists, belies the actual violence inherent in sm discourse and practice' (Lewis and Adler 1994, 435). Without detailing how, empirically, they arrived at their conclusions, they elaborate their standpoint: '[S/m's] separation of the sexual from the emotional, social and political aspects of lesbian lives, coupled, moreover, with a liberationist vision of the sexual experience itself, negates any regard for the future of commitment beyond the single sexual encounter ... the long-term relationship is excluded from the realm of fantasy' (ibid.). Here we see the inference of causation: (violent) s/m porn flagrantly promotes the casual, recreational, snappy, and guiltless fuck and as such jeopardizes the lesbian reader's ability to differentiate good from evil. By combining the super-valuation of long-term lesbian unions with essentialist notions of lesbians' inherent nurturing, egalitarian, and monogamous 'nature,' Lewis and Adler not only reinforce highly conservative notions of proper sexual conduct; they scapegoat s/m porn as a 'creeping colonization' in the absence of any data that confirm their fear of a lesbian s/m epidemic. (Certainly in Canada, with lesbian pornography routinely snatched at borders and from bookstores, alarmist dread of colonization seems laughably misplaced.)

American Ann Scales is a self-avowed radical feminist who recently analysed obscenity legislation in Canada: 'Butler is the law. It is still the best that any nation on earth has done so far to protect women from the harms of pornography – that specific propaganda that constructs women as *expendable* (Scales 1994, 363–4) (her emphasis).[23] Having enjoined 'all gay men and lesbians to withdraw from the war on *Butler*,' and having announced her support for Judge Paris's decision in *R. v. Scythes*, Scales goes to great lengths in the *Canadian Journal of Women and the Law* to meditate on her disgust for lesbian s/m porn (ibid., 350). She refers to Trish Thomas's 'Wunna My Fantasies' as a 'positive-outcome rape story' and suggests that it is as 'violent' and 'dehumanizing as what is common in mainstream pornography' (ibid., 375). In one of a series of bald generalizations *à la* Malamuth in *R. v. Scythes*, Scales states: 'Though the genders may be rearranged in gay and lesbian pornography, if the turn-on requires domination and subordination, then those materials affirm the social hatred of women ... The value enacted, therefore, even in some gay and lesbian materials, is that it is socially acceptable, indeed, desirable, to turn women (or their surrogates) into things, to deprive us of our selves, and to screw us to death' (ibid., 365). Scales maintains a paternalistic position in speaking for the 'victimized' bottom instead of letting the bottom speak for herself.

Of the multiple, unpacked assumptions at work in Scales's piece, one is that s/m lesbians are falsely conscious dupes who stupidly, selfishly, and violently poison the sexual climate and put (non-s/m) women at risk of annihilation. Another assumption, and one shared by Herman, Lewis, Adler, and others, is the claim that the image itself does the screwing: a literalist reading of pornography as a practice innately harmful to women. Winding down, Scales concludes: 'Lesbians have a powerful argument about our need to build and expand our interpretive communities ... But does the building of the interpretive, supportive community require trafficking in what would otherwise be pornography? Put in a less loaded way, can't we have sex without tolerating abusive sex, or what we want to call "depictions" thereof?' (Scales 1994, 381). First, I interpret Scales to be saying that the one and only by-product of reading pornography is real, live, hurtful sex. Second, she seems to yearn for an uncontaminated space populated by female bodies that manifest extra-discursive innocence free from the taint of sexually explicit texts, and free from all base desire to communicate (and fantasize) about sex, turn-ons *and* turn-offs. Like her anti-porn colleagues, Scales appears unable or unwilling to imagine women (and lesbians) as other than victims of textually mediated male oppression, hate, and torture.

In October 1993, on a panel organized in Toronto by Media Watch – the Canada-wide feminist advertising watchdog – well-known lesbian anti-porn advocate Susan Cole reinscribed the judgmental dichotomy of good girl/bad girl (and her own identification with goodness) by confessing that she did not protest the police seizure of *Bad Attitude* in the spring of 1992 because she could not, 'in good faith,' endorse the 'torture and pain inflicted by one woman on another.' I argue that the reading 'It's two women hurting each other' smacks of simplistic, moral indignation and a rigid refusal to *learn about* the actual particulars of s/m sex and fantasy.[24] Moreover, it closes off insight into how one's own sexual fantasies may contain elements of the same power that is honestly and formally played with in s/m imagery. Several months later in Toronto, New York art critic Liz Kotz argued that a 'tactically motivated disavowal of the dark, troubling registers of sexuality, including aggressive s/m,' will only result in constricted notions of pleasure, sex, and the body (Kotz 1994). I agree. Habitual genuflection to the negative frame of s/m, snuff, and kiddie porn, such as that exercised by the anti-porn feminists above, prohibits self-reflexive dialogue about the murky, scary, contradictory zone of sexual desire between the ears where force, raw aggression, surrender, and control often pervail.

I have no quarrel with the right of anti-porn feminists to publicize their positions. What I object to is the use of established and influential scholarly journals and conferences – authority-ascribing fora – to broadcast views that grant validity and credibility to moral claims *under the guise of social science.* In feminist anti-s/m tracts, a roaring silence surrounds how 'harm' or 'actual violence' is defined, calculated, and measured; instead, we find s/m porn advanced as a fully transparent and seamless category – the receptacle of all that is distastefully vile and injurious. The minds and bodies of queer (and straight) writers and readers of lesbian s/m porn are never present in feminist critiques of the sub-genre. In a recent issue of the *Canadian Journal of Law and Society,* legal scholar (and LEAF member) Karen Busby avowed: 'LEAF is committed to affirming the social and sexual identities of lesbians through law' (Busby et al. 1994, 184). And yet I deduce from LEAF's implicit anti-s/m stance that the social and sexual identites of lesbians are not all equal and, as such, are not equally defensible in court (or anywhere else). In my view, common to all feminist denouncers of lesbian s/m porn and practice is the standpoint of *not knowing.* In the place of knowledge, we find conjecture about what lesbian s/m fantasy is, how it works, and whom it 'harms.' But on what grounds might 'harmful materials' be distinguished from 'non-harmful materials'? Who decides? And how do these very questions reveal capitulation to the power of law, that is, *Butler,* to set the terms of debate and the parameters of 'truth'? Foucauldian theorist David Halperin reminds us that, '["truth"] licenses "experts" to describe and objectify people's lives, especially the lives of those who, for whatever reason, happen to find themselves most fully exposed to the operations of disciplinary power' (Halperin 1993, 88). Crown attorneys and judges seeking to criminalize lesbian (and gay) pornographers need look no further than this recent wave of feminist academic 'truth' about s/m for arguments that perfectly buttress the letter of Canadian obscenity law. In what follows, I show how some queerly located sexperts are leading us in radically other directions.

Cracking the Whip

Just over ten years ago, in the pathbreaking Canadian anthology *Women*

Against Censorship, Lorna Weir and Mariana Valverde advised: 'Our strategies for creating lesbian culture cannot be achieved through the law, police and courts. We do not need a legal defence as much as a cultural offense' (Valverde and Weir 1985, 105). In the same volume, critic Varda Burstyn called for 'pluralistic work that reflects the variety of sexual lifeways that exist in our society' (Burstyn 1985a, 156). In 1997, lesbians, gays, bisexuals, transsexuals, and transgenders continue to struggle to combat the internalized shame, fear, and self-hatred we are taught in a heterosexist, gender-bound, and homophobic culture. Part of this struggle necessitates access to a vast range of images that name lesbian sexual difference and celebrate the diversity and complexity of our sexual, emotional, intellectual, and spiritual selves.

Simply stated, the production of sexually explicit images highlights what is specific and unique to lesbian and gay communities: our same-sex desire. Erotic images validate our sexuality as one healthy, meaningful, and empowering part of our lives as lesbians (and gay men). Sexually explicit images produced by and for lesbians challenge the barriers of sexual fear, inhibition, ignorance, and shame by unapologetically foregrounding lesbian desire, and thus expanding the realm of knowable human sexual expression. Lesbian writer Pat Califia describes why she wrote *The Lesbian S/M Safety Manual* (1988): 'The purpose was to educate women who do s/m with other women about ways to fulfil fantasies about dominance and submission in ways that are emotionally and physically safe, provided that both partners are consenting adults and both of them find these types of fantasies mutually pleasurable' (cited in Fuller and Blackley 1995, 58). Mistress Patricia Marsh, a professional dominatrix in New York, remarks on the therapeutic value of s/m: 'Some people who are into s/m either as dominants or submissives are people who were abused and it is their way of healing. It is their way of owning it again; it is healing for them to get over the powerlessness they had in the abuse situation. It is a way of becoming powerful and saying I want this experience and I am turning it into pleasure' (cited in Bell 1995, 125).

Still, depictions of lesbian sexuality remain hard to find. Philosopher Marilyn Frye wryly observes the enduring 'inarticulate' character of lesbian sex (Frye 1988), and theorist Judith Roof remarks on the 'inconceivability of lesbian sexuality' (Roof 1991, 245). In Canada, the challenge to make lesbian sexual desire visible and speakable is being led by intrepid video and filmmakers Midi Onodera, Lorna Boschman, Kika Thorne, Candi Pauker, Shani Mootoo, Joyan Saunders, Margaret

Moores, Lynne Fernie, Aerlyn Weissman, Almerinda Travassos, and Kathy Daymond (see Bell, this volume); photographers Li Yuen, Cyndra MacDowall, Ellen Flanders, Heather Cameron, Jennifer Gillmor, and the duo Average Good Looks; poets Dionne Brand, Brenda Brooks, Chrystos, Daphne Marlatt, Betsy Warland, and Carolyn Gammon; visual artists G.B. Jones, Shonagh Adelman, Buseje Bailey, the Kiss & Tell collective, Cynthia Lo, and Stephanie Martin; writers Donna Barker, Marusia Bociurkiw, Sarah Sheard, Mona Oikawa, Tamai Kobayashi, Ingrid MacDonald; and performance artists Gwendolyn, karen augustine, Elaine Carol, Lisa Lowe, Lorri Millan, and Shawna Dempsey, among many others.[25]

Willing to push the limits of their own sexual imaginations, many of these artists explore sexual turf that is uncomfortable and unfamiliar: dykes with dicks, inter-racial lesbian sex, the anatomy of orgasm, dykes who do boys, group sex, anonymous and casual sex, leather, bondage, and s/m. In part, this new wave of work signifies the moxie of a generation of young lesbians and bisexuals determined to rebel against their symbolic 'mothers' and the positive-image school of lesbian and feminist image-making (Creet 1991a). In her introduction to *Macho Sluts*, Pat Califia notes:

'Feminist erotica' that presents a simplistic view of lesbian sex and two women in love in a bed who embody all the good things that patriarchy is trying to destroy isn't very sexy. This stuff reads as if it were written by dutiful daughters who are trying to persuade Mom that lesbian sex isn't dirty, and we really are good girls after all. It isn't challenging or stirring enough. The auto-erotically inclined lesbian reader deserves more bang for her buck. And Mom is never going to believe that nice girls put their hands in other girls' panties, anyway ... Lesbian writers have got to loosen up, drop our drawers, spread our cheeks, stick out our tongues, get nasty. (Califia 1988, 13)

Those who have actually seen lesbian s/m imagery (not an easy task) do not all describe it in glowing terms. In a culture still searching for images that reinforce individual and community pride and strength, efforts made to explore power, domination/submission, role-playing, costuming, and so on are often viewed as counter-productive, if not damaging. Some feel that exposing 'dirty laundry' needs to be avoided for fear of ceding ground to the fundamentalist and political right wing and their anti-woman, anti-homosexual, and racist ideologies. Others are afraid that the images may serve to reinvigorate age-old sexological descriptions of female homosexuals as sexually insatiable, promiscuous, aggressive, jealous, rough, and self-loathing perverts. In 1954, popular American psychoanalyst Frank Caprio named lesbians as unhappy, sexually maladjusted and prone to extreme jealousy, sexual immaturity, and sadomasochistic tendencies. He concluded that '[lesbians] can be restored to normal sex outlook by sympathetic and expert treatment, usually at the hands of a psychiatrist or psychoanalyst who believes in cure' (Caprio 1954, 171, 294).

Vancouver's Kiss & Tell visual art collective comment: 'We love making representations of our own sexuality. What we don't love is how state censorship denies our rights and threatens our queer culture. Making lesbian sex art isn't safe. It's not invisible and it's not always nice' (Kiss & Tell 1994, 1, 12). They talk about how their collaborative show, 'True Inversions,' was used to spread homophobic hatred and to threaten arts-council funding in 1992 in the province of Alberta (ibid., 59–74). And yet even in the current climate of severe 'obscenity chill,' the drive to render lesbian eroticism a movable threat stubbornly pushes ahead (Barclay and Carol 1992–3, 18–28).

Within the past five years irreverent risk-takers have launched sex magazines *Lezzie Smut* (Vancouver), *Lickerish: polymorphous queer candy* (Toronto), and *Frighten the Horses* (San Francisco) and the fanzines *SMACKS*, *BIMBOX*, and *Pussy Grazer*. The editors of Vancouver's *Lezzie Smut* lay out their publishing objective in their first editorial in September 1993:

This is a magazine about sex. About dyke sex. About what we do in bed (on the floor, in the elevator, when no one's looking on the bus. When they are looking). What we do, what we would like to do, what we are afraid of doing. We made it for you, to get you off, to get you thinking, to get you to write, take pictures, take chances. We made it for us too, because we wanted smut. We wanted flesh skin lips sex. And shucks, gals, as we all know porn for women by women is hard to come by on this side of the border. We made it because it's the best way to fuck over canada customs, to refuse to let them limit our desires. We made it because we are exhibitionists. We made it because this city needs a space for dykes to see themselves. A sex rag. Something to whack off to. (*Lezzie Smut* 1993, 5–6)

When I interviewed her in early 1994, then co-editor/publisher of *Lickerish: polymorphous queer candy* Jennifer Gillmor cited the 1993 obscenity ruling against *Bad Attitude* (which continues to publish her photographs) as instrumental in her decision to launch her own queer sex magazine (Gillmor 1994). 'Lickerish' was chosen as the title because it means 'eager to taste or enjoy, greedy, desirous, tempting the appetite, having or suggesting lustful desires.' In the editorial in the first issue, Gillmor and co-editor Janet Lee Spagnol state: 'some publications have been banned in Canada. [We were] frustrated as consumers knowing that virtually all of our pornography is imported and therefore, not specifically culturally relevant to us. *Lickerish* is our statement against the criminalization of art and desire. The recognition of the frustration was our catalyst in deciding that we need our own forum in Canada for explicit work by women and men from varying sexual deviations ... We sexual beings often seem most brimming with creativity when flooded with feelings of lust and passion' (Gillmor and Spangol, 1994, 1).

Lesbian s/m porn mounts a potent counterclaim *because* it performs excessive female sexuality and iconography in defiance of residual, Victorian definitions of (white, bourgeois) femininity. Images like those in *Bad Attitude* may disturb, dismay, or disgust viewers. I am not always comfortable with descriptions of sexual acts in lesbian-made porn, and I recognize that sexually explicit words and pictures are not uniformly liberatory. It is important and necessary to challenge sexist and racist portrayals of women in all pornographic disourse. At the same time, I predict that unless collective, loud-mouthed support is secured for alternative sexual discourses such as lesbian s/m fantasy, 'we-deviants' can anticipate successive rulings whereby legislators decide for us what is 'degrading,' 'dehumanzing,' and 'obscene.' The libidinal scope of Canadian lesbian cultural workers sketched above is proof of their high-amped assault on the moral certitudes of the status quo. This work alone will never hobble obscenity law, but it does help to seed a context from which to better explain and critically defend radical sexual pluralism in the future (Weeks 1991).

In 1997, as in the late nineteenth century, sexuality remains a site of contested meanings. Today, more and more feminists want space and language to describe sexual techniques, etiquette, fantasy, and vocabulary from the pivotal standpoint of female sexual subjectivity. It is possible that these new spaces may afford women different ways of configuring their own sexual identities and practices (see Smith 1995, 202). As such, repressive legal discourse that squeezes off conversations and blots out depictions seems patently premature (Tisdale 1994, Strossen 1995). The foregrounding of sexual and moral peril in an already erotophobic climate serves to reinforce, even heighten, feelings of sex-related pessimism and shame. Cindy Patton defines erotophobia as:

'The terrifying, irrational reaction to the erotic which makes individuals in society vulnerable to the psychological control of cultures where pleasure is strictly categorized and regulated' (Patton 1986, 103). My view is that rather than classify s/m fantasy and other non-conformist sexual tastes morally bad and dirty, hence punishable by law, we need to decriminalize depictions of consensual sex across a range of desires and discourses.

Knowledge of lesbian s/m image-making expands and positively deepens the range of female sexual possibilities across the spectrum of sexual preferences. At the same time, African American theorist Jackie Goldsby has pointed out that white narratives, icons, and ideologies have prevailed in the field of lesbian and gay sexual representation (Goldsby 1990, 15). However, increasing numbers of lesbians and gay men of colour, including Isaac Julien, Kobena Mercer, Donna Barker, karen augustine, Laverne Monette, and Dionne Brand are entering the scene as producers and critics of s/m imagery, and of sexually explicit materials in general.[26] Many have located their criticisms of s/m imagery (especially bondage, whipping, body marking) in specific histories of African American, Caribbean Canadian, black British, and Jewish persecution. Still, as the writings of Tina Portillo (1991), Donna Barker (1988), and Kobena Mercer (1991, 1992), and the films of Isaac Julien and Richard Fung attest, there is no agreement about what s/m means, how the signs might be used, and whether or not they are recoverable from racist and sexist trappings. Nor is there uniform support among producers and critics of colour for state sexual censorship as a solution.

Concluding Thoughts

Religious and medical prohibitions against homosexuality combined with state criminalization of homosexual practices (including consensual activities) in Canada until 1969 have made it difficult for gay men, lesbians, and bisexuals to openly experiment with, and to celebrate, their sexual difference.[27] Today, the age-old equation of homosexuality with sin, sickness, and/or criminality continues to drive many queers to secrecy and shame. Morally conservative discourse on obscenity in Canada continues to be vengefully formulated through coalitions of anti-porn feminists and neo-conservatives: the Coalition for Family Values, members of the Reform Party, Canadians for Decency, Citizens United for Responsible Education (CURE), REAL women, and the Conference of Catholic Bishops, among others.[28] Over fifty years ago, during the

Third Reich in Germany, lesbians, single mothers, and prostitutes were gassed as 'anti-social women' alongside Jewish peoples in Nazi death chambers. Decades later, in the 1990s, lesbian makers and readers of s/m fantasy have been reclassified in law as criminals *predisposed to anti-social behaviour*. To communities of lesbians shaped by the historical legacy of persecution and invisibility, the remaking of the 'lesbian pervert' in obscenity rulings is an all-too-familiar twist of the knife.

In order to fight repressive state, medical, and religious discourses and practices, lesbians, gays, bisexuals, and friends need to pursue alliances with all communities who have experienced histories of intimidation – for example, coalitions amongst Black, Asian, and First Nation communities and communities of sex-trade workers, the disabled, and AIDS activists. Ambitiously, we need to persuade queers and queer-positive supporters that state sexual regulation has an impact on all of our sexualities, not just on those of perverts. Scapegoating the 'deviants,' turning around to leave them holding the sexuality bag, marks a selfish, short-sighted betrayal. Moreover, I believe that we stand to benefit collectively from combining protests against state sexual censorship with organized action against the dismantlement of the Canadian welfare state, racist immigration policies, intensified regulation of sex-trade workers, and the coordinated reassertion of 'family values.'

Even though most s/m porn represents heterosexual women dominating and disciplining men (McClintock 1993, 211), disciplinary modes of state control such as sexual censorship laws instruct the systematic harassment of producers and consumers of queer images; hundreds of thousands of taxpayers' dollars are dedicated to processes of containment and normalization. In her 1993 case study of three lesbian and gay bookstores in Canada – L'androgyne in Montreal, Glad Day Bookshop in Toronto, and Little Sister's in Vancouver – Catherine Jones concluded that the personal costs of being subjected to, and demoralized by, death threats, fire bombs, and the scrutiny of police and customs officials are immeasurable.[29] In January 1996, Justice Kenneth Smith of the BC Supreme Court ruled that Canada Customs officials contravened the Charter of Rights and Freedoms in their regulation of lesbian and gay materials, but he did not declare sections of the *Customs Act* unconstitutional, which may mean business/censorship as usual.[30] Bookstore workers and anti-censorship activists suspect that Project P (the joint Metro Toronto Police and Ontario Provincial Police anti-porn squad) is primed to raid Glad Day Bookshop in Toronto again, this time for trafficking material that openly condones cross-generational sex – the newsletter of the North American Man/Boy Love Association NAMBLA. Admittedly, perceptions of NAMBLA among lesbians and gay men are extremely mixed. For example, the NAMBLA organization was banned from the 1994 Stonewall Anniversary parade in New York City, and welcomed in the counter-parade of sex radicals and AIDS activists. Whether Project P raids Glad Day for stocking the NAMBLA bulletin or not, full-fledged moral panics over youth sexuality have raged over the past two years.

In general terms, I feel strongly about increased access to materials that foreground the plurality of perverted and inverted desires. I want pornographies or eroticas that figure multi-sexual, multi-abled, multi-racial, and generationally mixed bodies, all wet and sticky. Perhaps more than anything, I would like to hear a lot more talk about what people like sexually and what they/we might want to find on fields of representation. In particular, I look forward to stepped-up sexual commentary from lesbians, gays, and bisexuals of colour. It behoves lesbian and feminist academics such as Didi Herman who have made public their concern about devoting so much time to 'this tired [sex] debate' when 'there are far more important things to worry about in the world,' to reconsider their own investments in the legal sanctioning of hetero-normativity (Herman 1994, 25). I argue that as long as the state/moral regulation of lesbian sexual materials persists, there will be a need for action on multiple fronts, including the fight for expanded access to the production and dissemination of alternative sexual discourses. In this case, I hardly consider battles for access to resources a luxury, indulgent pastime, or 'fetishism' (ibid., 24).

More than eighty years after Dr Howard Kelly's equation of 'good women' with sexual ignorance, we have only had a peek at what a lesbian, bisexual, or straight feminist sexual imagination might hold, or in what terms it might be conveyed. Today it perturbs me to think that sex-positive sparks such as *Bad Attitude* magazine may be extinguished before their chance to ignite into flame. In this chapter I have shown how and why the defence team headed up by lawyer Clare Barclay failed to save *Bad Attitude* from the trap of feminist-informed obscenity law designed to 'protect women from harm' and legislate 'women's equality.' In the Ontario Court, *Butler* was deployed by the Crown, and by Judge Paris, to adjudicate contesting epistemologies: a troublingly conservative, moralistic, and sex-negative feminism won the day in February 1993. In *R. v. Scythes*, lesbians who fantasize and practise s/m are scapegoated as the monsters from whom (all) women need and deserve protection. Indeed, we may conclude that these 'bad' lesbians – like the 'congenital inverts,' 'sex variants,' and 'bulldaggers' who preceeded them – are not women, and as such, their equality before the law need not be promoted or protected. *R. v. Scythes* confirms that s/m lesbians have become super-markers of female deviance and pathology, split off from 'good' women (and even 'good' lesbians) who uphold the sanctity of long-term, monogamous, loving relationships and nuclear families. Upon extending the logic of this binary stance, we find that those of us who defend *Bad Attitude* and publications like it can only appear as unintelligible, anti-feminist heretics. Moreover, under this regime, our challenges to the defective social-science data that structure Canadian obscenity law amount to nothing more than non-scientific prattle.

In the end, to the extent that lesbian s/m discourse impinges uncomfortably on what the unqueer centre postulates as 'normal' and 'natural,' it will continue to be prohibited as surely as its prohibition is eroticized in the service of (illicit) fantasy. Ironically, it is the very limits of bourgeois morality and gendered propriety that fantasy, lesbian s/m fantasy in particular, loves to manipulate and disrupt. I submit that the scope of the feminine sexual imaginary is all the more rich because of it.

Notwithstanding Diana Fuss's homo rereading of mainstream women's magazines, I for one refuse to be content with sucking 'lesbian content' out of *Elle, Vogue, Cosmopolitan,* and *Mirabella* or, for that matter, *Hustler, Penthouse,* and *Forum* (Fuss 1992, 713–37). I don't want to squirrel away my illegal desires until it is safe to do otherwise. Instead, I intend to continue pushing for lesbian criminality in all of its glorious manifestations, both real and imagined.

NOTES

* This summary statement was made by Crown Attorney Charles Granek as part of his final argument in the *R v. Scythes* obscenity trial, 18 December 1992.
1 Patricia McVicar, in Ontario Provincial Police report of the charges under the Canadian Criminal Code (R.S.C. 1985) for possession (s.163(2a)) and sale (s.163(2a)) of obscene material, in *R. v. Scythes* (16 February 1993), Toronto (Ont. Ct. Prov. Div.) [unreported], 5–6. McVicar was not responding to a complaint about either the bookstore or *Bad Attitude*.
2 On campaigns against venereal disease, see Cassel 1988. On the homo-purges

of the 1950s, see Kinsman 1995 and Kimmel and Robinson 1994. On crime comics and romance literature in the 1950s, see Adams 1994.

3 In his final 'Summation,' Crown Attorney, Charles Granek said this about my testimony: 'I think it's important to recognize the bias that [Dr Ross] has in terms of these issues and I merely cite to Your Honour in my cross-examination the comments that she was making about her views of censorship, how there ought to be a rather liberal opening up to some pretty serious types of articles that I was questioning her about' (Granek 1992b, 43)

4 Carole Vance is cited as identifying s/m as the epicentre of harm in feminist anti-porn politics in Fuller and Blackley 1995, 58.

5 Here I'm adapting the provocative insights of Judith Butler, worked up in her essay 'Critically Queer' (1993), 20–2.

6 I am not suggesting here that lesbian s/m is only a set of campy, theatrical tastes or aesthetics. It clearly involves much more than stylish codes, though the codes themselves are integral to the shaping of s/m identities and practices.

7 In her article 'Here, Clitty, Clitty' (1995), Marie Caloz tackles the trend in lesbian consumption of gay-male video pornography. She writes: 'It might seem a trifle odd that the pussy-down set would go hard for nine-inch males dicking it out. But it makes sense. Off-the-rack lezzie smut comes in two varieties – and little of it has to do with the real thing. Either you get islands of silicon implant bobbing in a sea of coiffed peroxide blonds, spreading it for the straight guy who can hardly believe his luck, or it's the kind of porn dykes tend to put out for themselves: an epic lifetime of foreplay riding on a tide of meaningful Bergmanesque glances and Hallmark card sentiment. When you finally get to the main event, the credits roll. The wet factor rating is definitely sub-Saharan' (p. 49).

8 For a provocative recasting of femme sexuality through analysis of what it means to 'get fucked,' see Cvetkovich 1995.

9 Pat Califia has recently drawn attention to the fact that tops need to be more aggressive about asking for what they want and stop acting like a 'bunch of codependents held hostage by rapacious bottoms.' See Califia 1992. Also on the dynamics of s/m, see contributions to John Preston's edited collection, *Leatherfolk* 1991). I want to thank Tim Timberg for pointing out that in much feminist and legal discourse, the bottom in s/m porn is seen as equivalent to the essentialized woman/victim in heterosexual porn. However, if bottoms/women are empowered and consent to sexual play, there is no degradation and humiliation – a very frightening concept for institutionalized heterosexism.

10 For an early discussion of this topic, see Valverde and Weir 1985.

11 Only after I wrote this section did I discover that 'Jessie' was Califia's first published piece of pornographic fiction. In *Restricted Entry: Censorship on Trial* (1995), this is how she talks about it: 'That story was a breakthrough for me as a writer. I was able to complete it. I was eventually able to share it with others and it became more than a work of fiction. It became an organizing tool. It became a way to signal to other women who might be interested in the sexual practices that there was someone else ... who was available to discuss those things with them. And it gave other women permission, whether they were writers or not, to start to think about and make that sexuality more public' (p. 59).

12 Several months before the trial, my partner and I had a little spat about why I had 'wasted my money' purchasing Madonna's *Sex*. Little did I know that I'd later be using it as sure-fire evidence of changing community standards about pornography in an Ontario court.

13 In the appendix to their volume, *Restricted Entry: Censorship on Trial*, Janine Fuller and Stuart Blackley include a detailed description of Memorandum D9-1-1.

14 In her MA thesis, Kirstie Lang analyses the debates surrounding the controversy generated by the exhibition of Robert Mapplethorpe's retrospective, 'The Perfect Moment' in the United States in 1989–90. See Lang 1995.

15 For analysis of the obsessive figuring of lesbian bodies in sexological photography in the 1930s, see O'Brien 1994.

16 For more detailed discussion of the dynamics of heterosexual s/m, in particular, the role of women as dominatrices in commercial s/m, see McClintock 1993, 211.

17 In a disturbing, MacKinnon-esque research paper on gay male pornography, Canadian Christoper Kendall makes the argument that 'harms-based research' on the 'effects of heterosexual pornography ... [offers] findings that are equally applicable within the context of gay male pornography' (Kendall 1993, 38). Kendall references Malamuth's testimony in *R. v. Scythes* as a way of buttressing his own conclusions that gay male porn promotes 'shared degradation,' 'contributes to the real abuse of real people,' and 'normalizes male sexual aggression' (p. 58).

18 It is important to note that *R. v. Butler* states that the audience to which sexually explicit material is addressed is not relevant to the determination of community standards (1992, 477–8).

19 By contrast, the courtroom at the British Columbia Provincial Court (Vancouver) during the Little Sister's bookstore's month-long challenge to Canada Customs censorship was routinely packed. This reflects the bookstore's almost ten-year battle to defend lesbian and gay literature from 'prior

restraint' and destruction at the Canada/U.S. border; it reflects the case's high profile in national and international media; it reflects the 'celebrity roster' of literary stars who testified for the bookstore (such as Jane Rule, Pat Califia, Nino Ricci, Pierre Berton); and it reflects the high level of queer and queer-positive community involvement – emotional, political, and financial – in the case itself.

20 For some of the key, recently published texts that address questions of sex, pornography, and censorship, see Gibson and Gibson, eds 1993, Smith 1993, Assiter and Avedon, eds 1993, Kiss & Tell, eds 1994, Goldsby 1993, augustine 1994, Segal and McIntosh, eds 1992, Gwendolyn et al. 1994, L. Williams 1990, McCormack 1993b, Butler 1990, B. Brown 1993, Lacombe 1994, and Adelman 1994.

Very little critical writing has been published on lesbian sexual images and texts, particularly s/m. Exceptions include Creet 1991a and Henderson 1992.

21 Here, I use the terms surprising and sex-negative because Herman's stance on s/m porn and practice seems internally inconsistent with her on-going, trenchant exploration of lesbian and gay identities, communities, and legal battles for freedom from discrimination. There is clearly something about s/m and the way it touches hot buttons that warrants further inquiry. See Herman's thoughtful analysis of the Christian Right's anti-homosexual discourse: '"Then I Saw a New Heaven and a New Earth": Thoughts on the Christian Right and the Problem of "Backlash,"' forthcoming in Leslie Roman and Linda Eyre, eds, *Dangerous Testimonies: Struggles for Equality and Difference in Education* (New York: Routledge).

22 My thanks to Leslie Roman for helping me think through the implications of treating s/m porn as equivalent to lived genocide.

23 On the surface, it seems surprising that Ann Scales testified on behalf of Little Sister's bookstore in their case against Canada Customs in October 1994. Joe Arvay, counsel for the bookstore, felt that Scales would be a useful witness, given her well-known heralding of *R. v. Butler* as a feminist victory. Indeed, in part because Scales was conveniently disqualified on the stand from commenting on the links between pornography and harm to women, Arvay was successful in artfully managing her articulation of pro-lesbian/gay, anti-censorship statements.

24 Susan Cole told me after the panel at Harbourfront that she now considered herself to be anti-censorship given her recent foray into writing and staging a play, 'Fertile Imagination.' That she made this comment in private and retained her public, pro-censorship stance is both perplexing and unsettling.

25 On recent trends in lesbian and feminist sex-related art practice, including the work of Canadians G.B. Jones and Kiss & Tell, see Adelman 1995.

26 On issues of race, racism, and pornography, see Goldsby 1993, Mercer 1992 and 1991, augustine 1994, Fung 1991 and 1993, Barker 1988, and Portillo 1991. Ever-irreverent, British black gay filmmaker Isaac Julien has made a short film, *The Attendant* (1993), that deliberately complicates debates about race/racism and s/m representation. He has also written about his film in 'Confessions of a Snow Queen' (1993).

27 For a more detailed examination of state and religious discourses on homosexuality see Kinsman 1996.

28 On CURE's Sue Careless's trip to Ottawa to drum up support for their anti-homosexual campaign, see Oldham 1993. For more on CURE, see Pegis 1993. In part, CURE has focused energy on protesting the Toronto Board of Education's new set of curriculum guidelines, a resource manual designed to combat homophobia and heterosexism. For one teacher's positive response to the Board's resource guide, see Ricker-Wilson 1993. The Toronto Board's curriculum guide is in direct contrast to Saskatchewan's Teen-Aid program designed by the province's Pro-Life Association and taught yearly to more than 20,000 students in 203 primary and secondary schools. The program extols chastity/abstinence, the sanctity of marriage, and negative views on homosexuality. See Mitchell 1993.

29 See Jones 1993. Also, see Brown 1993a, and Hough 1994. And for more on Canada Customs, see Johnston 1993 and Gillmor 1993. On the Little Sister's court challenge to Canada Customs, see Leiren-Young 1994, Dafoe 1994, and Fuller and Blackley 1995.

30 On the ruling in the Little Sister's bookstore challenge to practices of prior restraint by Canada Customs officials, see Cernetig 1996 and Rupp 1996.

5

On ne peut pas voir l'image
[The image cannot be seen]

SHANNON BELL

The virtuous: how they crave to be hangmen Let the Dead Bury the Living Criminals put on judges robes at night and slip out of their cells to commit murder in the name of justice. (Kroker and Weinstein 1994, 110)

When truth-telling is important, I write autofiction. Through a glory whole to eternity: Should I go to jail for sucking a fifteen and three quarter year old's cock and giving her money? Am I already in jail in the shared fate of the men rounded up in the most recent of recurrent sexual/moral panics? Have all the great concerns of humanity – truth, beauty, equality, eros – been reduced to the age of a sphincter muscle? 'The description and activities are degrading and without any human dimension. The dominant characteristic is the undue exploitation of sex. I find it to be obscene,' said the judge (*Glad Day Bookshop* 1992, 19). What I saw in *Advocate Men* was a bunch of guys posing, strutting, dicking around; I find it to be a campy powerful perversion of heteroliberal values; yeh, some men like to take it up the ass, some girls like to give it up the ass. The picture, said the judge, has 'no real human dimension,' no 'real human relationship' (ibid., 18, 16); but wait, I saw an interconnection of other with other, I saw chinese food after the shoot, I saw perrier, cigarettes off camera and buddies standing around watching and supporting. 'Pictures don't lie. Pictures tell it all,' said the London Chief of Police (CBC 1994, 12). They may speak but what do they say?

'Dad, how come the photographs are always black and white [heterosexual and over eighteen]? Didn't they have color film [and fags and dykes and fifteen-and-three-quarter-year-old persons] back then? Sure they did. In fact, those old photographs are in color. It is just the world was black and white then. Really? Yep. The world didn't turn color until sometime in the 1930's, and it was pretty grainy color for a while, too. That's really weird. Well, **Truth is stranger than fiction**. But then why are old paintings in color?! If the world was black and white, wouldn't artists have painted it that way? Not necessarily, a lot of great artists were insane. But ... But how could they have painted in color anyway? Wouldn't their paints have been shades of gray back then? Of course, but they turned colors like everything else did in the '30s. So why didn't old black and white photos turn color too? Because they were color pictures of black and white, remember? **The world is a complicated place**.[1] Whenever it seems that way, I do a porn shoot, and I write philosophy, I do both/and. I am ensouled body and I am embodied soul. Through a glory [w]hole to eternity.

Porn/Philosophy are living: the aesthetics of existence. And Kant, the great heteroliberal modern philosopher of morals can be used to theorize the pornographic. **Truth is stranger than fiction**.

How many philosophical systems, legal critiques, and political theories do you need to resolve that the depiction of bondage scenes, flagellation, three or more persons ass-fucking, a 39-thirty-year-old woman holding a teddy-bear and playing with her clit are okay, perhaps a bit boring, but okay. And even if not okay in some way, to some people, not necessarily criminal. The Answer: None.

Ethics/Morality/Politics: Categories in Crises, People in Prison

Truth is everywhere. There is merit and importance in Catharine MacKinnon's critique of pornography: it is important to recognize that some women and some men can feel degraded and dehumanized by depictions of people 'enjoying humiliation,' 'tied up,' gagged, whipped, whipping, 'reduced to body parts,' 'presented in scenarios of degradation, injury,' 'penetrated by objects or animals' (MacKinnon 1993, 121–2, n.32). Other women and men see S/M parody. Yet if I have been tied up and beaten against my will, without my consent, or if I connect these parodic images to the rape and slaughter of Bosnian women,[2] then they are harmful. If another viewer having had dungeon experience sees the depictions as taking place in a controlled environment where fears, fantasies, and desires are played out, it is therapy. 'The pictures tell it all.' MacKinnon is not simply the straw woman to be defeated in every anti-censorship/pro-porn writing. Students in my Women's Studies course, 'Pornography: A Post-modern Feminist Look,' said that although they might agree with the actual positions of the anti-censorship feminists presented in such collected works as *Sex Exposed* and *Dirty Looks*, they were tired of reading their cleverly constructed miscritiques of radical feminist positions on pornography. Women are harmed in pornography, and women grow making it (Bell 1994, 1995).[3] Seeing one sex as horny and available when you go to the corner store could be taken to reflect the gender inequality in society. Or maybe it could show what Camille Paglia sees: 'the sexual power women wield over men' (Paglia 1992, 66). Maybe it could be both/and.

The problem with MacKinnon, and with the Women's Legal Education and Action Fund who so strongly support *Butler*, is that their standpoint is presented as the **Truth** about porn, the one Truth to be enforced by Law. For MacKinnon and other key anti-pornography theorists, pornography is 'sexual reality' (MacKinnon 1987, 149); pornography 'is not imagery ... it is not a distortion, reflection, projection, expression, fantasy, representation, or symbol' (ibid., 149). MacKinnon positions this construction of pornography as 'the feminist view' (ibid., 148) and the feminist view *à la* MacKinnon is that pornography 'is a form of forced sex ... an institution of gender inequality' (ibid.). MacKinnon's position is one of certainty: this is what pornography is, this is what it does; women who disagree or partially agree are either collaborators or suffering false consciousness.[4] Vying for dominance with the anti-pornography radical-feminist position is a postmodern feminist position that sees pornography not as a singular reality but as a discourse of sexual representation composed of many different genres[5] that are open to many readings and thus many truths. Multiple meanings reside in the same image/text; '**ALL TRUTH IS CROOKED**' (Nietzsche 1977, 251).

Between pro-*Butler* (pro-censorship/anti-pornography) and anti-*Butler* (anti-censorship/pro-pornography) are competing ethical positions. When one comes across such a contested concept as pornography, it has to be located on a larger and greater contested terrain: ethics. The pornography debate is contingent on how we see truth, justice, and ethics. This essay (ab)uses philosophy to embrace pornography on the terrain of ethics. A word of warning: abusing philosophy is most useful in conjunction with the actual making of porn and engaging in porn resistance, thus the final section of this paper – 'Sexual Parrhesia: A "Truth" to Pornography?' – which consists of two pornosophy texts: 'Making pornography' and 'On ne peut pas voir l'image.'

The *Butler* Decision: An Aside

Two things happen with *Butler*: (1) the emphasis shifts from obscenity (sexually explicit) to abnormality (perversion);[6] (2) the intent of the law slips from punishment of those who offend decency to protection of populations. The *Butler* decision is an equality ruling that protects vulnerable populations from the harm of the obscene. *Butler* is the context in which the new so-called Child Porn Law is situated (see introduction); so-called because it brazenly classifies adolescents and young adults as 'children.'

(Ab)using Philosophy

Marjorie Garber uses the concept 'category crisis' as a way of 'disrupting and calling attention to cultural, social, or aesthetic dissonances' (Garber 1993, 16). While Garber is specifically applying the concept to the position of the transgendered person, the concept and the manner in which she deploys it is applicable to pornography and youth sexuality, for both pornography and youth sexuality produce and are produced as category crisis. Garber defines category crisis as 'a failure of definitional distinction, a borderline that becomes permeable, that permits of border crossings from one (apparently distinct) category to another' (ibid., 16). Like transvestism and transsexuality, which Garber positions as the 'third sex,' pornography and youth sexuality 'challenge the easy notions of binarity' (ibid., 10): in the case of the third sex, it is the binarism of gender that is challenged; for pornography it is the binarisms of pornography/art, pornography/erotica, pornography/philosophy; for youth sexuality it is the binarism of youth/child, youth/adult. The slash – '/' – of the binary division is a sliding space of ambiguity, a space that constantly shifts and changes, a space of play/philosophy/punishment: the space of both/and. The majority of sexual depictions are somewhere in-between pornography and art, are both pornography and art, both pornography and erotica, both pornography and philosophy; most of the boys charged with making youth porn are somewhere in-between youths and children, are somewhere in-between youth and adulthood. Sex with persons fourteen and over is legal providing the adult is neither in a position of authority or paying (with money or in some other manner); taking or possessing pictures of persons under eighteen or posing as under eighteen is illegal. In the spectacle of the London 'Porn Ring' the distinctions between youth and child completely collapsed

(CBC 1994, 42); 'seventeen year olds at the height of their sexual powers are called children' (ibid., 38).

What lurks in this space of ambiguity, where the 'crisis of category' (Garber 1993, 17) – pornographic/aesthetic, pedophilic/ordinary lovers – resides and resonates, is the structuring binary division of ethics and morality. Traditionally, the link between pornography and philosophy has been morality. The Law is based on a Kantian concept of morality, but life must be lived in accordance with a Foucauldian concept of ethics. Morality, according to Kant and neo-Kantian liberals, is a code or universal rule of behaviour that enforces and is enforced by the Law. This code is premised on a transcendent moral principle: the capacity of the human mind to form categorical imperatives. Kant gives two structuring imperatives: 'Act only on the maxim whereby thou canst at the same time will that it should become a universal law' and 'Act to treat humanity whether in thine own person or that of any other, in every case an end withal, never as a means only' (Kant 1927, 46–7). Kant posits a moral subject who because she is rational acts according to these two transcendent principles. Kantian morality is located in rational obedience to a universal rule of behaviour cum universal law. How does the subject know the moral principles and the derivative *rules*? They are given as the subject is given; this is the dominant Kant, the Kant of modernism, the Kant of the *First Critique of Judgement*: rules, established criteria, determinate judgments. There is no way out (except in art, perhaps). Behind Kant stands Augustine and way over on the left/right beside him lies Sade; but it is Saint Augustine all the way down/up. 'Lodged in the subterranean levels of liberalism' (Connolly 1993, xii), there is what William Connolly identifies as 'the Augustinian Imperative,' an intrinsic moral order that can be authoritatively represented in human law. There are two models or themes of morality in the Augustinian script: morality as obedience to a transcendental command from a God or a Law of Nature and morality as conforming to an intrinsic design or structure of things (ibid., 33–7). Clearly, Kantian morality corresponds to the first script. The manifest content of morality is historical. Grand concepts like 'categorical imperative' are brought down into a specific moral economy so that they can be operationalized; the myth is that it is the concept which structures specific practices of praise and blame, reward and punishment. 'A moral economy constitutes a set of equivalences between thought, words, action, freedom, responsibility, desert, and punishment' (ibid., 132).

A depiction of a woman, arms in wrist cuffs tied over her head, ankles bound to the base of a ladder, having her pussy whipped by a second woman is 'degrading and dehumanizing' (*Butler* 1992, 479). It places woman, as a category, in 'subordination, servile submission or humiliation' (ibid.). The image goes 'against the principles of equality and dignity of all human beings' (ibid.). The image is 'harmful to society, particularly to women' (ibid.). Never mind that the activity depicted is consensual: 'sometimes the very appearance of consent makes the depicted acts even more degrading or dehumanizing' (ibid.). Never mind that the image was derived through a discussion among the two women in the scene and the female photographer. Persons making the scene, persons selling the scene must be punished. A depiction of a woman, arms in wrist cuffs tied over her head, ankles bound to the base of a ladder, having her pussy whipped by a female youth or young woman (or older woman posing as) under eighteen years of age is 'child pornography.' Persons making the image 'are guilty of an indictable offence and liable to imprisonment for a term not exceeding ten years' (s.163.1 C.C.C.); persons selling the images are 'guilty of an indictable offence and liable to imprisonment for a term not exceeding ten years'; (ibid.); persons buying the image are 'guilty of an indictable offence and liable to imprisonment for a term not exceeding five years' (ibid.). And, however they may describe their experience, the persons making the image are taken as simply unaware of the harm they are causing, or suffering, or both. Do you think that the image will pass the 'internal necessities test' [the artistic defence]? *Naw. Tilt your head up, let the light flow onto your face. That's it, that's it. Always shoot in black and white. Look young, look real young, grab a teddy. Let's give it all the codes as an homage to obscene camp: yes, the bathroom tile, you tied to the pipes, me dripping hot wax on your breasts, shoot my shadow, play with the light, champagne for pouring, a whip for texture, place the teddy and possum as onlookers. We got it baby.*

The Augustinian imperative presupposes what Kant's categorical imperative presupposes: that is, for everything 'bad' that happens there is a responsible moral agent who must be blamed and punished. Without punishment there is no order; and order is at the centre of the two Augustinian scripts.

Friedrich Nietzsche and Michel Foucault, reclining alongside Sade, notice an 'arbitrary cruelty ... installed in those moral economies that take themselves to embody the will of god, a Law of laws, an Intrinsic purpose in Being, or a fictive Contract [the Rawlsian original position]' (Connolly 1993, 132). 'One knows my demand of [pornographers][7] that they place themselves beyond good and evil – that they have the illusion of moral judgement beneath them. This demand follows from an insight first formulated by me: that there are no moral facts whatever. Moral judgement has this in common with religious judgement, that it believes in realities which do not exist' (Nietzsche 1977, 119). But wait, even if '[t]here are no moral phenomena at all' (ibid., 104) and 'all truth is crooked,' (ibid., 251), there is **just** gaming,[8] there is an ethical interpretation of phenomena. Morality decomposes into ethics, where Michel Foucault and William Connolly argue it has to lie: 'Morality is too crude, ruthless, and blind to do the job we pretend it accomplishes. It covers up its own ineptitude in the interest of accomplishing ... [its] social task ... Morality, then, is in tendency immoral' (Connolly 1993, 135).

All truth is crooked. What occurs, and what perhaps has always occurred, in any moral economy is the moralization of self and demoralization of the other. Identity/difference: identity acquires definition when what is different from it is set out there on its outside, when it takes on desir-able attributes that are distinguishable from the other's undesirable attributes. The modern homosexual, the modern prostitute, were mapped and encoded in law around the same time and by some of the same laws during the latter half of the nineteenth century (Weeks 1991b; Bell 1994). It was this codification of the homosexual and the prostitute that constructed heterosexuality and female sexuality: the good woman (wife, mother, daughter) was defined in opposition to the whore. The characteristics of the good woman and of the noble heterosexual man have never been formulated in law. They just are what the whore and the queer are not. Today, the 'good' homosexual closest to the heterosexual norm of normal officially monogamous relationships, the homosexual who is in the home, is putting as much distance between himself and the homosexual who pays sixteen or seventeen year olds for sex, who buys a safe-sex video produced and enacted by three young guys (two fourteen year olds and a twenty-two year old); at the very least, the home-osexual just lets the equation that depictions of sexuality between youths and an adult equal obscenity and exploitation go unchallenged. 'We are just like you, we are queer taxpayers, we are concerned about the same social-sexual problems as you are, we want them imprisoned and/or "rehabilitated," just as you do.' It Kant be otherwise. Identity/difference is duplicated inside the category homosexual to produce an internal dichotomy: virtuous homosexual/pervert.

Definitions of the self depend on the projection of unwanted parts of the self onto an other who then has to be controlled, blamed, and punished in order to hold the integrity of the self. A number of recent publications appeal to the lesbian and gay movement to repudiate its abnormal extremes and line up with the normal majority as the inevitable and legitimate price of full acceptance into American society.[9] President Clinton, in response to Newt Gingrich's accusation that he was a 'counterculture McGovernik,' said, 'I am a middle-aged man who's worked very hard in his life to be a mainstream American, and I think I've done a reasonable job of it' (Willis 1994). Canadians try, perhaps even harder, to be mainstream Americans: the *Butler* decision was a rewrite and redirection of the Minneapolis Ordinance, which connected the concepts of harm, coercion, degradation, and dehumanization with obscenity. What got turned down in civil law in the States sprang up in Canada as criminal law. Women's equality and power will be achieved at the expense of bad women or women suffering false consciousness; women's equality and dignity will be achieved at the price of not listening to women who insist upon not realizing how victimized we are. All truth is crooked.

The *Butler* decision and the so-called Child Porn Law[10] are the manifest content of a moral economy in which the structuring principle is identity/difference, moral self/immoral other, its imaginary core is an intrinsic moral order in which everything undesirable must be identified as abuse and harm, which can and must be prevented by law.

What is harm? S/M porn, inter-generational sex, youth sexuality, prostitution? Harm is the closing of communication: the Canadian law against 'communicating.' We have a 'debate,' a brief, stifled debate; the loser is criminalized and goes to jail. 'Every truth is an established truth, the truth of a certain institution or institutional complex' (Connolly 1993, 136). 'Every discourse among interlocutors is a struggle against outsiders, those who emit interference and equivocation, who have an interest in that the communication does not take place. But in the measure that communication does take place and that statements are established as true, it designates outsiders as not making sense, as mystified, mad, or brutish, and it delivers them over to violence' (Lingis 1994, 135). '[W]hat concerns us in another is precisely his or her otherness,' (ibid., x), what we go after is difference; attacking 'carrion bodies with carrion utterances.'[11] But not just any difference; it is sexual difference, sexual 'deviance' that opens to moral paranoia; moral paranoia closes communication and delivers discussion and deviants over to violence.

Moral paranoia is the energy force of what Stuart Hall, Jeffrey Weeks, and Gayle Rubin have theorized as moral panics (see introduction and Gotell in this volume). Moral panics seem to arise cyclically and in times of what Rubin identifies as 'unthinkable destruction' (Rubin 1984, 267). Arthur Kroker and Michael Weinstein characterize the dominant political system at the end of the millennium as liberal fascism, 'where capitalism and its homicidal double: fascism' (Kroker and Weinstein 1994, 63) are united. '[L]iberal fascism – the growth of fascism as a tumor under an exhausted skin of liberal rhetoric' (ibid., 90). Great Britain, the United States, and Canada have new crime legislation and Canada, the United States, and Great Britain have new sex-crime legislation. 'Through the bunker state liberal fascism excludes surplus bodies (immigration), through the austerity state it uses debt reduction and high unemployment to control labor and minimize social programs, and through the security state it submits bodies to testing and surveillance. *Under liberal fascist ideology everything done to victims is for their own good or is regrettable action that is necessarily performed for an obvious over-riding human(itarian) interest. The dominant mood of liberal fascism is cynical piety'* (ibid., 65; emphasis added).

'At times such as these, when we live with the possibility of unthinkable destruction ... people become dangerously crazy [paranoid] about sexuality' (Rubin 1984, 269). The disease of paranoia manifests as a 'panic-anxiety that one's selfhood could be destroyed' (Sagan 1991, 26) by an evil other. There is obsession with poisoning: pollution, purging the body politic of the elements that pollute it, the cleansing of those who corrupt society, control at all borders of who can enter, walk the streets, and leave. The psychological mode of action in paranoia is projection: 'the attribution to external figures of motivations, drives or other tensions that are repudiated and intolerable in oneself' (ibid., 19). The moral self, the immoral other.

Sex, morality, and paranoia coalesce in moral panics. Fears attach to some sexual activity or population; these fears are channelled into political action and social change. The standard targets are pornographic materials, prostitutes, and erotic deviants. The moral sex panic of the 1950s was anti-homosexual; the moral sex panic of the mid-1980s linked pornography, prostitution, and child sexual abuse.[12] The moral panic of the 1990s is recombinant: it focuses on pornographic materials (*Butler* and the so-called Child Porn Law) and targets erotic deviants: S/M practitioners, lesbians, gay men, prostitutes/hustlers under eighteen, hebephiles. The hysteria mounts the closer the sexual activity gets to or can be portrayed as getting to children. Perhaps that is why 'seventeen year olds at the height of their sexual powers are called children' (CBC 1994, 38) in the London porn panic. The media played up the hysteria with repeated references to the 'Child Porn Ring.' We heard that '[m]ore than 800 videotapes have now been seized in this child-pornography ring' (ibid., 43); only later and less flamboyantly to learn the tapes were 'mostly Hollywood movies, National Geographic Specials and programs taped off television' (ibid., 44). In fact, 'none of the 800 tapes has been charged. What has been charged in the haul ... is one eight-millimeter film, some albums of snapshots, and some gay magazines of the sort you can buy in any bookstore' (ibid.). The fact that the seized videotapes were not chargeable as child porn or any type of porn did not in the least affect their currency in the child-porn panic: the London chief of police gave a press conference surrounded by hundreds of seized tapes. 'Pictures don't lie. Pictures tell it all' (ibid., 12). This image of the chief of police surrounded by what was represented as child porn[13] got provincial funding for 'Operation Guardian,' the province-wide joint-forces child-pornography task force. 'The Child Porn Ring' became 'The Child Porn Network' as the budget of the Ontario Police Taskforce to crack down on child porn rose. The 'Child-Porn Probe Spreads.'[14]

What is the 'truth' of the Child Porn Panic in southern Ontario, primarily London? The facts become jumbled as to what precisely the men have been arrested for and charged with. The police/media story presents the criminal charges as being for crimes involving sex with 'children.' The court records, however, tell a different story:

Of the more than 400 charges laid against 52 men so far, only 40 are for 'sexual interference,' which involves incidents with boys below 14. There is one charge of making 'child' pornography; there are 20 charges of possession of child pornography.

The bulk of the other 90 percent of the charges (just under half) are for using the services of teenage prostitutes above the legal age of consent. Sex for money is legal in Canada, providing the prostitute is not under the age of 18. [It is legal to have] sex with someone between 14 and 18, but it becomes a crime if [the person 18 or over] gives the juvenile anything that can be construed as payment[.]

[Many of the men have been charged with anal sex with a person under 18.] At the time the [Child Porn Scare] was getting underway, it was illegal for persons under 18 to have anal intercourse. This stands in contrast to Canada's general age of consent of 14 for oral or vaginal sex ... The discrepancy was ... ruled unconstitutional in August 1993 by Canada's lower courts. [T]he London police would lay some 40 charges of anal intercourse subsequent to that ruling, claiming that they were entitled to do so because the government was appealing the decision.

In May 1995, some 19 months into the London investigation and after at least 14 men were charged under [the law against anal intercourse for persons under 18, s.159 of Canada's Criminal Code], the Ontario Court of Appeals upheld the decision declaring the law unconstitutional ...

The ruling rendered invalid all the anal intercourse charges laid by police. But the damage was done. Men had gone to jail and lives were ruined. [These men] will forever be seen as the men who had anal intercourse with 'little children' in the 'kiddie porn ring.' (Couture 1995, 16–17; Hannon 1995, D1, D5)

Andrew Sorfleet, Toronto sex-worker activist, documents how the media and the police collaborated to set in motion the child-pornography panic. 'On January 15, 1994 both the *Toronto Star* and the *Toronto Sun* ran stories announcing Matthew McGowan's arrest. The reports and headlines fed directly to the newspapers by the police, suggested that the arrest was the result of a seizure of videotapes (plural) which "included child porn ... violence, degradation, and dehumanizing acts," and "videos show[ing] explicit, degrading and sometimes violent sex acts involving young male victims ranging from prepubescence to their early teens"' (Sorfleet 1993–4). The newspapers lead the reader to think that Matthew is charged with making child pornography; towards the end of the *Toronto Star* article, one line establishes that Matthew is actually charged with two counts of making obscene material, a charge no doubt premised on Hayes's ruling that casual gay sexual encounters are 'degrading and without human dimension' (*Glad Day Bookshop* 1992, 18). It was only when I interviewed Matthew that I realized he was charged under *Butler*'s reinterpretation of obscenity law.

Sorfleet continues: 'Here are some facts. In May, last year, before the youth porn law was passed, McGowan, 22 at the time, and his 14-year-old boyfriend of many months, borrowed a video camera and made a video with another 14-year-old friend from the boy's stroll. They were above the age of consent. The tape shows the three youths playing sexually, with a lot of verbal negotiation and consent, including discussions about safe sex. It is obviously a home movie and in no way resembles any kind of commercial production' (Sorfleet 1993–4, 10). 'Police are using the law to arrest people who are the most vulnerable and least likely to be able to launch a defence or to have any support within the broader community,' Sorfleet maintains (ibid.). 'It is clearly a homophobic attack on gay street youth. This law is also being used to attack the gay community and stifle any discussion about sexuality' (ibid.). 'It is also now apparent that, because of selective prosecution ... a law that was designed to protect youth is now causing youth extreme harm' (ibid., 9). Harm is the ending of discussion, the closure of communication.

How do we open communication between the hangmen and the accused, between the virtuous and the criminalized, between communicating positions in which one side has the power of the law, the police, the media, the 'helping' professionals; the other, perhaps the power of their own lived ethics, perhaps nothing but a will for erotic/sexual integrity, perhaps nothing. What is needed is a shift from teleological morality in which practices are connected to transcendent and/or intrinsic purpose, such as a law or a categorical imperative, to a-teleological ethics, the shift of Foucault and Connolly. Fifteen or more years ago Michel Foucault noted that 'the idea of morality as obedience to a code of rules is now disappearing, has already disappeared. And to this absence of morality corresponds, must correspond, the search for an aesthetics of existence' (Foucault 1988, 49).

What Foucault didn't take fully into account is that remnants of the archaic code are, as Connolly contends, 'lodged in the subterranean levels of liberalism' (Connolly 1993, xvi) – morality as 'cynical piety' (Kroker and Weinstein 1994, 65). One of Foucault's main philosophical projects and practical aims was to pursue ethics 'understood as a style of comportment' (Flynn 1988, 114), the art of living and dying. At the time of his death Foucault talked about ethical *parrhesia* and the *parrhesiastic* contract. *Parrhesia* is truth-telling; the *parrhesiastic* contract, truth-telling in the presence of another, and true life *parrhesia* is an aesthetics of existence, 'a truth one does or lives rather than says' (ibid., 113). Ethics, for Foucault, is the underside of Western morality: ethics is 'a very strong structure of existence without any relation with the juridical per se, with an authoritarian system, with a disciplinary structure' (ibid., 115). Foucault is opening a space for a plurality of truths, styles of life, points of resistance (ibid., 112). He is countering the history of truth that imagines an unification of truths in a developmental totality: Truth (ibid.). The *parrhesiastic* contract is a contract between equals, at least for the duration of the truth-telling; it is not the therapeutic contract of normalization in which one party provides the framework of Truth for the other party into which they must fit their truth. The imputation of false consciousness is not part of the contract. The *parrhesiastic* contract is listening and hearing what we may not want to hear. '[L]istening to a child, hearing him speak, hearing him explain what his relations actually are with someone, adult or not, provided one listens with enough sympathy

... [T]o suppose that a child is incapable of explaining what happened and incapable of giving his consent are two abuses that are intolerable, quite unacceptable' (Foucault 1988, 284).

Contrast this with the 'ground-breaking interviewing techniques' used by the London police, social welfare personnel and psychologists, therapists – the 'professionals' – to get 'scared young victims to 'fess up and tell police what's been going on' (CBC 1994, 38). The ground-breaking interviewing techniques hinge on therapeutic statements such as 'I don't believe you had a choice in the matter.' The youth: 'I could have said no, if I had wanted to.' Police social worker: 'Yeah, but he's twenty-eight.' Youth: 'So?' Police social worker: 'And you're a kid of what? Fifteen? Sixteen? Seventeen? Don't you think it is weird for him to be having sex with a person of your age?' Youth: 'Mm-hm.' Police social worker: 'That's what I'm getting at ... he's used you for these acts ... Did you ever feel used by him?' Youth: 'Sometimes, I guess' (ibid., 39–40). As the research coordinator at the London Family Court Clinic explains: 'victim impact statements are written by clinicians who have a lot of experience in child victimization.' There is 'the victim's version of the story' and 'what we think it means' (ibid., 40). Truth as clinical interpretation. **All truth is crooked.** In John Greyson's video examination documenting the London porn panic, *After the Bath*, a London Children's Aid social worker says of the youth: 'Many of them did not see what had happened to them as abusive, they didn't picture the people, the adults involved as abusers. They felt that they had participated in activities where they got something for it. They felt they knew what they were doing' (Greyson 1995). Discounting the youths' own testimony, the social worker says: 'The big task is to identify that it was abusive' (ibid.). London youth talking to CBC journalist: 'They wanted me to say to the judge that I feel I was a victim' (CBC 1994, 18). 'They tell us we're victims, hurt by this, not thinking that we may not be that stupid' (ibid.).

Until the CBC series, the boys did not speak for themselves and the men were not interviewed. The rationale: 'Pictures don't lie, pictures tell it all.'[15] What do the pictures tell? The pictures tell the viewer that people under eighteen and over fourteen (except in one case, an eleven year old) suck cock and have anal intercourse, with each other and with people over eighteen, sometimes with more than one person at once. The truth of the pictures is filled in by the meaning they hold for the viewer. When I see the pictures I see teenage boys engaging in sex with each other and with men; when the London chief of police sees the pictures, he sees child abuse, he sees 'children used like pieces of meat' (CBC

1994). Is it because he has never sucked the cock of a fifteen year old, a seventy year old, is it because he has never had sex for the camera, sex with at least two others for fun and money? What if he had? Could s/he see different truths in the pictures by listening to the speech of those making the images? Foucault argues, like Lyotard (in fact, this is Lyotard's concept of justice), for case-by-case truth; Foucault is arguing for 'listening to' and 'trusting' the child's testimony; for recognizing that children are capable of subjecthood and of consent/non-consent. Foucault is speaking about listening to children, he does not specify an age; in London and Toronto the 'children' are fourteen to seventeen. In Canada it is legal for fourteen year olds to have sex. The age of consent is fourteen. However, not for anal sex until May 1995, when the Ontario Court of Appeal struck down section 159 of the Criminal Code, not if the person eighteen or over is in a position of trust or authority (s.153(1) C.C.C.), and not if money, gifts, food, or lodging is received from a person eighteen or over when sex has occurred (s.212(4) and s.150.1(5) C.C.C.). The eighteen year old can go to jail.

What happens in liberal fascism is that the debatable, the discussable, is made undebatable, is a univocal reflection of a moral economy of equivalence. In place of the moral economy, Foucault and Connolly propose 'ethical sensibility' premised on care of self and becoming, rather than knowing oneself and being. Care of oneself was a dominant moral principle in antiquity: it produced a self-governing, relational self: 'The precept "to be concerned with oneself" ... was one of the main principles of cities, one of the main rules for social and political conduct and for the art of life' (Foucault 1988b, 20). Care as the operative principle of an ethical sensibility translates as 'the care of what exists and might exist; ... a sharpened sense of reality; ... a readiness to find what surrounds us as strange and odd, ... a certain determination to throw off familiar ways of thought and to look at the same things in a different way; ... a lack of respect for the traditional hierarchies of what is important and fundamental' (Foucault 1988, 328). Listen: 'I sucked the cock of a fifteen year old boy, he bought me dinner and lent/gave me twenty bucks, he had money, I was broke, I was twenty-nine' [I, the author]. Listen: 'Yes, I went looking for sex ... it was all consensual ... I see something wrong with what I did because it seems to be socially unacceptable. That's the only reason ... it's kind of embarrassing ... I don't see myself as a victim – the men treated me with respect, they helped me out in trouble' (CBC 1994, 21) [I, the London hustler].

This 'lack of respect for the traditional hierarchies of what is important and fundamental' (Foucault 1988, 328) for William Connolly becomes a practice, a politics of 'agonistic respect.' Agonistic respect is 'a social relation of respect for the opponent against whom you define yourself, even while you resist its imperatives and strive to delimit its spaces of hegemony' (Connolly 1993, 155). Agonistic respect is not liberal tolerance (although in the current condition of liberal fascism liberal tolerance is appealing), where liberal tolerance lets the other be as an 'other' [liberal fascism rounds up the predictable suspects], agonistic respect is an active relation of interdependence and strife between identities. Identity and difference are contested. One 'identif[ies] traces in the other of the sensibility one identifies in oneself and locate[s] in the self elements of the sensibility attributed to the other' (ibid., 157). We share in one another's fate; it is the Rawlsian original position without closure. Agonistic respect 'folds contestation into the foundations of the identity from which liberal tolerance is derived and delimited' (ibid., 156). Connolly calls it a politics of critical pluralism. But why not put some care back into democracy and name it radical democracy; it is what some refer to as deep democracy. What it entails is the principle of care, manifest as the activity of listening, listening to all, all the way. Radical democracy is listening to all others and all parts of the self; not only 'legitimate' parts but also 'inappropriate' parts – criminals, pornographers, prostitutes, murderers, philosophers, S/M practitioners, schizophrenics, and on and on. The debate has no conclusion. How do we know if someone is harmed? We listen. 'On October 8th, 1993 it was announced that a 14-year-old [street youth] was being held in a psychiatric facility, because he had attempted suicide twice. The Crown stated that there was "a direct link between the boy's suicide attempts and his appearance in the homemade videos because of guilt and shame." But it was police investigations that made this home movie public, [Sorfleet 1993–4, 9] and the young man's private life public' (Sorfleet and Bearchell 1994, 10).

How do we judge harm? The same way we listen: case by case. 'Let us be just' (Lyotard and Thebaud 1985, 19). '[T]ruth is not ontological truth, it is ethical' (ibid., 60). And all truth is crooked.

Justice consists of resisting the insistence of certain language games or narratives to provide the rules for other language games, or narratives; that is, to become metalanguages or grand narratives; to be ontologized truths. Some fourteen year olds making a gay sex video perhaps are harmed, some perhaps are not: 'When they made the video all three boys were above the age of consent for sex, which is fourteen. They had

had sex with other boys many times before. They made the video of their own free will and for their own fun. They had safe sex only. And at the time they made the video the new child porn law did not ... exist' (SWAT 1993). Is the harm in the filming, in the sex acts themselves, or is it in how 'the standard' of the 'community' re-presents the acts: 'violent sex acts,' 'young male victims,' 'degrading'? (O'Neill 1994). McGowan presents a different picture: '[T]here is a lot of stuff happening on this video that if you didn't see the pictures and you only heard the sound track, you would think it is **just** people having a good time, laughing and talking. Max Allen played it on CBC radio' (McGowan 1994, interview). I 'would ... tolerate other Canadians being exposed to' (*Butler* 1992, 478) this video; in fact, if Canadians actually saw oral and anal intercourse between three young male friends – yes they could also be female – maybe many would not find it degrading and dehumanizing. Maybe many would see it as **Just** Sex. Is it that the public has been 'desensitized' (*Butler* 1992, 481) so that they are not able to see 'any real human relationship' (*Glad Day Bookshop* 1992, 25), and are trained to overlook 'the human dimensions'[16] in same-sex play that involves more than two people (ibid.)? What if one were to judge case by case?: 'if you didn't see the pictures and you only heard the sound track, you would think it is just people having a good time, laughing and talking' (McGowan 1994, interview).

A society is just if no one game dominates the other games and becomes a grand narrative. But, of course, there are many grand narratives or metalanguages: liberalism (liberty), democracy (equality), law (criteria, determinate judgements), heterosexuality (the privilege of defining yourself in relation to an opposite sexual other). One 'ought to be pagan'[17] (Lyotard and Thebaud 1985, 59); there are always many prescriptions, one cannot live in community without many prescriptions. 'Let us be pagan' (ibid., 19), let us 'maximize as much as possible the multiplication of small narratives' (ibid., 59). According to the narrative of young male hustlers, the video is not degrading and dehumanizing; to quote Matthew: 'I want to make it very clear that the video is not obscene in my eyes. There isn't any violence; there is not whipping or anything like this. It is very vanilla sex. It is very funny, we are laughing' (McGowan 1994, interview). Matthew went underground in the time between the September arrest of one of the young males and 15 January 1994, when he decided to return to Canada to fight the impending charges. He explained the video to *Eye Magazine* reporter Gemma Files, under the pseudo-name John Doe. He says: 'The three of us went off and had a ball, taking turns with the camera, talking and smiling and joking around and hugging and playing with each other's dicks. Nobody's drunk, nobody's stoned. It's all safe sex, with condoms. All three of us have had enough sex with other men and boys to know what we're doing and what we like, and all three of us were old enough to have sex with each other legally. But making a video of it or even having a video of it is now illegal. We made the video before the law was passed, so it wasn't illegal when we made it. But they arrested and charged my friend anyway for making "obscene material" under the new law' (Files 1994). This statement about these events was submitted to the *Globe and Mail*'s 'Facts and Arguments' section by Maggies, the Toronto prostitutes' rights action group, only to be turned down with the statement that they 'could not publish it' (ibid.).

The real issue in justice, according to Lyotard, is terror. Terror is the interruption of the social bond by death in all its forms: repression, hunger, violence, unemployment, jail, dehumanization, harm. Terror is the fear of one language game becoming hegemonic and imposing its concept of justice. Some sexual others live in terror; terror produced by the very heteroliberal values that proclaim justice, equality, and dignity.

'Prescriptives, taken seriously, are never grounded: one can never reach the just by a conclusion'[18] (Lyotard and Thebaud 1985, 17). What is degrading to some persons is not to many others. 'Degrading, obscene, dehumanizing' are empty categories that get filled with the content of homophobia, whorephobia, ageism, sadomasophobia, transgenderphobia, and fear of difference.

I'll take the strategy of paralogy (Lyotard and Thebaud 1985): a practice that counters a metalanguage game like the Law, a practice that defers consensus, that produces dissension and undermines the search for commensurability. Are the images art, social commentary, pornography, a ruse, three young males playing, two middle-aged girls playing?

As a judicial strategy, I'll take the Kant of the Third Critique: the Kant of aesthetic judgments, Kant concerned with beauty in which the particular itself is so complex that it can't be brought under a universal. Judgment is a case-by-case judging of the manner in which each unique complex set of events hangs together. 'Everyone knows how beautiful young people are and how beautiful their bodies are' (Ginsberg 1994). What we do with beauty we can do with justice. We judge the same way we listen: on a case-by-case basis.

At the level of moral philosophizing, I'll take the Rawlsian 'original position' (justice as fairness) sexualized. Justice for Rawls is the first virtue of the social; it is equivalent to truth in thought. I'll abide by the prescriptions of the potentially pagan Rawls. Rawls's social contract takes place in an imaginary original position of blind equality where justice is discussed and determined; it is an ongoing process. Of course, the original position is hypothetical; but Rawls holds that as a society we can get there when we combine justice as fairness with the veil of ignorance. We all choose our social fates together, but behind the veil of ignorance. Individuals are to agree to a set of practices that will govern the basic structure of society, they are to choose these principles on the grounds of self-interest. The rational persons, however, in the original position, don't know their identities, they don't know what they do for a living, how intelligent they are, what their abilities are; they don't know what their own conception of the good is; they do know that they have a conception of the good and that it will differ from others (Rawls 1971). What is under erasure in the discussion of justice in the original position is all knowledge of the features that distinguish one person from another.

No one in the original position knows their sexual orientation, the object of their desire; no one knows if they will be straight, gay, bi, a chicken, a chickenhawk, a male, female, or transgendered person. A society of sexual justice has to take all these positions into account: 'we share one another's [sexual] fate' (Rawls 1971, 102).

At a recent anti-censorship panel in Toronto,[19] a gay client charged with paying for sex with someone under the age of eighteen told how hurt and astounded he was at the cops' idea that the sex he had with the hustler was exploitative. In Canada it has lately been made a criminal offence to pay or provide any other consideration in exchange for sex with someone under the age of eighteen, even though the age of consent is fourteen – as if money made an otherwise tolerable act so intolerable that prison must be part of the answer. Giving money might be ok, sexual intercourse without money might be ok, but mixing sexual and economic liquids is bad.

I looked at the hustlers on the stage, I looked at the boys and girls in the under-18 sex videos illegally shown at the event. I looked at the client. It was clear who had more power. Not the client. Justice as Fairness is premised to benefit the least advantaged. Men are going to jail for paying for sex with someone seventeen and a half years old: it is not illegal for a young person to sell sex, but it is only legal to pay someone for sex if they are at least eighteen years old. The onus is on the customer and the older person to demonstrate that they took 'all reasonable steps to ascertain the age of' the young person (s.150.1(5) C.C.C.). The maximum penalties for breaking the age-of-consent laws (relating to anal intercourse [until May 1995] and payment for sex) range from five to fourteen years in prison. The age-of-consent laws changed in 1989 without much fanfare. The new laws sat on the books until the new 'child-porn' law was passed. At that point the consent laws began to be enforced, almost like an ex-post-facto law, to clients of male hustlers. **Tricking with Philosophy** is a dangerous business. *Do you have a driver's licence? Show me your driver's licence? What bars do you go to? Do they let you into the baths? Are you eighteen? Do you have a birth certificate? When is your birthday? Get in!*

Sexual Parrhesia: The Ethics of Truth-telling and the Morality of Liberal Fascism – The Charging of Matthew McGowan

This is a composite text of *sexual parrhesia* beginning with the official tale of the charging of Matthew McGowan as presented in the *Toronto Star*, followed by Matthew's truth as published in *Eye Magazine* and told to me in an interview; intercut (text in italics) is McGowan's poetry. Included is another truth, the 'final truth' of The Charging of Matthew McGowan as delivered by Judge Bovard in his 'Ruling on Committal to Stand Trial' based on preliminary hearing evidence. This text connects with the second text of *sexual parrhesia*: **The Charging of Two Johns.** Again the official tale as told in the *Toronto Star* and *X-tra!* is presented alongside two other truths: one from a john of some twenty-five years, the other an excerpt from an interview with the famous beat poet and young-man lover Allen Ginsberg. The texts – *Sexual Parrhesia*: **The Charging of Matthew McGowan** and *Sexual Parrhesia*: **The Charging of Two Johns** – cum full circle: from the young Matthew McGowan, the most famous hustler in Canada and burgeoning beat poet, to Allen Ginsberg, the most famous beat poet and young-man lover in North America.

'Man faces porn charges after videotapes seized'

A former worker at a Cabbagetown drop-in centre for prostitutes faces child pornography charges after a large seizure of sexually explicit videotapes involving young boys.

A group of people made, traded, bought and sold videotapes showing young boys engaging in sex, said Detective Terry Wark of the Metro police morality bureau.

'It was mostly the work of pedophiles ... very secretive,' Wark said yesterday.

The arrests are part of their ongoing Project P investigation into the making and distribution of child pornography in Metro, Wark said.

In late August, police raided two downtown apartments ... They seized thousands of pornographic tapes, including a significant number involving children.

Police said the videos showed explicit, degrading and sometimes violent sex acts involving young male victims ranging from prepubescence to their early teens.

Matthew Howard McGowan, 23, of no fixed address, turned himself in to police yesterday. He was charged with two counts of making obscene material.

McGowan ... had been living in New York City. A warrant was issued for his arrest last September. (O'Neill 1994)

Matthew and his friends made two videos; they were found in the August porn raid amongst what the police numbered as 'thousands of pornographic tapes.' 'As pornography goes, the videotapes in question are strictly low-to-no-tech: A trio of horny boys in tube-socks, fading in and out of focus while cracking constant jokes about proper sex flick etiquette. Condoms appear, are fumbled with, used and discarded' (Files 1994). The videos' significance: 'What this basically means is that we finally have consensual, loving Canadian pornography,' says journalist and anti-censorship activist Max Allen. 'Except that we also have a new law under which the people making it are being arrested' (ibid.).

Interview with the young Matthew McGowan, the most famous hustler in Canada and burgeoning beat poet

Shannon: You have been charged with making obscene material. What did you make?
Matthew: I made a so-called pornographic video of myself and two other people. I now am twenty-three; at the time I was twenty-two; the other people were both fourteen. I want to make it very clear that the video is not obscene in my eyes. There isn't any violence; there is no whipping or anything like this. It is very vanilla sex. It is very funny, we are laughing. In fact, there is a lot of stuff happening on this video that if you didn't see the pictures and you only heard the sound track, you would think that it is just a couple of people having a good time, laughing and talking. Max Allen played it on CBC radio.

Shannon: Why is it considered obscene?

Matthew: I guess the cops consider it obscene under the 1992 Butler ruling which seems to have made explicit homosexual sex obscene, especially when there are more than two people present.

I am going merely on assumption as to why the video is considered obscene because it has been a month and a half since my bail hearing and my lawyer has yet to receive disclosure of the evidence. The video's 'obscenity' may have to do with the fact that two people in it are under eighteen and it is illegal to make sexual images of people under eighteen since the new so-called child pornography law, even though the age of consent is fourteen.

Shannon: What was your bail hearing like? I heard it took three days.
Matthew: My lawyer told me before I even came back into the country 'this hearing is going to be all about information. It is going to be like a boxing match, an information session for both sides; hopefully, we will be the ones walking away with more information.' It was like a bad Perry Mason flick. The Crown Attorney kept going off on these tangents; the Judge chastised him a number of times saying 'this is useless information. It has nothing to do with what is happening and I think you had better get back on track.' The Crown Attorney asked me questions such as 'Do you know who George Hislop [the grandaddy of the T.O. gay movement] is?' The next question was 'How many videos did you give him?'

My mother came to court, my boyfriend, many of Maggies' staff, and some anti-censorship people from York University. There were different types of people there all the time, I believe that their presence had an impact on the case.

I am out on bail on my own recognizance so I am responsible for my own actions.

Shannon: I guess you have to stay in the city, can you still work?
Matthew: I can still work as long as I don't break the law, I could work from home. Remember that while prostitution isn't illegal, soliciting and communicating are, a hustler any age can be arrested for communicating.

Shannon: You went to the U.S. for four months. Why did you leave and why did you return?
Matthew: When I first decided that I should leave I was aware that the police were looking for me. It was also brought to my knowledge that

there were no warrants for my arrest and I did not have to speak to the police which meant that if I left the country at this point I was not fleeing prosecution.

I went to New York State and I ended up in New York City. New York City for me when I first got there was scary, very, very scary. Here are some of my notes about the way I felt in New York City, I wrote this particular piece in a stairwell, this will give you an idea of how I was feeling.

Oblivion
What a wonderful way to escape one's own painful reality.

A life, a life,
my kingdom for a life.
Scrutinizing situations in a stairwell, while stoned
What a stupid sentiment,
senseless, yet seductive,
Contemplating companions
while in compromising circumstances.
To care or not to care?
Is this a relevant question?
Feelings of futility while flanked by felonies
for foolish folly while fucking with friends.
Intellectualizing incredible indiscretion
induced by overindulgence.
Pretending to be passive
while pondering predicament
pending prosecution,
precariously placing pleasure before pain,
possibly prolonging proceedings
while praying profusely for poetic justice.

Sitting in a stairwell stoned.
Feeling sorry for being stupid,
but sad for being forced into solitude.

I had some really hard times when I was in New York. I was alone in a big city with nobody other than myself to look after me and that scared me. I was so utterly alone. I had left everything that I ever had behind me, I just walked away from it all. I wrote a lot of stuff, it says:

My life is pretty well ruined because my name had been in the paper, the big daily paper.

I guess I got my wish, or at least half of it,
I am now famous, hah!
Been less than two weeks and already I have given up,
I do things that I tried so hard to put off to the side.
And now with the change I cannot get bad habits out of my mind.
I have again been caught up in the party, party, party.
Hopefully I will remain sane.
I feel myself slipping a little more, as the news gets worse.
I am trying to make the best of the worst.
This it the most frightening situation that I have ever been in.

Then, of course, I go off on some really heavy tangents:

I do not like my life. I wish I had the courage to kill myself because this is becoming over-
whelming. I am not sure I can stand prolonged exposure. I wish very much that I was
not scared to die ... I wish there was something else, I wish I knew because the circum-
stance has become too much for my relatively simple and loving personality.

I am not a sexual monster.
I am not a predator.
I only have sex with the completely willing and to the best of my knowledge
I have never coerced anyone.

Now I am a fugitive for having sex[.]

Shannon: The label pedophile was thrown around in connection with you; the term immediately brings to mind sex with six year olds.
Matthew: The word pedophile wouldn't have bothered me, but the word 'diddler' really, really has a heavy impact on me because I am of the jail culture. When you say the word 'diddler' I think of a person playing around with some two year old kid, that is my immediate response.

Shannon: Why did you come back to Toronto?
Matthew: Why? It was an informed decision, but it was a damned hard decision to make because the people around me made it very clear to me that they could not guarantee my freedom when I came back. I said 'It is something that I really have to do now.' I had come to the conclusion that the longer I stay away the worse off I am going to be later on, and so I started getting support from people who I needed support from. Without that support I would never have come back. These people include

Maggie's, my mother, my boyfriend Matthew, a number of my friends who are not gay, who are actually very, very straight, they ended up being very supportive. However, I have also lost a lot of friends over this.

Shannon: Is that because of the newspaper coverage?
Matthew: It is because of the inaccuracy.

Shannon: What is the inaccuracy?
Matthew: That I was charged with making 'child pornography' when in fact I was charged with making something that is obscene. The papers made it sound like I was beating up little children. The police met me coming off the ramp of the airplane.

Shannon: The famous picture of you being taken into custody at the police station, which was on the front page of the local papers, when was that taken?
Matthew: That was taken behind 52 division. I have something to say about that picture. I was sitting in the police car when we drove up and you could see the press from quite a ways back. The police officer that was with me, his name is Detective Constable Pat Nevin, said to me 'You can cover your head now.' I said 'I refuse to cover my head, I have nothing to hide.' The police normally drive a police car into the 52 division station and close the garage door before the person in custody gets out of the car, which makes it hard for the press to get a picture. But because I made that statement to that cop, he had the driver stop the car, he took me out of the car and walked me to the station, so the press could take pictures. It was an intimidation tactic. The cops were trying to intimidate me so much so that I would just back off, which I refuse to do.
     When I turned myself in I walked into protective custody which was suppose to protect me, I was in that range for about four or five minutes and I walked out with a black eye and my nose was broken.

Shannon: Are a lot of the boys working boy town under eighteen? If so then I guess the date can get arrested for paying for sex with someone under eighteen.
Matthew: Some of the guys are, some aren't.

Shannon: What is your take on the media's repeated claim that the johns of people under eighteen are victimizers?

Matthew: I am sure that that may be the case once in a while, but not very often. When I do a date it is on my terms. Almost every single date that I have ever pulled, I have thought that I got the better end of the stick than them. They were paying to do things with me. That is definitely an ego boost. The money is good.

I came out of the closet at sixteen. If I had known about hustling I would have done it. I know I would have been on that corner every night, I would have been selling it real hard.

Shannon: Who is victimizing, then?
Matthew: The cops.

Shannon: Who are your clients?
Matthew: There are all kinds. One of my better clients is married with two children. He is very up front with his wife about the fact that he likes sex with boys. He is very up front about the fact that he is bisexual and about what he wants to do sexually. He says 'this is what I want to do, you in? Okay, good, let's go.'

My clients come from all walks of life: I have a number of upper class guys, a Justice of the Peace, I have middle class guys, I have working class guys and I have clients who live in single rooms and are poor.

Shannon: What is a good client for you?
Matthew: A person that you can have a good time with even when you are not working and he is not paying. Someone you can hang around with and enjoy talking to.

Shannon: You have worked in Toronto, New York, San Francisco. What are some of the differences in the hustler scene?
Matthew: In New York there is a somewhat different scene than in T.O.; there is a bar called Rounds. Really upper class, upper scale, young guys who want to make $150 a pop for a date go to Rounds. It is $10 for young guys just to walk in the door, $5 for older men. The scene is very, very competitive. All the preppie guys give you nasty glances if you talk to someone they were talking to. For someone like myself, who is not aggressive when it comes to dates, the place was not that great. I wait for someone to come to talk to me. If they don't talk to me, I don't talk to them. I bide my time, I stare at them, when someone comes over to talk to me, that's cool. I make a lot of money this way.

I made a lot of money at another place called Julius, it is a lower class bar but I made more money at Julius than I did at Rounds. I cater to the type of person who likes to sit around, shoot the breeze, hang out, have a nice conversation. I can have a conversation about anything. While in New York, I met a man who liked to take me out for dinner and drinks, he didn't want sex.

Shannon: Why do older men spend money on boys and not have sex on the agenda?
Matthew: They like the company of a young man.

The 'Final Truth' of the Charging of Matthew McGowan

'My ruling in this case is that the video tapes in question are not obscene,' said Bovard J. (Bovard 1995, 3). As a spectator in court I saw McGowan the hustler leaning on a car (nobody can lean on a car the way a hustler can); I heard Matthew the poet reading me his prose:

People will say things about me and a boy called Joel. Me and Joel will never get to say anything back. These people will call us some evil things publicly, but we will only get to respond to them privately ...

I refuse to stand by and let someone decimate my character, and falsely accuse me of coercion in sex in any way, shape, or form. Something I find deplorable.

Broken dreams, a broken past, the future is uncertain.

I remembered McGowan the political activist addressing the Toronto March 1994 rally to repeal the youth-porn law: 'The police have got to stop this cruel witch-hunt before they ruin any more young people's lives and reputations ... What we're calling for is the repeal of these repressive, homophobic laws, the release of the young men who have been identified by the circulation of still photos made from discarded videos, and at the very least an apology to those people who have had their private lives made public by some overzealous cops who have a hard-on for arresting young male hustlers' (Kinsman 1995, 14). My mind drifted to the boy bars of Amsterdam, four in the morning, boys playing pinball, hawks sitting at the bar watching with that indifferent cool desire, me watching the hawks watching the boys, aware that desire is the joker in the deck, me wanting the hawks wanting the boys. Just behind consciousness and time, the eternal prison seduction: hawk-hand holding a smoking reef raised to the lips of another, roughly circling and parting lips, space, soul to impaling finger/penis/eternity. McGowan saying, 'I am of the jail culture'; McGowan in that in-between phase: part hawk, part boy. A more common phase than straight culture might suppose; John Greyson's video *After the Bath* discloses that 'six of the men who appeared in the [London] videos were charged with anal sex and sexual interference with boys under fourteen, except these six men were age sixteen to twenty-one themselves, sometimes as young as their alleged victims. Indeed all six will testify as alleged victims of other men charged' (Greyson 1995). My mind shifted to that hetero-cult film *Casablanca* and the fifties masculinist prototype Rick, of course played by Bogart. Rick: 'I'm the only cause I'm interested in.' That haunting mantra-line transfigures as it touches the words of Walt Whitman, the grand American poet, one of whose personae was probably chicken-queen: 'I contain multitudes' (Whitman 1981, 74). The thought circle loops to a November 1993 Anti-Censorship Panel at Harbourfront where the Toronto prostitute/performance artist Gwendolyn told the audience, 'I am those boys in jail!'

In his ruling Bovard J. identified the issues: first, 'are the video tapes obscene,' and the sub-issue that had to be decided in order to make that determination: 'what is the definition of children, as that term is used in *R. v. Butler*' (Bovard 1995, 3). Bovard J. reviewed the evidence:

The accused was charged with making two sex video tapes. Both tapes depict various consensual sexual activities between the accused, who is an adult, and two boys [J.S. and M.D.] who were fourteen years old ...

I viewed the video tapes in Court ... The first one depicts M.D. lying down in shorts on a bed with a beer bottle in his hand. A pair of unknown hands are seen rubbing his body and touching his penis, part of his underpants are moved to the side thereby exposing one of his testicles. There is music playing in the background.

M.D. is then shown lying naked on the bed. J.S. is seen performing fellatio on him. One of them exposes his anus, and anilingus is performed on him by the other. Then both are shown lying on the bed, one on top of the other. They are both naked.

J.S. continues to play with M.D.'s anus, fingering it lightly on the surface. As they lay there their genitals are exposed. Then the accused is seen performing fellatio on M.D. and masturbating. Then the accused is seen masturbating himself while lying next to M.D. and playing with M.D.'s genitals. The accused then performed anilingus on M.D.

The second video showed the accused naked, performing fellatio on M.D., and he and J.S. caressing M.D. and performing fellatio on him. It also showed M.D. masturbating himself ...

Acts of anilingus by the accused on M.D. are shown while M.D. laid on top of

J.S. and was fingering him in the anus. Then J.S. and the accused are seen slapping M.D. lightly on the buttocks while M.D. lies on top of J.S. ... The spanking is done in a playful way ...

In the next scene M.D. and J.S. are naked lying on their backs on the bed. J.S. has a knife and playfully simulates cutting his own testicles with the knife. Both of them have knives, and are playing with them by rubbing them against their bodies. (ibid., 4–6)

Bovard J. established that he finds 'all of the sexual acts depicted on the video ... consensual' (ibid., 6–7). The question is whether or not the videos are obscene under s.163(8). At the end of his ruling Bovard J. categorizes the two videos as being in the third category of pornography produced in *R. v. Butler*:[20] 'explicit sex that is not violent and neither degrading or dehumanizing ... and will not qualify as the undue exploitation of sex unless it employs children in its production' (ibid., 8). That the videos are category three pornography is an assumption Bovard J. works from throughout his argumentation.

Beginning with the sub-issue, the key in Bovard J.'s ruling is what or who is a child. He states: 'There is no general definition of "child," in the *Criminal Code*, nor was it defined by the Court in *Butler*. And "child" is not defined in the *Criminal Code* with reference to section 163(1)(a)' (Bovard 1995, 9), the section McGowan was charged under. Section 163(1)(a) reads:

Every one commits an offence who

(a) makes, prints, publishes, distributes, circulates, or has in his possession for the purpose of publication, distribution or circulation any obscene written matter, picture, model, photograph or other thing whatever[.]

Before examining the age that denotes child in the Criminal Code, Bovard J. positions child as contested category, a term whose meaning eludes according to context, a category-in-crisis; a lived category that since the child-pornography law has been reified to refer to anyone under eighteen. Bovard J. contends: '[Child] is one of those terms that everyone thinks they know the meaning of, but no one can define clearly for all circumstances. Its definition varies in different legal and non-legal contexts' (ibid.). The currency invested in the term/category in the McGowan case is great; 'category-in-crisis, men-in-jail.' Bovard J. says: 'In the case before me, if "child" is understood to include someone who is fourteen, then according to *Butler*, the videos before me are obscene, even if they fall into category three, since children were used in their production. If "child" does not include someone who is fourteen, then they are not obscene, because in the absence of that the accused, and the two persons in the video tapes with him were all consensually doing something that was legal at the time' (ibid., 9).

Bovard J. begins by citing the recent Ontario Court of Appeal ruling (*R. v. M. (C.)* 1995), which 'struck down Section 159 of the Criminal Code which made it an offense for anyone under 18, and not married, to have anal intercourse' (Bovard 1995, 9). Then, in the ancient tradition of *parrhesia*, there is a moment of truth-telling that shatters the presumption at the heart of the child-porn law: that society can know when childhood ends and adulthood begins, that this moment is the same for everyone, and it is precisely at age eighteen. The Protagorean proposition *nothing is one thing* – all things are relational to the core, meaningful only in different ways in different contexts – retrieved and recycled by Foucault and Lyotard, can be heard in Bovard J.'s words: 'It is difficult to determine whether at 14 years old the two persons in the video are among the persons that would fall into the category of children as the term is used in *Butler*. It is somewhat artificial to state an age at which a young person stops being a child. Persons develop at different rates. One person can demonstrate the characteristics we associate with a child at the age of seventeen, sixteen, or fifteen. On the other hand, some persons at those ages have developed more rapidly, and do not demonstrate those characteristics. So at what age is a person no longer a child?' (ibid., 10).

'So at what age is a person no longer a child?' Bovard J. recalls the *Oxford English Dictionary* definition of child: 'a young person of either sex below the age of puberty. One who is considered to have the characteristic manners or attainments of a child' (Bovard 1995, 10). Bovard J. goes to the sections in Part V of the Criminal Code, 'Sexual Offences, Public Morals and Disorderly Conduct,' that mention young persons: 150.1(1), 152, 153(2), 160(3), 161(1), 173(2), 170, 171, 172. He claims: 'I searched these sections hoping to find an answer to my question' (ibid., 11). His finding was that only s.172 includes age fourteen as child, all the other sections make a distinction between a young person below fourteen and over fourteen. While s.172 is the only section in which the term child is defined, the section specifies that the definition is 'for the purposes of this section' (ibid., 12). 'Section 153(2) defines "young person," as a person 14 years of age and more, but under 18 years' (ibid.). He cites the *Young Offenders Act*, in which "child" is defined as a "person who is, or in the absence of evidence to the contrary, appears to be under the age of 12 years."' (ibid., 13). Bovard J. acknowledges that had s.163.1, the Child Pornography Law, which came into force on 1 August 1993, been in place his reasoning would have been different. He concludes his ruling statement by saying: 'As things stand today, by passing section 163(1). Parliament has spoken clearly that it wants to extend its protection via the *Criminal Code* to all young persons under 18. *And I agree with that*. In the light of this development, it is a quirky thing to have to decide this case on the law as it existed before Section 163.1 was passed. However, the accused cannot be made subject to the law on a retroactive basis. He is subject to the law as it existed' (ibid., 15).

Although Bovard J. made an ethical ruling based on the law of the time and the acknowledgment that child is a category-in-crisis, although he came close to arguing for a case-by-case assessment, he closes by supporting the chronological reification of child/non-child. One is left questioning the morality behind a justice system that would have placed McGowan in jail if one of his friends had been thirteen and three-quarters or if the videos had been produced on 2 August 1993.

Sexual Parrhesia: The Ethics of Truth-telling and the (im)Morality of Unknown Flesh – An Interlude

Pier Paolo Pasolini [reflecting on Boy 2, a sixteen-year-old]:

Now, you see, he will go back home to his father who is drunk and out of work. His father beats him and calls him a monster. He's jealous of his son's growing prick. Me, I'm not jealous. I love the little monster. I just want to give the kid a soccer ball and if he wants ... [looking off] and I think he does want, I'll make him come. [pause] When his father dies, they'll erect a monument and sing 'himmmmmms.' When I die – if some jealous father doesn't shoot me first – they'll call me pederast. Except for the boys. They'll call me Jack Palance. In fact, I do look a little like him. [He feels his face again] I do ...

They are all so different and yet the same, light or dark, large or small. When I love him it means I love ... the world ... Is not the world seventeen years old and very stupid? (Gilbert 1995, 37, 57)

The gift of a soccer ball travestied by Canadian law as payment for sex (s. 212(4) C.C.C.) is what would send Pasolini to jail. Not only would the infamous Italian rough tough Palance-like romo-sexual Pasolini be in jail, but so would Harry Stack Sullivan, the famous American psychiatrist, who brought the relational nature of the self into psychotherapy. The home-osexual Sullivan lived his entire life closeted with his lover James, whom he had met as a fifteen- or sixteen-year-old boy, probably a hustler.[21] Under Canadian law, Sullivan could have been jailed at any time. 'Through the summer of 94 nearly 3 dozen men were charged under SCOOP. Both the police and the *London Free Press* kept calling it a child pornography investigation. Yet not one child porn charge was laid. Instead the men were charged with a range of sexual offenses, some dating back twenty-five years. These included buggery and gross indecency charges under archaic laws which were repealed or replaced in 1985' (Greyson 1995).

Sexual Parrhesia: The Ethics of Truth-telling and the Morality of Liberal Fascism – The Charging of Two Johns, A School Teacher, and an Alderman

'[A] veteran Scarborough public school teacher is the 34th person to be charged with sex offenses by a special joint police taskforce [Project Guardian] investigating child pornography in the London, Ont., area.' '[The man] faces three charges of obtaining sexual services of a person under 18 years of age.' 'Police said the latest charges involve two male prostitutes aged 16 and 17 who they allege were picked up on the streets of London and transported to a motel in Mississauga for sexual purposes in 1992 and 1993' (Josey 1994).

'Colleagues at the [school] board said [he] is a "well respected" teacher who is chairperson of his school. The chairperson is a senior teacher who helps other teachers with any curriculum or teaching problems' (ibid.).

'Police said [the teacher] was unmarried and lived with his parents' (ibid.).

The former St Thomas alderman said, 'I don't go around molesting children. I am not a diddler ... if the opportunity arises that I can have sex with a male prostitute ... I do' (Couture and Venizelos 1994). The former alderman was charged with eighteen charges of paying for the sexual services of a person under eighteen, five charges of gross indecency and five charges of anal intercourse with teenagers ranging in age from fourteen to seventeen (ibid.). The anal-intercourse restriction to over eighteen was declared unconstitutional by an Ontario Court judge. This ruling was being appealed, allowing police to continue to charge persons for engaging in anal intercourse with persons under eighteen. The age of consent for oral and vaginal sex is fourteen; for anal sex it was eighteen, until May 1995.

The '[f]ormer St Thomas alderman sat with his head bowed, trembling, and twice broke into sobbing before his three-and-a-half-year penitentiary sentence was handed down' (Couture 1994).

Justice Jeffry Flynn noted during the June 24 court session (held in London) that many of the acts were consensual, 'depraved as they are.' Justice Flynn asked: 'Would any right-thinking person accept this kind of activity?' 'If this man didn't put them [the teens] on the path to corruption – he certainly fostered it' (Couture 1994).

An Interview with John[22]

There certainly may be problems with intergenerational sex and youth prostitution – society certainly may be justified in regulating these activities. It may even be necessary to humiliate and imprison a highly respected Scarborough public-school teacher for giving money to a sixteen-year-old hustler for sex. It may even be that whatever affection, delight, friendliness, playfulness, respect, mutual aid, even devotion, might be found in these interactions are entirely cancelled, wiped out, voided, and transmuted into excrement by the harm.

What is incredible, though, is the straight mind's insistence that youth are directly harmed by the sexual involvement itself rather than by the social and cultural contextualization of this sexual involvement.

According to the straight story, only a child who has been subjected to incest or other abuse at a very young age – six to twelve, say – and who never learned that he could say 'no' – would go on to have sex with adults, with or without payment – as an older teenager, say fifteen to eighteen. If youngsters could say no, they invariably would say no.

In the straight story, there is not space for the many young persons who have never been abused in any way, who arrive at sex with adults from many different starting points, possibly including their enthusiastic sex lives with other young people.

The straight mind cannot admit that in most cases 'harm' to the young person is not an automatic result of sexual involvement with older people. If sex with an age peer doesn't directly cause feelings of having been 'used,' shame, nightmares, flashbacks, addiction, etc., etc., sex with people ten or twenty years older need not do so either.

The straight defender of youth can't confess: These are our youth, we don't really care what they think they want, we don't want them to have sex with adults, we don't want them to connect money with sex, we are revolted and disgusted by this, therefore we have said that sex with adults is always and under all imaginable circumstances harmful to young persons. We can't say that it is our responses of horror and revulsion that are upsetting to the youth; therefore, those attracted to them are deviants, sickos, who should be cured/punished like the homosexuals of the forties and fifties.

In the pre-Civil War United States, racists (that is, almost everyone) considered miscegenation (cross-racial sex) a crime 'because' of the harm it caused to the offspring of such unions, forced to grow up as 'mongrels' in a racist society. And they were right. Whites and blacks who produced children were by that fact abusing them.

We are the masters and mistresses of Empathy. We can't imagine how these sickos can ignore the feelings of youth.

It is indeed true that a young person may sooner or later experience profoundly unpleasant feelings and regret about their sexual misbehaviour, because of the horror it aroused in the straight parental generation.

The fact is, all youth belong to the straight parental generation, the mothers and fathers, psychiatrists, social workers, cops, and journalists, not to themselves. Adults sexually involved with youth cause great pain to adults not so involved.

Allen Ginsberg: Communicating

'I had a conversation with Andrea Dworkin in which I said, "I've had affairs with boys who were 16, 17, 18 ... What are you going to do, send me to jail?" And she said "You should be shot" ... The problem is, she was molested and hasn't recovered from the trauma. And she's taking it out on ordinary lovers' (Ginsberg 1994).

'They [legislators and police] might try going to the National Museum in Greece. The youth in between puberty and maturity is, for both men and women, one of the oldest aesthetic erotic contemplations in history. Everyone knows how beautiful young people are and how beautiful their bodies are. To forbid representation of that is ridiculous ... Really, the intention [of these laws] is to shut off all public discourse and all public communication – which will lead to real perversion' (ibid.).

Sexual Parrhesia: A 'Truth' to Pornography?

'Making Pornography' and 'On ne peut pas voir l'image' are responses to the 'unstated understandings of the truth about pornography' (See Cossman in this volume). Both representations [words and photographs] have been presented as performance texts: 'Making Pornography' was performed at the *Queer Sites: Bodies at Work, Bodies at Play* conference, University of Toronto, May 1993, and at *Dirty Pictures and Sweet Obscenities*, a two-day protest against censorship held as part of Toronto Pride Day weekend, June 1993; 'On ne peut pas voir l'image' was exhibited by twenty Toronto art/theatre/performance spaces from 10 September to 22 October 1994, and was the artist project in *Fuse Magazine* (Vol. 18, no. 1, 1994) as a protest response to section 163.1 of the Criminal Code, the 'Child Pornography' law. The art action took place in conjunction with the court case of artist Eli Langer. 'Making Pornography' could be charged under *Butler*; 'On ne peut pas voir l'image' could be charged under the 'Child Pornography' law. The representations mix lesbian sexuality, sadomasochism, and youth sexuality, the contested sites of the new obscenity. These are recombined with philosophy [wisdom] and poetry [eros].

Making Pornography

There are two predominant positions on lesbian pornography (see Ross, this volume): one is that no image produced in the dominant pornographic medium be reproduced; the other is that these images be taken to their extreme, destabilizing the heterosexual scenarios. The first is a position of substance; the second is a position of camp, of performance over substance: porno as mimicry.

What happens when hetero-gendered codes – dress, gesture, posture, and sexual activity – are reworked in a lesbian frame? What happens when you mime the mime that heterosexuality has written on male and female bodies and you are both female (as takes place in butch/femme role playing)? What happens when you mix the codes (butch and femme) on one female body? When you play with the more and more popular S/M images? What happens when you both play daddy boys or boyfriends, imaging gay male pornography?

Three performing porno images.

Image One
A woman has her ankles bound to a ladder, arms in wrist cuffs tied over her head; the woman is wearing work boots, a long slinky cocktail dress,

she has a shaved head. The second woman, wearing a leather mini-skirt, platform ankle boots, and a gangsterish fedora, is simultaneously exposing the first woman's sex and holding a knife to it. (See p. 234.)

Image One and a half

The roles reverse; the female gangster now has on one of those grown-up dresses (lace and taffeta) that little girls play dress-up in, she is lying on her back holding a teddy; the previously tied woman has inserted a speculum into the girl/woman's vagina sideways and is inspecting her internal sex organ with a latex gloved hand.

What you have here is at the very least a destabilizing of codes. Is the gangster moll of *Image One* raping, castrating, slashing the woman fixed to the ladder or is she cutting her sexuality loose from male inscription that has perpetuated these crimes against women? Is the act an act of dehumanization and thus obscene, or is it an act of rehumanization and thus sacred? Or is it simultaneously both? In *Image One-and-a-half* has the fairy child through her/his apparently incompetent mime of doctor recoded the medical instrument as a sexual toy and with a twist of the wrist and a turn of the speculum exposed the girl's sex and her sexual power, undercutting the doctor's power in the official gynecological examination?

Image Two

Two women same size, same body type and shape, slightly different moustaches, both clad in leather pants, one wearing a Greek fisherman's hat, one wearing work boots, the other cowboy boots, redo scenes from Tom of Finland, the famous subcultural gay leather man excess artist of the fifties to seventies. They pose and wrestle. They do some general bad-attitude spanking and sneering around. (See p. 235.)

What do you have here? Two women parodying two gay men parodying the excess of masculinity. Judith Butler argues that drag is not an imitation of any original; rather it is a parody of the idea of there being any original (Butler 1990). Gender, as Butler puts it, is 'the repeated stylization of the body, a set of repeated actions within a highly rigid regulatory frame that congeal over time to produce ... a natural sort of being' (ibid., 33). Gender is imitation without any original, and drag, as the imitation of imitation, reveals the imitative non-essense of gender. Occurring in this representation is the repetition of the performance twice removed (remember, gender requires a performance that is repeated); the 'meanings' associated with all three 'identities' lesbian/gay/hetero, are rendered indistinct. It gives new meaning to Marlon Brando's lament in *On The Waterfront*: 'I wanted to be a somebody.'

Image Three
A trace to the old burlesque tradition, but the return is bent: the role of
the vaudeville showgirl was to raise desire in her audience. Here on an
old trunk, a woman in classic showgirl attire – feather boa, garters,
seamed nylons, and pumps – is receiving pleasure from her female
friend who is in 1990s leather boy gear. (See facing page.) Here is a slippage of time periods and genres: the object of desire in one period
becomes the satisfied sexual subject in the hand of a new transgender
icon. Beside the pair, for those in the know, is the faint outline of Judy
Garland in male tramp drag sitting on a show trunk singing 'I was born
in a trunk in the Princess Theater' in Alexander, Manitoba. Her tramp
undermined the showgirl image; it takes a leather boy to resexualize her.

P.S.   Pussy Phrenology: Or How Old Is That Pussy in the Picture?
The so-called Child Pornography law in Canada, s.163.1 of the Canadian
Criminal Code, makes it illegal to possess, produce, sell, or distribute
sexually explicit images of a person who is or is depicted as under the
age of eighteen in films, magazines, videos, and computer-generated
images; it also makes illegal written materials that 'advocate' having sex
with a person under the age of eighteen.

When you see a pussy, you need to ask, 'How old is that pussy in the
picture?' This essay does not advocate lawbreaking; it advocates recon-
sideration of the law.

On ne peut pas voir l'image

She is five,
She is fifteen,
She is forty.
She is a boy child
    a girl child
    a woman.

Her defiant gaze catches the spectator
with the savvy of the veteran sex worker,
with the anger of the wilful child,
with the hurt of the erased adolescent,
with the power of a woman in control of her pleasure.

She has been abused?
She has been loved?

She is desiring.
She is desired.
She is ugly.
She is sexy.

She uses the image?
The image uses her?

Whatever you say she is, she is not.

Kath Daymond
Shannon Bell

NOTES

1 'Calvin and Hobbes,' *Toronto Star,* 5 November 1994, Comics.
2 MacKinnon has documented the interconnection between rape and pornography in the Serbian soldiers' filmed rape of Bosnian women. 'Turning Rape into Pornography: Postmodern Genocide,' in *Mass Rape* (1994).
3 See my books *Reading, Writing, and Rewriting the Prostitute Body* (Bloomington: Indiana University Press, 1994) and *Whore Carnival* (Brooklyn: Autonomedia, 1995); porn stars Veronica Vera, Annie Sprinkle, and Candida Royalle discuss the imperfection of porn as a sexual medium and how they grew in it.
4 See MacKinnon, 'On Collaboration,' in *Feminism Unmodified* (1987).
5 What I am terming a postmodern feminist position on pornography had its origin in the infamous 1982 Barnard 'Scholar and Feminist' conference, resulting in *Pleasure and Danger: Exploring Female Sexuality,* edited by Carol Vance (1984). More recent texts include Lynne Segal and Mary McIntosh, eds, *Sex Exposed: Sexuality and the Pornography Debate* (1992, 1993); Pamela C. Gibson and Roma Gibson, *Dirty Looks: Women, Pornography, Power* (1993); and Shannon Bell, *Reading, Writing and Rewriting the Prostitute Body* (1994).
6 As Cossman points points out in chapter 3, the sexualities attracting attention are gay and lesbian, sadomasochist, and youth sexualities.
7 I have replaced philosophers with pornographers.
8 This is a reference to Jean-François Lyotard's concept of justice as set forth in his book *Just Gaming* (1985).
9 Kirk and Madsen 1989 and Bawer 1993. Kirk and Madsen warn the gay community: 'We're assumed to consist entirely of extreme stereotypes: men ultrawishy and ultraviolet, Frankenstein thug-women with bolts on their necks, mustachio'd Dolly Parton wanna-bes, leather-men in boots and whips, ombudsmen of pederasty squirling their ombudsboys – all ridiculous, deranged, or criminal. And when we are *finally* allowed to rally and march, to lay our case before the cameras of the straight American public, what do we do? We call out of the woodwork as our ambassadors of bad will all the

screamers, stompers, gender-benders, sadomasochists, and pederasts, and confirm Amercia's worst fears and hatreds' (p. 144). They advise: 'When you're very different, and people hate you for it, this is what you do: *first* you get your foot in the door, by being as *similar* as possible; then, and only then – when your one little difference is finally accepted – can you start dragging in your other peculiarities, one by one' (p. 146). Kirk and Madsen juxtapose 'drag queens and pederasts' to 'the rest of us'; they state: 'the rest of us are working our butts off to convince straights that, in all respects other than what we like to do in bed, we're exactly like folks' (p. 147).

Bawer echoes Kirk and Madsen's concern for heterosexual acceptance; he restates: 'The marchers who make the Gay Pride Day march embarrassing to many homosexuals ... represent the same small but vocal minority of the gay population that has, for a generation, played no small part in shaping and sustaining most heterosexuals' notions of what it means to be homosexual ... I've remarked that many heterosexuals think of homosexuality in terms of "practice" or "activity," but this is at least partly because the subculture-oriented gays center their lives on their sexual orientation and because a generation of gay activists have made the right to engage with abandon in certain kinds of activity their principle cause' (p. 160).

10 The new Canadian so-called Child Porn Law, June 1993, is an extension and expansion of the U.S. child-porn bills, *The Child Sexual Abuse and Pornography Act* (1986) and *The Child Protection and Obscenity Enforcement Act* (1988); it was under the former that such artists as Jock Sturges, Robert Mapplethorpe, and Alice Sims were charged and people became afraid to take nude photos of children, adolescents, and late teens. The latter bill required proof that all actors/models producing sexually explicit material were eighteen or over; the proof requirements were applied retroactively over the previous ten years.

11 This is a borrowed trace from Alphonso Lingis's chapter 'carrion body carrion utterance' in *The Community of Those Who Have Nothing in Common* (1994).

12 Both the *Badgely Report* on child sexual abuse (Canada, Committee on Sexual Offences Against Youths and Children, 1985) and the *Fraser Commission Report* (Canada, Special Committee on Pornography and Prostitution, 1985) found evidence of extensive child sexual abuse in Canada and pointed to a consensus in society on the need for dealing immediately with the issue. See Lacombe 1988, 112.

13 *Toronto Star*, 22 October 1993. On 19 March 1996 all pornography charges relating to this seizure were withdrawn. The man charged, 'who was a high school teacher, lost his job, was evicted from his apartment and said he was

subjected to public humiliation because of inaccurate media coverage' (Couture 1996, 11). He has filed a lawsuit seeking damages 'as a result of what documents call the false presentation of ——— as a child pornographer' (ibid.).

14 4 June 1994, front-page headline.

15 London chief of police; CBC, 1994, 12.

16 Judge Hayes ruled that casual gay sexual encounters are 'degrading and without human dimension' *Glad Day Bookshop v. Canada*, [1992] O.J. No.1466 (QL), 25.

17 'What makes paganism? It consists in the fact that each game is played as such, which implies that it does not give itself as the game of all the other games or as the true one.' Lyotard and Thebaud 1985, 60.

18 Thebaud questions Lyotard: 'You say: "It is unjust." How can you say it, if you do not have a representation of what justice ought to be, unless you derive this prescription of acting against from something else?' Lyotard responds: 'No. I do not think that it can be derived. I think that one can try to derive it. It can be derived in Kantian fashion; it can be derived in Hegelian fashion; it can be derived in Christian fashion. There is thus a whole slew of possible motifs. I mean "motif" almost in the sense of embroidery.' Lyotard and Thebaud, 1985, 69.

19 The panel was organized to provide information about the new child porn law, the charging of the Toronto hustler and image producer Matthew McGowan, artist Eli Langer, the clients in London. Examples from commercial films and erotic videos of what is now classified as 'child pornography' were displayed on video monitors. A video entitled *Bobby and Monica* produced by Butlerfilms Canadian Video for a test case to challenge section 163.1 of the Canadian Criminal Code, which outlaws representations of sex involving people fourteen to eighteen years old, was shown. The forum was held at the 519 Community Centre in Toronto, June 1994.

20 The videos could not be placed in the first category of pornography, explicit sex with violence, Bovard J. reasons: 'I do not think the spanking nor the knife scenes qualify as actual or threatened violence. These acts were done in a playful and joking manner. No harm was done nor threatened, and there was a mood of laughter and joking around during the scenes. M.D. who is being spanked was asked twice if it hurt, and he said no' (Bovard 1995, 14). The videos do not lie in the second category of pornography, explicit sex without violence, but which subjects people to treatment that is degrading or dehumanizing. Bovard J. states: 'Nor do I find the videos depict acts which subject any person to treatment that is degrading and dehumanizing. I think that although the scenes depicted are of dubious taste, the community would

tolerate others being exposed to them, because I infer from the material itself ... that the degree of harm ... that could flow from such exposure, would be at a tolerable level' (ibid., 14–15).

21 In his corrective to Helen Swick Perry's biography of Sullivan, Michael Allen documents through interviews with Sullivan's colleagues, students, and friends: 'Sometime in 1927, [Sullivan] met a young man named James Inscoe. Jimmie, who later took Sullivan's surname, was about 15 or 16 years old at the time. Although Helen Perry wrote that nobody could tell her how Harry met Jimmy, she confessed to me when we met one quiet fall afternoon in her Cambridge, Massachusetts, apartment, that Jimmie had been a "male hustler" in Washington D.C. Shortly thereafter, Jimmie, who was to become Sullivan's secretary, housekeeper, office manager, and longtime companion, moved into Sullivan's suburban Maryland home. Harry and Jimmie made a home together in Maryland and New York City, for twenty-two years, until Harry's death in 1949. Jimmie's place in Sullivan's life was complex and ambiguous; to Sullivan's colleagues, he was "Harry Stack's foster son," although they had no official or legal relationship; among Sullivan's friends, Jimmie was known simply as "the man who came to stay"' (Allen 1995, 9).

22 This is part of a longer interview with John, a bisexual client of prostitutes and hustlers; the full interview is published in Bell 1995.

References

Adams, Mary Louise. 1993. 'Precedent-Setting Pulp: Women's Barracks Was Deemed "Exceedingly Frank."' *X-tra!*, 3 September, 21.

– 1994. 'The Trouble With Normal: The Social Construction of the Teenager in Post-War Ontario.' Ph.D. dissertation, OISE, University of Toronto.

Adelman, Shonagh. 1994. *Skin Deep*. Toronto: A Space Gallery.

– 1995. 'Girrly Pictures.' *Border/Lines* no. 37: 28–35.

Allen, Carol, and Rosamund Elwin. 1993. *Getting Wet: Tales of Lesbian Seduction*. Toronto: Women's Press.

Allen, Michael. 1995. 'Sullivan's Closet: A Reappraisal of Harry Stack Sullivan's Life and His Pioneering Role in American Psychiatry.' *Journal of Homosexuality* 29, no. 1.

Allison, Dorothy. 1988. 'Her Thighs.' Chapter in *Trash*. Ithaca, NY: Firebrand Books.

Arcand, Bernard. 1991. *The Jaguar and the Anteater: Pornography and the Modern World*. Toronto: McClelland and Stewart.

Assiter, Alison, and Carol Avedon, eds. 1993. *Bad Girls and Dirty Pictures: The Challenge to Reclaim Feminism*. London: Pluto Press.

Attorney General of Canada. 1991. 'Factum of the Respondent.' *Butler v. R.*, [1992] 1 S.C.R. 452, [1992] 8 C.R.R. (2d) 1.

Attorney General of Manitoba. 1991. 'Factum of the Respondent.' *Butler v. R.*, [1992] 1 S.C.R. 452, [1992] 8 C.R.R. (2d) 1.

augustine, karen/miranda. 1994. 'Bizarre Women, Exotic Bodies and Outrageous Sex: Or if Annie Sprinkle Was a Black Ho She Wouldn't Be All That.' *Border/Lines* 32 (Spring): 22–4.

Backhouse, Constance. 1991. *Petticoats and Prejudice: Women and Law in Nineteenth Century Canada*. Toronto: Women's Press.

Bad Attitude: Lesbian Erotic Fiction. 1991a. Vol. 7, no. 4.

– 1991b. 'Editorial: Gay Bashing.' Vol. 7, no. 4: 2.

Barber, Karen, ed. 1991. *Bushfire*. Boston: Alyson Publications.

Barclay, Clare. 1992. 'Summation.' *R. v. Scythes* (16 January 1993), Toronto (Ont. Ct. Prov. Div.) [unreported] 6–24.

Barclay, Clare, and Elaine Carol. 1992–3. 'Obscenity Chill: Artists in a Post-Butler Era.' *Fuse* 16, no. 2 (Winter): 18–28.

Barker, Donna. 1988. 'S & M Is an Adventure.' *Fireweed* no. 28: 115–21.

Bartholomew, Amy. 1992. 'Achieving a Place for Women in a Man's World.' Draft paper, Carleton University, Ottawa.

Bawer, Bruce. 1993. *A Place at the Table: The Gay Individual in American Society*. New York: Poseidon Press.

Bearchell, Chris. 1983. 'Art, Trash and Titillation: A Consumer's Guide to Lezzy Smut.' *The Body Politic*, May, 29–33.

– 1993. 'Gender Bender: Cut That Out.' *This Magazine* 26 (January–February): 40.

Bell, Shannon. 1993. 'Katie Bornstein: A Transgeneral, Transsexual, Postmodern Tiresias.' In *The Last Sex: Feminism and Outlaw Bodies*, ed. Arthur Kroker and Marilouise Kroker. New York: St Martin's.

– 1994. *Reading, Writing and Rewriting the Prostitute Body*. Bloomington: Indiana University Press.

– 1995. *Whore Carnival*. Brooklyn: Autonomedia.

Berger, Ronald, Patricia Searles, and Charles Cottle. 1991. *Feminism and Pornography*. New York: Praeger.

Bergman, Brian. 1994. 'The Battle over Censorship.' *Maclean's*, 24 October, 26–9.

Bergman, David. 1993. 'Introduction.' In *Camp Grounds: Style and Homosexuality*, ed. David Bergman, 3–18. Amherst: University of Massachusetts Press.

Blizzard, Christina. 1992a. 'Gay Pap Appalling Tax Waste.' *Toronto Sun*, 25 January, A14.

– 1992b. 'Gay Flier Furor: Pamphlet Says Homosexuality "Natural."' *Toronto Sun*, 25 September, A4.

– 1992c. 'Gay Case for Fliers Is Bizarre.' *Toronto Sun*, 29 September, A14.

– 1992d. 'Personal Problem? Yes, It Is.' *Toronto Sun*, 15 October, A16.

Boffin, Tessa, and Jean Fraser, eds. 1991. *Stolen Glances: Lesbians Take Photographs*. London: Pandora.

Bornstein, Kate. 1994. *Gender Outlaw: On Men, Women and the Rest of Us*. New York: Routledge.

Bovard J. 1995. 'Ruling on Committal to Stand Trial.' Ontario Court (Provincial Division). Toronto, 23 October.

Bright, Susie. 1990. *Susie Sexpert's Lesbian Sex World*. San Francisco: Cleis Press.

– 1992. *Susie Bright's Sexual Reality: A Virtual Sex World Reader*. San Francisco: Cleis Press.

British Columbia Civil Liberties Association. 1991. 'Factum of the Intervenor, the British Columbia Civil Liberties Association.' *Butler v. R.*, [1992] 1 S.C.R. 452, [1992] 8 C.R.R. (2d) 1.

Brodie, Janine. 1994. 'Politics on the Boundaries: Restructuring and the Canadian Women's Movement.' Eighth Annual Robarts Lecture, York University, North York, Ont., March.

Brown, Beverly. 1993. 'Troubled Vision: Legal Understandings of Obscenity.' *Perversity: a journal of culture/theory/politics* 19 (Spring): 29–44.

Brown, Eleanor. 1993a. 'Customs Targets Gay Book Distributor.' *X-tra!*, 28 May, 13.

– 1993b. 'Harassment Escalates.' *X-tra!*, 24 December, 1.

– 1994. 'Hustler Speaks Out on Obscenity Charge.' *X-tra!*, 13 May, 11.

Brown, Wendy. 1991. 'Feminist Hesitations, Postmodern Exposures.' *differences: a journal of feminist cultural studies* 5 (Spring): 63–84.

Brownmiller, Susan. 1975. *Against Our Will: Men, Women and Rape*. New York: Simon and Schuster.

Burstyn, Varda. 1985a. 'Beyond Despair: Positive Strategies.' Chapter in *Women Against Censorship*. Vancouver: Douglas and McIntyre.

– 1985b. *Women Against Censorship*. Vancouver: Douglas and McIntyre.

Busby, Karen. 1994. 'LEAF and Pornography: Litigating on Equality and Sexual Representations.' *Canadian Journal of Law and Society* 9, no. 1 (Spring): 165–92.

Butler, Donald V. 'Factum of the Appellant.' 1991. *Butler v. R.*, [1992] 1 S.C.R. 452, [1992] 8 C.R.R. (2d) 1.

Butler, Judith. 1990. 'The Force of Fantasy: Feminism, Mapplethorpe, and Discursive Excess.' *differences: a journal of feminist cultural studies* 2 (Summer): 105–25.

– 1992. 'Contingent Foundations.' In *Feminists Theorize the Political*, ed. Judith Butler and Joan Scott, 3–21. New York: Routledge.

– 1993. 'Critically Queer.' *GLQ: A Journal of Lesbian and Gay Studies* 1, no. 1: 20–33.

Cairns, Alan. 1991. 'Constitutional Minoritarianism in Canada.' In *Canada: State of the Federation 1990*, ed. R. Watts and D. Brown. Kingston, Ont.: Institute of Intergovernmental Relations.

Califia, Pat. 1981. 'Feminism and Sadomasochism.' *Heresies, The Sex Issue* 12; reprinted in Pat Califia, *Public Sex: The Culture of Radical Sex*, 165–74. San Francisco: Cleis Press 1994 (cited to first printing).

– 1988. *Macho Sluts*. Boston: Alyson Publications.

– 1992. 'The Limits of the S/M Relationship, or Mr. Benson Doesn't Live Here Anymore.' *Out/Look* (Winter): 15–21.

– 1993. '*Sex* and Madonna, Or, What Do You Expect From a Straight Girl Who

Doesn't Put Out on the First Five Dates?' In *Madonnarama: Essays on Sex and Popular Culture*, ed. Lisa Frank and Paul Smith, 169–84. San Francisco: Cleis Press.

Califia, Pat, and Janine Fuller. 1995. Introductions in *Forbidden Passages: Writings in Canada*. Pittsburgh: Cleis Press.

Caloz, Marie. 1995. 'Here, Clitty, Clitty: Fag Porn Is Fast Becoming the Choix du Jour for Lesbians.' *X-Tra!*, 24 November, 49.

'Calvin and Hobbes.' 1994. *Toronto Star*, 5 November, Comics.

Campbell, Robert, and Leslie Pal. 1989. *The Real Worlds of Canadian Politics*. Peterborough, Ont.: Broadview.

Canada. Committee on Sexual Offences Against Children and Youths. 1985. *Report of the Committee on Sexual Offences Against Children and Youths: The Badgely Report*. Ottawa: Government of Canada [Dept. of Justice].

Canada. House of Commons. Standing Committee on Justice and Legal Affairs. 1978. *Report on Pornography*. Ottawa: Queen's Printer.

– House of Commons. Standing Committee on Health, Welfare, Social Affairs, Seniors and the Status of Women. 1991. *The War Against Women*. Hull, Que.: Supply and Services Canada.

– Special Committee on Pornography and Prostitution. 1985. *Pornography and Prostitution in Canada: Report of the Special Committee on Pornography and Prostitution: The Fraser Commission Report*. Vols. 1 and 2. Ottawa: Minister of Supplies and Services.

Canadian Advisory Council on the Status of Women. 1988. *Pornography, An Analysis of Proposed Legislation (Bill C-54)*. Ottawa: Candian Advisory Council on the Status of Women.

Canadian Broadcasting Corporation. 1993. 'Feminism and Censorship.' *Ideas*, CBC Radio Works, Toronto, October.

– 1994. 'The Bedrooms of the Nation.' *Ideas*, CBC Radio Works, unpublished radio transcripts, Toronto, October.

Canadian Civil Liberties Association/Manitoba Association for Rights and Liberties. 1991. 'Factum of the Intervenors, the Canadian Civil Liberties Association and the Manitoba Association for Rights and Liberties.' *Butler v. R.*, [1992] 1 S.C.R. 452, [1992] 8 C.R.R. (2d) 1.

Canadian Panel on Violence Against Women. 1993. *Changing the Landscape: Ending Violence Achieving Equality*. Ottawa: Canadian Panel on Violence Against Women.

Caprio, Frank. 1954. *Female Homosexuality: A Psychodynamic Study of Lesbianism*. New York: The Citadel Press.

Carol, Elaine. 1995. 'The Chill Continues: Artists After Bill C-128.' *Fuse* 19, no. 1 (Fall).

Cassel, Jay. 1988. *The Secret Plague*. Toronto: University of Toronto Press.

Cernetig, Miro. 1996. 'Censorship Discriminates against Gays, Court Says.' *Globe and Mail*, 20 January, A1.

Charles, W.H. 1966. 'Obscene Literature and the Legal Process in Canada.' *Canadian Bar Review* 44: 243.

Cole, Susan. 1989. *Pornography and the Sex Crisis*. Toronto: Amanita.

Congress of Canadian Women. 1952. 'Proceedings of the Special Committee on Salacious and Indecent Literature.' Submission to the Senate, 25 June.

Connolly, William. 1993. *The Augustinian Imperative: A Reflection on the Politics of Morality*. London: Sage Publications.

Cossman, Brenda. 1993. 'How the State Created a Bunch of Paedophiles.' *X-tra!*, 12 November, 17.

Couture, Joseph. 1994. 'Topping Sentenced.' *X-tra!*, 8 July.

– 1995. 'London's Trials.' *The Guide: Gay Entertainment, Politics and Sex*, July.

– 1996. 'Project Guardian's Tiny Error ... Porn Bust Used for Political Purposes Has Fallen Apart.' *X-tra!*, 28 March, 11.

Couture, Joseph, and Kleri Venizelos. 1994. 'Politician Outed, Bath-house Targeted, Police Seeking "Sex Offenders" in Porn Sweep.' *X-tra!*, 15 April, 17.

Coward, Rosalind. 1982. *Female Desire*. New York: Grove Press, Inc.

Creet, Julia. 1991a. 'Daughter of the Movement: The Psychodynamics of Lesbian S/M Fantasy.' *differences: a journal of feminist cultural studies* 3, no. 2 (Summer): 135–59.

– 1991b. 'Lesbian Sex/Gay Sex: What's the Difference?' *Out/Look* no. 11: 29–34.

Crimp, Douglas, and Michael Warner. 1993. 'No Sex in *Sex*.' In *Madonnarama: Essays on Sex and Popular Culture*, ed. Lisa Frank and Paul Smith, 93–110. San Francisco: Cleis Press.

Currie, Dawn. 1992. 'Representation and Resistance: Feminist Struggles Against Pornography.' In *The Anatomy of Gender*, ed. D. Currie and V. Raoul. Ottawa: Carleton University Press.

Cvetkovich, Ann. 1995. 'Recasting Receptivity: Femme Sexualities.' In *Lesbian Erotics*, ed. Karla Jay, 125–46. New York: New York University Press.

Dafoe, Chris. 1993. 'Customs Opened Domestic Shipment.' *Globe and Mail*, 9 December, A1.

– 1994. 'Little Sister v. Big Brother.' *Globe and Mail*, 8 October, C1, C2.

de Grazia, Edward. 1992. *Girls Lean Back Everywhere: The Law of Obscenity and the Assault on Genius*. New York: Vintage Books.

Durham, Martin. 1991. *Sex and Politics*. London: MacMillan.

Dworkin, Andrea. 1981. *Pornography: Men Possessing Women*. New York: Perigee Books.

Eisenstein, Zillah. 1988. *The Female Body and the Law*. Berkeley: University of California Press.

Erwin, Lorna. 1988. 'Challenging Feminism: The Organized Antifeminist Back-lash.' *Resources for Feminist Research* 17, no. 3 (September).

Files, Gemma. 1994. 'Does the New Kid Porn Law Go Too Far? Gay Teens Argue Bill C-128 Has Homophobic Overtones.' *Eye Magazine*, 4 November, 10.

Fish, Stanley. *Doing What Comes Naturally: Change, Rhetoric and the Practice of Theory in Literary and Legal Studies*. Chapel Hill, NC: Duke University Press.

Flanders, Ellen. 1993. 'Feminism and Censorship.' *Ideas*, CBC Radio Works, Toronto, October, 9.

Flax, Jane. 1990. 'Postmodernism and Gender Relations in Feminist Theory.' In *Feminism / Postmodernism*, ed. L. Nicholson. New York: Routledge.

Flynn, Thomas. 1988. 'Foucault as Parrhesiast: His Last Course at the College de France (1984).' In *Final Foucault*, ed. James Bernauer and David Rasmussen. Cambridge: MIT Press.

Foucault, Michel. 1978. *The History of Sexuality.* New York: Pantheon.

– 1979. *Discipline and Punish.* New York: Vintage.

– 1980. *The History of Sexuality*, trans. Robert Hurley. New York: Vintage Books.

– 1988. *Politics, Philosophy, Culture: Interviews and Other Writings 1977–1984*, ed. Lawrence D. Kritzman. New York: Routledge.

Freedman, Jonathon. 1992. 'Testimony.' Transcripts from *R. v. Scythes* (16 January 1993), Toronto (Ont. Ct. Prov. Div.).

Frug, Mary Joe. 1992. *Postmodern Legal Feminism*. New York: Routledge.

Frye, Marilyn. 1988. 'Lesbian Sex.' *Sinister Wisdom* (Summer/Fall).

Fuller, Janine, and Stuart Blackley. 1995. *Restricted Entry: Censorship on Trial*. Vancouver: Press Gang Publishers.

Fung, Richard. 1991. 'Looking for My Penis: The Eroticized Asian in Gay Video Porn.' In *How Do I Look? Queer Film and Video*, ed. Bad Object Choices, 145–68. Seattle: Bay Press.

– 1993. 'Shortcomings: Questions about Pornography as Pedagogy.' In *Queer Looks: Perspectives on Lesbian and Gay Film and Video*, ed. Martha Gever, John Greyson, and Pratibha Parmar, 355–67. Toronto: Between the Lines.

Fuss, Diana. 1989. *Essentially Speaking: Feminism, Nature and Difference*. New York and London: Routledge.

– 1992. 'Fashion and the Homo-Spectatorial Look.' *Critical Inquiry* 18 (Summer): 713–37.

Gamble, Andrew. 1988. *The Free Economy and the Strong State*. London: MacMillan.

Gammon, Carolyn. 1992. *Lesbians Ignite*. Charlottetown, PEI: Gynergy Press.

Garber, Marjorie. 1993. *Vested Interests: Cross-Dressing and Cultural Anxiety.* New York: HarperCollins.

Gibson, Pamela C., and Roma Gibson, ed. 1993. *Dirty Looks: Women, Pornography, Power.* London: British Film Institute Publishing.

Gilbert, Sky. 1995. 'Pasolini/Pelosi, or The God in Unknown Flesh: A Theatrical Enquiry into the Murder of Filmmaker Pier Paolo Pasolini.' In *This Unknown Flesh.* Toronto: Coach House Press.

Gillmor, Don. 1993. 'Strange Customs.' *Saturday Night* (March): 31–3, 66–7.

Gillmor, Jennifer. 1992. 'In-Chief and Cross-Examination.' Transcripts from *R. v. Scythes* (16 January 1993), Toronto (Ont. Ct. Prov. Div.), 16–22.

– 1994. Interview with Becki Ross.

Gillmor, Jennifer, and Janet Lee Spagnol. 1994. 'Editorial.' *Lickerish: polymorphous queer candy* 1, no. 1 (Winter): 1.

Ginsberg, Allen. 1994. 'Nothing Human Is Alien.' Interview by Matthew Hayes. *X-tra!*, 15 April, 20.

Goldsby, Jackie. 1990. 'What It Means to Be Colored Me.' *Out/Look* 9 (Summer): 8–17.

– 1993. 'Queen for 307 Days: Looking B(l)ack at Vanessa Williams and the Sex Wars.' In *Sisters, Sexperts and Queers: Beyond the Lesbian Nation*, ed. Arlene Stein, 110–28. New York: Plume.

Gomez, Jewelle. 1987. 'Come When You Need Me.' In *The Leading Edge*, ed. Lady Winston, 161–71. Denver: Lace Publications.

Gotell, Lise. 1993. 'Feminism, Equality Rights and the Charter of Rights and Freedoms in English Canada.' Ph.D. diss., Dept. of Political Science, York University, North York, Ont.

– 1995. 'Litigating Feminist "Truth."' *Social and Legal Studies* 4, no. 1 (Winter).

– 1996. 'Policing Desire: Obscenity Law, Pornography Policy and Feminism.' In *Women and Public Policy in Canada*, ed. J. Brodie, 279–318. Toronto: Harcourt Brace.

Grace, Della. 1991. *Love Bites.* London: GMP.

Granek, Charles. 1992a. 'Cross-Examination of Jennifer Gillmor.' Transcripts from *R. v. Scythes*, 14 December.

– 1992b. 'Cross-examination of Becki Ross.' Transcripts from *R. v. Scythes*, 14 December.

– 1992c. 'Summation.' Transcripts from *R. v. Scythes*, 18 December.

Greyson, John. 1995. Videotape: 'After the Bath.' Toronto: Grey Zone Ltd.

Group Against Pornography. 1991. 'Factum of the Intervenor, Group Against Pornography.' *R. v. Butler*, [1992] 1 S.C.R. 452, [1992] 8 C.R.R. (2d) 1.

Gwendolyn, Karen/miranda augustine, Susan Cole, Becki Ross, Midi Onodera, and Karen Busby. 1994. 'Politics of Desire: Pornography, Erotica, Freedom of Expression: Proceedings of MediaWatch Panel, October 1993.' *Fireweed: A Feminist Quarterly* 42 (Winter): 22–40.

Halperin, David. 1993. 'Bringing Out Michel Foucault.' *Salmagund* no. 97 (Winter): 69–89.

Hannon, Gerald. 1995. 'The Kiddie-Porn Ring That Wasn't.' *Globe and Mail*, 11 March, D1, D5.

Hekman, Susan. 1990. *Gender and Knowledge: Elements of a Postmodern Feminism.* Boston: Northeastern University Press.

Henderson, Lisa. 1992. 'Lesbian Pornography: Cultural Transgression and Sexual Demystification.' In *New Lesbian Criticism*, ed. Sally Munt, 173–92. New York: Columbia University Press.

Henry, Buck. 1993. Introduction to *The Betty Pages Annual*, vol. 2. New York: Pure Imagination.

Herman, Didi. 1994. 'Law and Morality Re-Visited: The Politics of Regulating Sado-Masochistic Porn and Practice.' Paper delivered at the Canadian and American Law Society Association conferences, Calgary and Phoenix, June.

Hough, Robert. 1994. 'Degrading Customs.' *Globe and Mail*, 12 February, D1, D5.

Hunt, Margaret. 1990. 'The De-Eroticization of Women's Liberation: Social Purity Movements and the Revolutionary Feminism of Sheila Jeffreys.' *Feminist Review*, Spring: 23–46.

Hunter, Ian, David Saunders, and Dugald Williamson. 1993. *On Pornography: Literature, Sexuality and Obscenity Law.* New York: St Martin's Press.

Hustler. 1990. 'Stream of Cuntiousness.' March: 36–41.

– 1993. 'Nicki and Bronson: Aquavelvet.' Photographed by Matti Klatt. March: 96–104.

Jarvie, Suzanne. 1992. 'In-Chief and Cross-Examination.' Transcripts from *R. v. Scythes*, 14 December, 23–7.

Jeffreys, Sheila. 1994. *The Lesbian Heresy: a feminist perspective on the lesbian sexual revolution.* London: Women's Press.

Johnston, Lucinda. 1993. 'Saving Canada from "Betty Page."' *Canadian Bookseller*, February: 30–3.

Jones, Catherine. 1993. 'Patrolling the Borders: Censorship and Gay and Lesbian Bookstores, 1982–1992.' MA thesis, Dept. of Canadian Studies, Carleton University, Ottawa.

Josey, Stan. 1994. 'Teacher Charged in Child Porn Probe.' *Toronto Star*, 27 August.

Julien, Isaac. 1993. 'Confessions of a Snow Queen: Director's Notes on the Making of *The Attendant*.' *Cineaction: Radical Film Criticism and Theory* 32 (Fall): 5–9.

Kaihla, Paul. 1994. 'Sex and the Law: Judges Set the Standards.' *Maclean's*, 24 October, 30–1.

Kaminer, Wendy. 1992. 'Feminists Against the First Amendment.' *Atlantic Monthly* (November).

Kant, Immanuel. 1927. *Fundamental Principles of the Metaphysics of Morals.* London: Longmans, Green.

– 1951. *Critique of Judgement*. Trans. J.H. Bernard. New York: Hafner Publishing.

Keane, John. 1988. *Democracy and Civil Society*. London: Verso.

Kelly, Howard. 1913. *Medical Gynecology*.

Kendall, Christopher N. 1993. '"Real Dominant, Real Fun!": Gay Male Pornography and the Pursuit of Masculinity.' *Saskatchewan Law Review* 57: 21–57.

Kendrick, Walter. 1987. *The Secret Museum: Pornography in Modern Culture*. New York: Viking Press.

Kessler-Harris, Alice. 1987. 'Equal Employment Opportunity Commission v. Sears, Roebuck and Company: A Personal Account.' *Feminist Review* 25: 46–69.

Kimmel, David, and Daniel Robinson. 1994. '"Certain Sensitive Position": Anti-Gay Security Regulations and the Canadian Civil Service, 1955–1970.' Unpublished manuscript, Toronto.

King, Allison. 1993. 'Mystery and Imagination: The Case of Pornography Effects Studies.' In *Bad Girls and Dirty Pictures: The Challenge to Reclaim Feminism*, ed. Alison Assiter and Carol Avedon. London: Pluto.

Kinsman, Gary. 1987. *The Regulation of Desire: Sexuality in Canada*. Montreal: Black Rose Books. 2nd ed. 1996.

– 1994. 'Keep your fucking laws off our bodies: organizing to repeal the youth porn law.' *Parallelogramme* 20, no. 1.

– 1995. '"Character Weaknesses" and "Fruit Machines": Towards an Analysis of the Social Organization of the Anti-Homosexual Purge Campaign in the Canadian Federal Civil Service, 1959–1964.' *Labour/Le Travail* 35 (Spring): 133–61.

Kinsman, Gary, and Deborah Brock. 1985. 'Porn/Censor Wars and the Battlefields of Sex.' In *Issues of Censorship*. Toronto: A Space Publication.

Kirk, Marshall, and Hunter Madsen. 1989. *After the Ball: How America Will Conquer Its Fear and Hatred of Gays in the '90s*. New York: Penguin.

Kiss & Tell, eds. 1994. *Her Tongue on My Theory: Images, Essays and Fantasies*. Vancouver: Press Gang Publishers.

Knopff, R., and F.L. Morton. 1992. *Charter Politics*. Scarborough, Ont.: Nelson.

Kotz, Liz. 1994. 'Keeping Secrets and Other Stories: On Lesbian Representation.' Panel presentation, A Space Gallery, Toronto.

Kroker, Arthur, and Michael Weinstein. 1994. *Data Trash*. Montreal: New World Perspectives.

Lacombe, Dany. 1988. *Ideology and Public Policy*. Toronto: Garamond.

– 1994. *Blue Politics: Pornography and the Law in the Age of Feminism*. Toronto: University of Toronto Press.

Landsberg, Michele. 1992. 'Canada: Antipornography Breakthrough in the Law.' *MS Magazine*, May/June.

Lang, Kirstie. 1995. 'Freezing the "Perfect Moment."' Unpublished MA thesis, Department of Curriculum Studies, University of British Columbia.

LEAF. 1990. 'Outreach the Focus of Cross-Canada Coalitions.' *LEAFLines* 4, no. 1 (November).

– 1991a. 'Factum of the Intervenor, Women's Legal, Education and Action Fund.' *Butler v. R.*, [1992] 1 S.C.R. 452, [1992] 8 C.R.R. (2d) 1.

– 1991b. 'Keegstra, Andrews, Smith and Taylor: Supreme Court Upholds Prohibitions on Hate Literature.' *LEAFLines* 4, no. 2 (March).

– 1992. 'Butler: Supreme Court Upholds Obscenity Law.' *LEAFLines* 5, no. 1 (Summer): 14.

– 1993. 'LEAF's Policy of Outreach and Diversification.' *LEAFLines* 5, no. 3.

Leiren-Young, Mark. 1994. 'Breaking the Ties That Bind: Can a Small Bookstore Take on the Feds and Win?' *Georgia Straight* 25 (7–14 October): 11, 13, 15, 17.

Levan, Andrea. 1995. 'Responding to a Social Problem: The Canadian Panel on Violence Against Women.' In *Women and Public Policy in Canada*, ed. J. Brodie. Toronto: Harcourt Brace.

Lewis, Reina. 1994. 'Dis-Graceful Images: Della Grace and Lesbian Sado-Masochism.' *Feminist Review* no. 46 (Spring).

Lewis, Reina, and Karen Adler. 1994. 'Come to Me Baby or What's Wrong with Lesbian S/M.' *Women's Studies International Forum* 17, no. 4: 433–41.

Lezzie Smut. 1993. 'Editorial: Show Us Yours.' Vol. 1, no.1 (September): 5–6.

Linden, Robin Ruth, et al., eds. 1982. *Against Sadomasochism: A Radical Feminist Analysis.* East Palo Alto, Calif.: Frog in the Well Press.

Lingis, Alphonso. 1994. *The Community of Those Who Have Nothing in Common.* Bloomington, Ind.: Indiana University Press.

Loach, Loretta. 1993. 'Bad Girls: Women Who Use Pornography.' In *Sex Exposed: Sexuality and the Pornography Debate*, ed. Lynne Segal and Mary McIntosh. New Brunswick, NJ: Rutgers.

Lyotard, Jean-François. 'Note on the Meaning of Post.' In *Postmodernism: A Reader*, ed. Thomas Docherty, 47–50. New York: Columbia University Press.

Lyotard, Jean-Francois, and Jean-Louis Thebaud. 1985. *Just Gaming.* Trans. Wlad Godzich. Minneapolis: University of Minnesota Press.

McAllister, Debora. 1992–3. '*Butler*: A Triumph for Equality Rights.' *National Journal of Constitutional Law*: 118.

McBride, Stephen, and John Shields. 1993. *Dismantling a Nation.* Halifax: Fernwood.

McClintock, Anne. 1993. 'Maid to Order: Commercial Fetishism and Gender Power.' In *Dirty Looks: Women, Pornography, Power*, ed. Pamela C. Gibson and Roma Gibson, 207–32. London: British Film Institute Publishing.

McCormack, Thelma. 1993a. 'If Pornography Is the Theory, Is Inequality the Practice?' *Philosophy of the Social Sciences* 23, no. 3 (September).

- 1993b. 'Keeping Our Sex "Safe": Anti-Censorship Strategies vs. The Politics of Protection.' *Fireweed: A Feminist Quarterly* 37 (Winter): 25–34.

McGowan, Matthew. 1994. Interview with Shannon Bell.

McIntosh, Mary. 1993. 'Liberalism and the Contradictions of Sexual Politics.' In *Sex Exposed: Sexuality and the Pornography Debate*, ed. Lynne Segal and Mary McIntosh, 155. New Brunswick, NJ: Rutgers.

MacKinnon, Catharine. 1982. 'Feminism, Marxism, Method and the State: An Agenda for Theory.' *Signs: Journal of Women in Culture and Society* 7: 515.

- 1983. 'Feminism, Marxism and the State: Toward a Feminist Jurisprudence.' *Signs: Journal of Women in Culture and Society* 8: 635.

- 1987. *Feminism Unmodified: Discourse on Life and Law.* Cambridge: Harvard University Press.

- 1989. *Towards a Feminist Theory of the State.* Cambridge: Harvard University Press.

- 1993. *Only Words.* Cambridge: Harvard University Press.

- 1994. 'Turning Rape into Pornography: Postmodern Geonocide.' *In Mass Rape: the War Against Women in Bosnia-Herzegovina*, ed. Alexandra Stiglmayer. Lincoln and London: University of Nebraska Press.

MacKinnon, Catharine, and Andrea Dworkin. 1985. 'Model Anti-Pornography Law.' In 'Against the Male Flood: Censorship, Pornography, and Equality.' *Harvard Women's Law Journal* 8: 24.

- 1994. Statement by Catharine A. MacKinnon and Andrea Dworkin Regarding Canada Customs and Legal Approaches to Pornography, 26 August.

McLaren, John. 1991. 'Now You See It, Now You Don't: The Historical Record and the Elusive Task of Defining the Obscene.' In *Freedom of Expression and the Charter*, ed. David Schneiderman. Toronto: Thomson.

Madonna. 1992. *Sex.* New York: Time Warner Books.

Malamuth, Neil. 1992. 'In-Chief and Cross-Examination.' Transcripts from *R. v. Scythes*, 14 December, 3–78.

Manchester, Colin. 1988. 'Lord Campbell's Act: England's First Obscenity Statute.' *Journal of Legal History* 9: 223.

Martin, Luther, Huck Gutman, and Patrick Hutton, eds. 1988. *Technologies of the Self: A Seminar with Michel Foucault.* Amherst, Mass.: University of Massachusetts Press.

Mercer, Kobena. 1991. 'Skin Head Sex Thing: Racial Difference and the Homo-erotic Imaginary.' In *How Do I Look? Queer Film and Video*, ed. Bad Object Choices, 169–210. Seattle: Bay Press.

- 1992. 'Just Looking for Trouble: Robert Mapplethorpe and Fantasies of Race.' In *Sex Exposed: Sexuality and the Pornography Debate*, ed. Lynne Segal and Mary McIntosh, 92–110. London: Virago.

Merck, Mandy. 1993. 'From Minneapolis to Westminster.' In *Sex Exposed: Sexuality and the Pornography Debate*, ed. Lynne Segal and Mary McIntosh. New Brunswick, NJ: Rutgers University Press.

Mitchell, Alanna. 1993. 'Faith, Hope and Chastity.' *Globe and Mail*, 18 February, A1.

Mitchinson, Wendy. 1991. *The Nature of Their Bodies: Women and Their Doctors in Victorian Canada*. Toronto: University of Toronto Press.

Mort, Frank. 1987. *Dangerous Sexualities*. London: Routledge and Kegan Paul.

Nazarieff, Serge. 1988. *Jeux de Dames Cruelles, 1850–1960*. Berlin: Taco.

Nead, Lynda. 1992. *The Female Nude: Art, Obscenity and Sexuality*. London: Routledge.

– 1993a. '"Above the Pulp-Line": The Cultural Significance of Erotic Art.' In *Dirty Looks: Women, Pornography, Power*, ed. Pamela C. Gibson and Roma Gibson. London: British Film Institute Publishing.

– 1993b. 'The Female Nude: Pornography, Art and Sexuality.' In *Sex Exposed: Sexuality and the Pornography Debate*, ed. Lynne Segal and Mary McIntosh. New Brunswick, NJ: Rutgers University Press.

Nestle, Joan. 1987. *A Restricted Country*. Ithaca, NY: Firebrand Books.

Newton, Esther. 1993. 'Role Models.' In *Camp Ground: Style and Homosexuality*, ed. David Bergman, 39–53. Amherst: University of Massachusetts Press.

Nietzsche, Friedrich. 1977. *A Nietzsche Reader*, ed. R.J. Hollingdale. London: Penguin Books.

O'Brien, Kelly. 1994. 'Turning Deviant Bodies into Visible Objects of Knowledge: A Look at the Way *Sex Variants* Sees Lesbians.' Unpublished manuscript, Toronto.

Oldham, Jim. 1993. 'Spreading the Word: CURE Founder Travels to Ottawa to Sow New Seeds.' *X-tra!*, 30 April, 11.

O'Neill, Dottie. 1994. 'Man Faces Porn Charges After Videotapes Seized.' *Toronto Star*, 15 January, A14.

Paglia, Camille. 1992. 'Rape and the Modern Sex War.' In *Sex, Art, and American Culture*. New York: Vintage Books.

Pally, Marcia. 1994. *Sex and Sensibility: Reflections on Forbidden Mirrors and the Will to Censor*. Hopewell, NJ: Ecco Press.

Patton, Cindy. 1986. *Sex and Germs: The Politics of AIDS*. Montral: Black Rose Books.

Pegis, Jessica. 1993. 'A Sick Body of Evidence: CURE Scrapes Bottom to Find "Scientific" Support for Its Homophobic Agenda.' *Xtra*, 3 September, 17.

Petchesky, Rosalind. 1984. *Abortion and Women's Choice*. Boston: Northeastern University Press.

Pidduck, Julianne. 1994. 'Feminist Rhetoric on Violence Against Women and the

Production of Everyday Fear.' Paper prepared for the York University Feminist Political Science Conference, North York, Ont.

Portillo, Tina. 1991. 'I Get Real: Celebrating My Sadomasochistic Soul.' In *Leather-Folk: Radical Sex, People, Politics and Practice*, ed. Mark Thompson, 49–55.

Preston, John, ed. 1991. *Leatherfolk*. Boston: Alyson Publications.

Rawls, John. 1971. *A Theory of Justice*. Cambridge: Harvard University Press.

Raymond, Janice. 1992. 'Pornography and the Politics of Lesbianis.' In *Pornography: Women, Violence and Civil Liberties*, ed. Catherine Itzin, 166–78. London: Oxford University Press.

Richardson, Bill. 1995. 'Of Fabulous Thighs and Delicate Eyes.' *Georgia Strait* 29, no. 1460: 17.

Ricker-Wilson, Carol. 1993. 'Tolerance in Our Schools Cannot Be One Dimensional.' *Toronto Star*, 13 April, A17.

Rodgerson, Gillian. 1993. 'Lesbian Erotic Explorations.' In *Sex Exposed: Sexuality and the Pornography Debate*, ed. Lynne Segal and Mary McIntosh. New Brunswick, NJ: Rutgers University Press.

Roof, Judith. 1991. *A Lure of Knowledge: Lesbian Sexuality and Theory*. New York: Columbia University Press.

Ross, Becki. 1991. 'Sex, Lives and Archives: Pleasure/Danger Debates in 1970s Lesbian Feminism.' In *Women Changing Academe*, ed. Sandi Kirby et al., 89–112. Winnipeg: Sororal Publishing.

– 1992. 'In-Chief and Cross-Examination.' Transcripts from *R. v. Scythes*, 3–109.

– 1993. 'Trish Thomas: Reborn in Porn.' *X-tra!*, 11 June, 27.

– 1995. *The House That Jill Built: A Lesbian Nation in Formation*. Toronto: University of Toronto Press.

Rubin, Gayle. 1984. 'Thinking Sex: Notes for a Radical Theory of the Politics of Sexuality.' In *Pleasure and Danger: Exploring Female Sexuality*, ed. Carol Vance. London: Routledge and Kegan Paul.

– 1987. 'The Leather Menace: Comments on Politics and S/M.' In *Coming to Power*, ed. Samois. Boston: Alyson Publications.

– 1989. 'Thinking Sex: Notes for a Radical Theory of the Politics of Sexuality.' In *Pleasure and Danger: Exploring Female Sexuality*, 2nd ed., ed. Carol Vance. London: Routledge and Kegan Paul.

– 1993a. 'Misguided, Dangerous and Wrong.' In *Bad Girls and Dirty Pictures: The Challenge to Reclaim Feminism*, ed. Alison Assiter and Carol Avedon. London: Pluto.

– 1993b. 'Thinking Sex: Notes for a Radical Theory of the Politics of Sexuality.' In *The Lesbian and Gay Studies Reader*, ed. H. Abelove et al. New York: Routledge.

Rupp, Shannon. 1996. 'B.C. Court's Ruling Falls Short, Bookstores Say.' *Globe and Mail*, 23 January, A9, A10.

Ryder, Bruce. 1995. *Sexuality and the Law: Cases and Materials*. Toronto: Osgoode Hall Law School.

Sagan, Eli. 1991. *The Honey and the Hemlock. Democracy and Paranoia in Ancient Athens and Modern America*. New York: Basic Books.

Scales, Ann. 1993. 'Submission to the Court.' *Little Sister's Book and Art Emporium v. Canada*, Vancouver, 30 August [unreported].

– 1994. 'Avoiding Constitutional Depress: Bad Atttitudes and the Fate of Butler.' *Canadian Journal of Women and the Law* 7: 349–92.

Scheier, Libby. 1988. 'Bill C-54: Tying Tongues.' *Saturday Night*, June.

Sedgwick, Eve. 1990. *Epistemology of the Closet*. Berkeley: University of California Press.

Segal, Lynne. 1993. 'Does Pornography Cause Violence? The Search for Evidence.' In *Dirty Looks: Women, Pornography, Power*, ed. Pamela C. Gibson and Roma Gibson, 5–21. London: British Film Institute Publishing.

Segal, Lynne, and Mary McIntosh. 1992. *Sex Exposed: Sexuality and the Pornography Debate*. London: Virago.

– 1993. *Sex Exposed: Sexuality and the Pornography Debate*. New Brunswick, NJ: Rutgers University Press.

Shaver, Frances. 1994. 'The Regulation of Prostitution: Avoiding the Moral Traps.' *Canadian Journal of Law and Society* 9, no. 1 (Spring): 123–46.

Singer, Linda. 1993. *Erotic Welfare*. New York: Routledge.

Smart, Carol. 1989. *Feminism and the Power of Law*. London: Routledge.

– 1990. 'Law's Power, the Sexed Body and Feminist Discourse.' *International Journal of Law and Society* 17: 194–210.

– 1993. 'Unquestionably a Moral Issue: Rhetorical Devices and Regulatory Imperatives.' In *Sex Exposed: Sexuality and the Pornography Debate*, ed. Lynne Segal and Mary McIntosh, 184–99. New Brunswick, NJ: Rutgers.

– 1994. 'Law, Feminism and Sexuality.' *Canadian Journal of Law and Society* 9, no. 1 (Spring): 15–38.

– 1995. *Law, Crime and Sexuality*. London: Sage Press.

Smith, Anna Marie. 1993. '"What Is Pornography?": An Analysis of the Policy Statement of the Campaign Against Pornography and Censorship.' *Feminist Review* 43 (Spring): 71–87.

– 1995. '"By Women, For Women and About Women" Rules OK?: The Impossibility of Visual Soliloquy.' In *A Queer Romance: Lesbians, Gay Men and Popular Culture*, ed. Paul Burston and Colin Richardson, 199–215. London and New York: Routledge.

Smith, Barbara. 1988. 'Sappho Was a Right-Off Woman.' In *Feminism and Censor-*

ship: The Current Debate, ed. Gail Chester and Julienne Dickey. London: Prism.

Snider, Laureen. 1990. 'The Potential of the Criminal Justice System to Promote Feminist Concerns.' *Studies in Law, Politics and Society* 10.

– 1994. 'Feminism, Punishment and the Potential of Empowerment.' *Canadian Journal of Law and Society* 9, no. 1 (Spring): 75–104.

Sorfleet, Andrew. 1993–4. 'Pornofire.' *Maggie's Line* (Winter).

Sorfleet, Andrew, and Chris Bearchell. 1994. 'The sex police in a moral panic: how the "youth porn" law is being used to censor artists and persecute youth sexuality.' *Parallelogramme* 20, no. 1.

Stewart, Susan. 1994. 'Porn Wars and Other Hysteries.' In *Her Tongue on My Theory: Images, Essays and Fantasies*, ed. Kiss & Tell, 5–26. Vancouver: Press Gang Publishers.

Strossen, Nadine. 1993. 'A Feminist Critique of "The" Feminist Critique of Pornography.' *Virginia Law Review* 79: 1099.

– 1995. *Defending Pornography: Free Speech, Sex and the Fight for Women's Rights*. New York: Scribner.

Stychin, Carl. 1992. 'Exploring the Limits: Feminism and the Legal Regulation of Gay Male Pornography.' *Vermont Law Review* 16: 857.

SWAT (Sex Worker Alliance of Toronto). 1993. Press release, distributed at the MediaWatch Panel, Toronto, October.

Tanguay, Brian. 1994. 'The Transformation of the Canadian Party System in the 1990s.' In *Canadian Politics*, ed. James Bickerton and Alain-G. Gagnon. Peterborough, Ont.: Broadview.

Taylor, Kate. 1993a. 'Show Breaks Sex Taboo.' *Globe and Mail*, 14 December, C1.

– 1993b. 'Child-Porn Law Used for the First Time.' *Globe and Mail*, 22 December, A5.

– 1993c. '"I'm Not a Pornographer", Charged Artist Says.' *Globe and Mail*, 23 December, A7.

Theakston, Greg, ed. 1994. *Betty Page Confidential*. New York: St Martin's Press.

Thomas, Trish. 1991. 'Wunna My Fantasies.' *Bad Attitude* 7, no. 4: 25–9.

– 1993. Interview with Becki Ross, Toronto, May.

Tisdale, Sallie. 1994. *Talk Dirty to Me: An Intimate Philosophy of Sex*. New York: Doubleday.

Toobin, Jeffrey. 1994. 'X-Rated.' *The New Yorker*, 3 October, 70–8.

Valverde, Mariana. 1985. *Sex, Power and Pleasure*. Toronto: Women's Press.

– 1989. 'Beyond Gender Dangers and Private Pleasures: Theory and Ethics in the Sex Debates.' *Feminist Studies*, no. 2 (Summer).

– 1991. *The Age of Light, Soap, and Water: Moral Reform in English Canada 1885–1925*. Toronto: McClelland and Stewart.

– 1996. 'Social Facticity and the Law: A Social Expert's Eyewitness Account of Law.' *Social and Legal Studies* 5, no. 2 (June): 201–17.

Valverde, Mariana, and Lorna Weir. 1985. 'Thrills, Chills and the "Lesbian Threat" or, The Media, the State and Women's Sexuality.' In *Women Against Censorship*, ed. Varda Burstyn, 99–106. Vancouver: Douglas and McIntyre.

– 1988. 'The Struggles of the Immoral: Preliminary Remarkson Moral Regulation.' *Resources for Feminist Research* 17, no. 3 (September).

Vance, Carole. 1984. 'Pleasure and Danger: Toward a Feminist Politics of Sexuality.' In *Pleasure and Danger*. Boston: Routledge and Kegan Paul.

– 1989. 'The War on Culture.' *Art in America* 77, no. 9: 39–45.

– 1993a. 'Feminist Fundamentalism – Women against Images.' *Art in America* 29 (October).

– 1993b. 'Negotiating Sex and Gender in the Attorney General's Commission on Pornography.' In *Sex Exposed: Sexuality and the Pornography Debate*, ed. Lynne Segal and Mary McIntosh. New Brunswick, NJ: Rutgers University Press.

Vega, Judith. 1988. 'Coercion and Consent: Classic Liberal Concepts in Texts on Sexual Violence.' *International Journal of the Sociology of Law* 16: 75–89.

Weeks, Jeffrey. 1991. *Against Nature*. London: River Oram Press.

– 1986. *Sexuality*. London: Tavistock Publications.

Whitaker, Reg. 1987. 'Neo-Conservatism and the State.' In *The Socialist Register 1987*, ed. R. Miliband and J. Saville. London: Merlin.

Whitman, Walt. 1981. 'Song of Myself.' In *Leaves of Grass and Selected Prose*, ed. Lawrence Buell. New York: The Modern Library.

Wicke, Jennifer. 1993. 'Through the Gaze Darkly: Pornography's Academic Market.' In *Dirty Looks: Women, Pornography, Power*, ed. Pamela C. Gibson and Roma Gibson. London: British Film Institute Publishing.

Williams, Linda. 1989. *Hard Core: Power, Pleasure and the Frenzy of the Visible*. Berkeley: University of California Press.

– 1990. *Hard Core: Power, Pleasure and the Frenzy of the Visible*. London: Pandora.

– 1993a. 'Pornographies On/Scene, or Different Strokes for Different Folks.' In *Sex Exposed: Sexuality and the Pornography Debate*, ed. Lynne Segal and Mary McIntosh. New Brunswick, NJ: Rutgers University Press.

– 1993b. 'Second Thoughts on Hard Core: American Obscenity Law and the Scapegoating of Deviance.' In *Dirty Looks: Women, Pornography, Power*, ed. Pamela C. Gibson and Roma Gibson. London: British Film Institute Publishing.

Williams, Toni. 1990. 'Re-Forming "Women's" Truth: A Critique of the Royal Commission on the Status of Women.' *Ottawa Law Review* 22: 725–59.

Willis, Ellen. 1994. 'One of Those Weeks: A Media Diary.' *Village Voice*, 22 November.

Wilson, Elizabeth. 1993. 'Feminist Fundamentalism: The Shifting Politics of Sex and Censorship.' In *Sex Exposed: Sexuality and the Pornography Debate*, ed. Lynne Segal and Mary McIntosh. New Brunswick, NJ: Rutgers University Press.

Winston, Lady, ed. 1987. *The Leading Edge*. Denver: Lace Publications.

Yeatman, Anna. 1990. *Bureaucrats, Technocrats and Femocrats*. London: Allen and Unwin.

List of Cases

Dominion News and Gifts (1962) v. R., [1963] 2 C.C.C. 103 (Man.C.A.).

Dominion News and Gifts (1962) v. R., [1964] S.C.R. 251, [1964] 3 C.C.C. 1 103.

Glad Day Bookshop v. Canada, [1992] O.J. No. 1466 (QL).

Langer. See R. v. Paintings ...

Little Sister's Book and Art Emporium v. Canada (Minister of Justice), [1996] B.C.J. No. 71, 19 January 1996.

Lushner v. Revenue Canada (Customs and Excise), [1985] 1 F.C. 85 (C.A.).

R. v. 931536 Ontario [unreported].

R. v. Adams, [1966] 4 C.C.C. 42 (N.S.Co.Ct.).

R. v. Brodie, [1962] S.C.R. 681, 132 C.C.C. 161 (cited to C.C.C.).

R. v. Butler, [1992] 1 S.C.R. 452, [1992] 8 C.R.R. (2d) 1 (cited to C.R.R. in chapter 3; cited to S.C.R. in chapter 5).

R. v. Cameron, [1966] 2 O.R. 777, [1966] 4 C.C.C. 273 (Ont.C.A.).

R. v. Close, [1948] V.L.R. 445 (New Zealand).

R. v. Curl (1727), 2 Strange 788, 93 E.R. 849 (K.B.).

R. v. Doug Rankine Co. (1983), 9 C.C.C. (3d) 53 (Ont.Co.Ct.).

R. v. Hawkins (1993), 86 C.C.C. (3d) 246

R. v. Hicklin (1868), 3 L.R.Q.B. 360.

R. v. Keegstra, [1990] 3 S.C.R. 697, 61 C.C.C. (3rd) 1.

R. v. M. (C.) (1995), 23 O.R. (3d) 629.

R. v. Oakes, [1986] 1 S.C.R. 103, 24 C.C.C. 321.

R. v. Paintings, Drawings and Photographic Slides of Paintings (20 April 1995), Toronto U219/94 (Ont.Ct.Gen.Div.) [cited as *Langer*].

R. v. Ramsingh (1984), 14 C.C.C. (3d) 230 (Man.Q.B.).

R. v. Red Hot Video (1985), 18 C.C.C. (3d) 1 (B.C.C.A.).

R. v. Scythes (16 January 1993), Toronto (Ont.Ct.Prov.Div.) [unreported].

R. v. Towne Cinema Theatres, [1985] 1 S.C.R. 494, 18 C.C.C. (3d) 193 (cited to C.C.C.).

R. v. Wagner (1985), 36 Alta.L.R. (2d) 301 (Q.B.).

R. v. Zundel, [1992] 2 S.C.R. 731, 75 C.C.C. (3rd) 449.

Index